ANTONY AND CLEOPATRA IN CONTEXT

ANTHEM PERSPECTIVES IN LITERATURE

Titles in the **Anthem Perspectives in Literature** series are designed to contextualize classic works of literature for readers today within their original social and cultural environments. The books present historical, biographical, political, artistic, moral, religious and philosophical material from the period that enable readers to understand a text's meaning as it would have struck the original audience. These approachable but informative books aims to uncover the period and the people for whom texts were written; their values and views, their anxieties and demons, what made them laugh and cry, their loves and hates. The series is targeted at high-achieving A-level, International Baccalaureate and Advanced Placement pupils, first-year undergraduates and an intellectually curious audience.

ANTONY AND CLEOPATRA IN CONTEXT

THE POLITICS OF PASSION

Keith Linley

ANTHEM PRESS

Anthem Press
An imprint of Wimbledon Publishing Company
www.anthempress.com

This edition first published in UK and USA 2015
by ANTHEM PRESS
75–76 Blackfriars Road, London SE1 8HA, UK
or PO Box 9779, London SW19 7ZG, UK
and
244 Madison Ave #116, New York, NY 10016, USA

Copyright © Keith Linley 2015

The author asserts the moral right to be identified as the author of this work.

All rights reserved. Without limiting the rights under copyright reserved above,
no part of this publication may be reproduced, stored or introduced into
a retrieval system, or transmitted, in any form or by any means
(electronic, mechanical, photocopying, recording or otherwise),
without the prior written permission of both the copyright
owner and the above publisher of this book.

British Library Cataloguing-in-Publication Data
A catalogue record for this book is available from the British Library.

Library of Congress Cataloging-in-Publication Data
Linley, Keith.
Antony and Cleopatra in context : the politics of passion / Keith Linley.
    pages cm
Includes bibliographical references and index.
ISBN 978-1-78308-377-0 (papercover : alk. paper)
1. Shakespeare, William, 1564–1616. Antony and Cleopatra. 2. Literature and society. 3. Social role in literature. 4. Kings and rulers in literature. 5. Man-woman relationships in literature. 6. Love in literature. 7. Politics in literature. I. Title.
    PR2802.L56 2015
    822.3'3–dc23
    2014048303

ISBN-13: 978 1 78308 377 0 (Pbk)
ISBN-10: 1 78308 377 8 (Pbk)

Cover image © Andrew_Howe/iStockphoto.com

This title is also available as an ebook.

CONTENTS

Introduction	vii
Prologue: The Setting	1

Part I. The Inherited Past

1. The Historical Context	9
2. The Elizabethan World Order: From Divinity to Dust	17
3. Sin, Death and the Prince of Darkness	53
4. The Seven Cardinal Virtues	71
5. Kingship	75
6. Patriarchy, Family Authority and Gender Relationships	93
7. Man in His Place	119
8. Images of Disorder: The Religious Context	125

Part II. The Jacobean Present

9. The Context of Tragedy	133
10. 'O'erflowing the Measure': Restraint and Excess	151
11. Infinite Variety: Isis or Strumpet?	167
12. Rome versus Egypt: Gendering the State	183
13. Literary Context	199
14. Political Context	221

Notes	233
Bibliography	245
Index	249

INTRODUCTION

About This Book

This book concentrates on the contexts from which *Antony and Cleopatra* emerges, those characteristics of life in early Jacobean England which are reflected in the values and views Shakespeare brings to the text and affect how a contemporary might have responded to it. These are the primary, central contexts, comprising the writer, the text, the audience and all the views, values and beliefs held by these three. The actions taken and words spoken by the characters do not all represent Shakespeare's own views, but they will have evoked ethical judgements from the audience in line with the general religious and political values of the time. There would have been a range of differing responses, though the fundamentals of right and wrong would have been broadly agreed. These primary contexts, this complicity of writer, audience and text and their shared mediation of the play, are the prime concern of this book.

Where relevant, the book also focuses on a range of secondary contexts. A play does not come into being without having a background and does not exist *in vacuo*. It will have its own unique features, but also characteristics inherited from its author as well as sources derived from and traits resembling the writing of its time. Other secondary contexts – the actors, their companies, the acting space, the social mix of general audiences – do not figure in this study except as occasional incidentals.

There are tertiary contexts too. There is the afterlife of the text (its printed form, how subsequent ages interpreted it on stage and changed it) – what is called its performance history. And there is the critical backstory, showing how critics of subsequent times bring their agendas and the values and prejudices of their period to analysis of the text. These are referenced incidentally where they seem useful and relevant, but are not a major concern. The 'Further Reading' list provides broad guidance on the critical and performance history and any scholarly edition of *Antony and Cleopatra* will cover these areas in greater detail.

This book is for students preparing assignments and exams for Shakespeare modules. The marking criteria at any level explicitly or implicitly require students to show a consistently well-developed and consistently detailed understanding of the significance and influence of contexts in which literary texts are written and understood. This means responding to the play in the ways Shakespeare's audience would have done. You will not be writing a history essay, but along with considering the play as a literary vehicle communicating in dramatic form, you will need to know something of how Shakespeare's audience might have reacted. A text is always situated in some way within its historical setting. The correlatives in this case would have been the classics (for the educated), the Bible, Christian ethics and the society of the day, the latter meaning they would view the play in the light of what had happened in recent history and what was currently happening in the court, in the city, in the streets, on the roads and in the villages. No one could watch Antony's foolishness and not think of King James. The conduct of rulers was of great interest to writers, preachers, politicians and the ordinary man in the tavern. No one could watch the power struggles on stage and not think of the court. Though the story is from ancient times its issues must have created a disturbing sense of recognition of the political concerns of Jacobean England.

The following material will enable you to acquire a surer grasp of this cultural context – the social-political conditions from which the play emerged, the literary profile prevailing when it was written, and its religious-moral dimension. The setting is pagan, but since the play was written in an age of faith, when the Bible's teachings and sermons heard in church formed part of every man and woman's mindset, it is vital to recreate those factors, for the actions of the characters would have been assessed by Christian criteria. You may not agree with the values of the time or the views propounded in the play, but you do need to understand how belief mediated the possible responses of the audience that watched the play in 1606. A key concept in this book's approach is that *Antony and Cleopatra* is full of sins, transgressions, boundary crossing and rule breaking – in the personal world and in the public and political arenas. Alerted to the transgressive behaviour of Antony in the opening scene, audience members who did not already know the story would expect he be punished. Though biblical values would be applied to the action, there is much more going on scene by scene than a series of echoes of or allusions to what the Bible says about virtue and vice. Interwoven are political concerns about rule (of the self, of a state), public service and the dangers of appetite unrestrained, with Antony caught between reason and appetite and Cleopatra representing appetite out of control.

What Is a Context?

Any document – literary or non-literary – comes from an environment and has that environment embedded in it, overtly and covertly. Its context is the conditions which produced it, the biographical, social, political, historical and cultural circumstances which form it, and the values operating within it and affecting the experience of it, including what the author may have been trying to say and how the audience may have interpreted it. A text in isolation is simply a collection of words carrying growing, developing meanings as the writing/performance progresses. It is two-dimensional – a lexical, grammatical construct and the sum of its literal contents. It has meaning, we can understand what it is about, how the characters interact, but context provides a third dimension, making meaning comprehensible within the cultural values of the time. Primary context is the sum of all the influences the writer brings to the text and all the influences the viewer/reader deploys in experiencing it. Knowing the cultural context enriches that experience. This book concentrates on the archaeology of the play, recovering how it would be understood in 1606, recovering the special flavour and prevailing attitudes of the time, and displaying the factors that shaped its meaning for that time and that audience. '*Antony and Cleopatra' in Context* offer the views, prejudices, controversies and basic beliefs buried in the play. These are the significations of society embedded in the text that, added together, make it what Shakespeare intended it to be – or as close as we can be reasonably sure. Recovering the mindset, nuances and values Shakespeare intentionally or unconsciously worked into *Antony and Cleopatra* and how his audience would have interpreted them means recreating the Elizabethan-Jacobean period. To achieve that a range of aspects is considered, but two key contextual areas dominate the approach of this book: the religious-moral and the socio-political. The audience would have interpreted the multiple transgressions represented in the play in terms of the scriptural upbringing most of them would have had and in the light of their ideas on how leaders should behave. Set among the movers and shakers of the Roman world, the play automatically activates considerations related to kingship, rule, loyalty, honesty in diplomacy and flattery of leaders. These were subjects constantly debated in pre–Civil

War England and have specific relevance to the hothouse court of James I. Sin, subversion, transgression and reversals abound in the play.

Part I looks broadly at the contemporary 'world view' – the inherited past which shaped how the Jacobeans thought about God, the world, sin, virtue, death, the Devil, the social structure, family, gender relationships, social change and political matters. Connections are made between the play and the wider literary world. Most importantly, the book considers the religious beliefs informing the likely judgements made of the actions in the play and suggests a number of socio-political allusions that gave the drama a topical dimension. It is not known where the play was first performed – at the Globe public arena, the Blackfriars indoor theatre or at court – but the audience would have seen many of their own and national concerns staged for consideration. Part II discusses contemporary contexts – politics, literature, authority and morality – that enhance and clarify some issues addressed in the play. It does this by looking, in separate chapters, at tragedy as a genre, at the central characters, at political matters uppermost in people's minds in 1606, and at the literary scene. Above all, the play engages with the theme of flawed leadership. It is a theme with which Shakespeare seems particularly concerned in the early 1600s and one which occurred in many of his previous works.

Crucial to the religious context are the moral frameworks against which conduct in the play would have been measured: the Ten Commandments, the Seven Deadly Sins, the Seven Cardinal Virtues, and the Corporal and Spiritual Works of Mercy – the ethical framework in which the action is set and by which it is to be judged. You need to absorb them thoroughly as they recur constantly (see Chapters 3 and 4). These ethical contexts decode the hidden nuances and inflexions of meaning by which a contemporary audience would have mediated their responses to the story of a famous Roman general and triumvir and his equally famous (or infamous) lover. There will have been many different responses, but in the area of religious and moral values there will have been many shared reactions.

A gulf always exists between what people are supposed to do or believe and what they actually do or believe. Machiavelli's version of the traditional 'mirror for princes' book claimed:

> I have thought it proper to represent things as they are in real truth, rather than as they are imagined. [...] The gulf between how one should live and how one does live is so wide that a man who neglects what is actually done for what should be done learns the way to self-destruction rather than self-preservation.[1]

Ignorance, indifference, rebelliousness, purposeful wickedness, laziness and weakness account for these discrepancies. No one in the audience would have missed the fact that Antony neglects his duty, makes foolish decisions and puts his personal obsession before his public responsibilities. Antony was certainly aware of the difference between his expected and his actual behaviour. Many would have condemned the Queen of Egypt as a promiscuous Machiavellian. Many, like Dryden when he wrote his version of their story, might have thought the world well lost in favour of such passion. Though he admitted 'the excellency of the Moral' (for 'the chief Persons represented were famous Patterns of unlawful Love'), he attempted to draw the characters as favourably as history allowed.[2] He altered history to the extent of bringing Octavia to Alexandria and found: 'I had not enough consider'd, that the compassion she mov'd to her self and Children, was destructive to that which I reserv'd for *Anthony* and *Cleopatra*; whose mutual love being founded upon vice, must lessen the favour of the Audience to them, when Virtue and Innocence were oppress'd by it.' Others would have seen it as the tragedy of lives sacrificed in a political conflict or as a black comedy of a fool for love, a charismatic figure destroyed by his weakness for a scheming vamp.[3]

Further Reading

Editions of the play with useful introductions and reading lists

All give textual history, discuss sources, raise key issues and review recent criticism.
Arden Shakespeare: *Antony and Cleopatra* (ed. M. R. Ridley, 1956).
Arden Shakespeare: *Antony and Cleopatra* (ed. John Wilders, 2004).
New Cambridge Shakespeare: *Antony and Cleopatra* (ed. David Bevington, 2005).
Oxford Shakespeare: *Antony and Cleopatra* (ed. Michael Neill, 2000).

Other critics

Shakespeare: Antony and Cleopatra: A Casebook (ed. John Russell Brown).
Antony and Cleopatra, New Casebooks (ed. John Drakakis, 1994).
Jonathan Dollimore, *Radical Tragedy: Religion, Ideology, and Power in the Drama of Shakespeare and His Contemporaries* (1984).
Juliet Dusinberre, *Shakespeare and the Nature of Women* (1979).
Alexander Leggatt, *Shakespeare's Political Drama* (1989).
H. A. Mason, *Shakespeare's Tragedies of Love* (1970).
Robert Miola, *Shakespeare's Rome* (1983).
Phyllis Rackin, *Shakespeare and Women* (2005).
Derek Traversi, *Shakespeare: The Roman Plays* (1963).

Journal articles

Clifford Davidson, '*Antony and Cleopatra*: Circe, Venus, and the Whore of Babylon', *Bucknell Review* 25 (1980).

Ronald R. Macdonald, 'Playing till Doomsday: Interpreting *Antony and Cleopatra*', *English Literary Renaissance* 15 (1985).

Christopher Wortham, 'Temperance and the End of Time: Emblematic *Antony and Cleopatra*', *Comparative Drama* 29 (1995–96).

Paul Yachnin, '"Courtiers of Beauteous Freedom": *Antony and Cleopatra* in Its Time', *Renaissance & Reformation* 26 (1991).

Note: All quotations from the play are from the M. R. Ridley Arden edition.

Prologue

THE SETTING

Majesty and love do not go together.[1]

The audience is restless and excited. This play promises much. It is history, Roman history. This means battles, political conflicts, personal rivalries, devious plots – and deaths. And it is a love story of fated celebrities, a tale of tragic grandeur about some of the great figures of the classical past. The story of Antony and Cleopatra intertwines with a seismic shift of power that was a turning point in the rise of the greatest empire the world had seen. It marks the end of the Republic and the beginning of the rule of the emperors. And mixed in with all the political machinations for power is perhaps one of the greatest love stories ever told. Perhaps. Passion, politics, blood – a heady mix. The hero is a man of legendary name, standing alongside Julius Caesar and Alexander the Great, a renowned figure from the classical world, a man who lost one-third of the world for the love of one of the most beautiful and fascinating women of all time. A man to be admired and envied, or pitied and mocked. As lovers, Antony and Cleopatra are spoken of in the same breath as Romeo and Juliet, Héloïse and Abelard, and Cathy and Heathcliff. Icons of love – tempestuous and passionate – their story symbolizes emotion triumphing over duty, the heart over the head, and the feminine over the masculine approach to life. They are charismatic, their lives and deaths are exotic – Antony's suicide by stabbing himself with his own sword and Cleopatra's by letting venomous snakes bite her. War, love and death: powerful themes, an exciting combination, and all bustled along in 42 scenes spanning a large part of the Central and Eastern Mediterranean. Exotic, foreign settings, a large cast of speaking roles and many more servants, spear carriers and extras, a fast-paced narrative, many short scenes, reported battles, three suicides – it all makes for an action-packed drama on top of the tense and sparky relationship of the title characters. Those who know the story anticipate drama, love and disaster among some of the great names of the past. And all the moving poetry one expects from Master Shakespeare.

This is one rather sentimentalized, biased and inaccurate view of the story. A politically aware audience would have seen it rather differently. Today we prioritize love, individuality and a work/life balance that preferences personal life and pleasure over mundane money earning, job satisfaction and public duty. In 1606/1607 the story offered different angles that are far from romantic and demonstrated what happens when two public figures allow their private wills to dominate their larger responsibilities. Many viewers would have already seen Antony on stage as the playboy turned hero in *Julius Caesar* (1599). But now his neglect of his political duties, his muddled mixing of pleasure and position and his humiliating submissiveness to a woman will have disastrous consequences. Antony might be seen as a magnificent figure but not too subtle, an instructive example of history's trickery – giving immense power to a man so weak, so besotted, as to desert his men in the middle of battle to follow the woman he loves. This is the dishonour a woman can bring to a man. The play is a triple lesson in how fate can give power to exactly the wrong people, how rule accorded to privilege and inheritance rather than ability and merit can be disastrous, and how the power of the privileged allows them to play with the fates of millions as if they did not count. These were all topical concerns for the Jacobeans. What is problematic, apart from any moral disapproval of Antony's adulterous philandering, is that he has position and power and his dereliction of duty, his thoughtless squandering of money, his inept political moves and his valuing of show over substance affects millions. The Jacobean court was full of libertine men. Many of them had undue power and influence – over servants, estate tenants, government departments and finances, judges and courts. The king himself was a thriftless profligate already racking up huge debts. From the standpoint of seventeenth-century orthodox thinking both leading characters are set upon a path (possibly definable as tragic) that should lead to extreme judgement and punishment. It is probable that many in the audience already knew the main thrust of the story, but unlikely that many would feel their ends were undeserved. There had been lust-lorn kings and dangerous queens on stage before. The interest lay in how Shakespeare would present the central characters, how he would intertwine the love and the politics, how he would delineate the personalities of the lovers. Many at the performance would probably regard Cleopatra as a devious, politicking strumpet, a typical untrustworthy woman, and Antony as a great fool hypnotized by a woman's wiles. From the very opening of the play, with Philo's 'Nay, but this dotage of our general's/O'erflows the measure', to the flurry of the closing scenes, their actions deviate from acceptable conduct in a multiplicity of ways. The opening lines thrust us into the heart of the play's key thematic concern. Though pagan Rome did not approach morality within the matrix of Commandments, sins and virtues of Shakespeare's time, there were many overlaps in personal and public ethics. Many in the audience would know, from their school or university training, of Cicero's and Plato's writings on honour and duty in both the civic and private spheres of life. They would readily identify the two lead characters as sinners on a large scale, charismatic but severely tainted and weak. They are a disaster, possibly a tragedy, waiting to happen. Antony is politically inept and a personal mess. He loses his third of the Roman world through elementary miscalculations and excessive adulation of an unreliable, neurotic temptress. From a Jacobean perspective Antony is both a flawed leader and a flawed man. In the moral context he transgresses by being an adulterer and fornicator – twice. His excessive indulgence in food and drink is gluttony, his lifelong womanizing is lust, his material wastefulness is excess and ostentation, his theatrical self-dramatization and grand gestures are vanity. He has a longing for grandeur, for a nobility and freedom of spirit, but ends up a hapless victim of Cleopatra and Caesar. Both he and his mistress are at the top of the social hierarchy, but fail to conform to the expectations of their rank and the duties that go with them. To political theorists the gestures and assumed persona of both protagonists are inappropriate, lacking moderation, humility and circumspection. In the political context both fail to exercise most of the qualities required in a leader. He is flamboyant, a larger-than-life leader, but at the same time a fool who makes costly military blunders and is obsessed with a woman to the detriment of balance and civic duty. She is a drama queen both in the sense that she makes her whole life an egocentric emotional drama with everyone else expected to play up to her whims and demands, and in the sense that she is a queen who loves to overdramatize herself as Isis or Venus – a deity of femininity. Neither balance nor moderation are much regarded today, but at the time they were essential in a governor or ruler. In Roman and Christian terms lack of control in private individuals would be condemned. In a public personage it was damnable, unforgivable. In a ruler of such a vast area of conglomerate states, his behaviour is monumentally ominous. While Antony's conduct triggers multiple identifications with King James, Cleopatra too falls under the same judgements. She endorses all the misogynistic stereotypes men and the church believed, and as a queen she distantly reflects many of the failings of the lately lamented but increasingly criticized Elizabeth.

There is no definitive evidence to suggest where the play was first performed.[2] Knowing the venue would give some indication of the likely social range of the spectators, for the public theatre, the private theatre and the court performance had different customers. That said, it is probable that all three types of audience would have responded to the political dimensions of the play as they tie in so closely with contemporary concerns. The acting space too would affect the staging, creating or diminishing the sense of the global scale of the action. A balcony above an inner room (as in the traditional Globe stage) would enable Antony to be hoisted into Cleopatra's monument for the final scenes. A record from the Lord Chamberlain's Office in 1669 asserts that it was 'formerly acted at the Blackfriars', but does not specify whether that was in 1606 or at any other time up to 1642, when Blackfriars was closed by Parliament (along with all public playhouses). Demolished in 1655, this private indoor space had intermittently, between 1608 and 1642, been the winter arena for the King's Men. The troupe had occasionally performed there earlier than 1608, presumably when bad weather closed the Globe or in other ad hoc situations and probably for a fee. Because of its higher entry price its audience was more upmarket than the public amphitheatres – a mix of bourgeoisie and the better sort. An Inns of Court student describes the range in *Satyres* (1617): '*Captain Martio*' (a soldier), 'A *Cheapside* Dame (a citizen's wife), a 'misshapen *Prodigall*', a 'world of fashions' (a peacock male), 'a *Woman* of the *masculine Gender*' (a male transvestite) and 'a plumed *Dandeprat*' (an insignificant nobody dressed up finely, possibly homosexual).[3] The author calls the audience 'this *Microcosme*, Man's Societie'. This is, however, an incomplete microcosm in so far as it omits the common sort who mostly frequented the open-air theatres. The types identified represent a range of stock characters commonly satirised in the City Comedies.

In February 1607 Barnaby Barnes's play *The Devil's Charter*, performed at court, seems to allude to Cleopatra's death as depicted by Shakespeare, when a character, the Borgia Pope, Alexander VI, applies two asps to the breasts of his victims, two sleeping princes. Plutarch reported a single snake biting her arm, but it had become traditional by Shakespeare's time that she let the asp bite her breast. It has more visual effect, is more dramatic looking, and potently resonates as a transgressive, inverted mother–baby image. Barnes's apparent allusion sets a date by which Shakespeare's play had been written and seen, but does no more than that. Also in 1607 Samuel Daniel published a revised version of his play *Cleopatra*. His earlier edition (1594) may have influenced Shakespeare's decision to handle the story.[4] Both works share details not in Plutarch. Shakespeare's play then encouraged Daniel, while revising his new edition, to insert some verbal borrowings, to use some of the character names and copy some of the stage business. This reinforces the probability that the play was staged before 1607. Daniel worked (February 1604–April 1605) as a licenser in the Stationers' Office so may have seen the play in manuscript during the vetting process. Barnes's reference (without the opportunity Daniel had had) suggests he had seen a performance.[5]

On 20 May 1608, Edward Blount acquired the rights to 'a booke Called Antony & Cleopatra'. If this is Shakespeare's play it sets an end date for its composition. Though acquired by Blount, the 'booke' appears not to have been printed as an individual text until it appeared in the 1623 Folio, from a transcript possibly based on Shakespeare's manuscript, but appears not to have left any record of performance other than Brathwait's reference in *The English Gentlewoman* (1631) to how 'the last Scene clozed all those Comicke passages with a Trajicke conclusion'.[6] This might have been a reaction to reading the play or seeing a performance. In 1616 a young Cambridge graduate, Rev. Robert Anton, wrote in *The Philosophers Satyrs* that women who 'gad' to 'base Playes' shall 'see the vices of the times' and specifically mentions '*Cleopatres* crimes'.[7] This, again, may not be a response to seeing the piece, but no more than a repetition of the customary view of the queen as an evil, sinful temptress.

The lack of evidence of performance suggests, though it does not prove definitively, that it was not popular and was not performed more than a handful of times. Clearly Dryden knew the text, and from 1677 onwards the story was performed in his simplified version, *All For Love*. Shakespeare's play re-emerges in 1759 when an abridged form was played at Drury Lane. Dr Johnson acknowledged the pacey action:

> This play keeps curiosity always busy, and the passions always interested. The continual hurry of the action, the variety of incidents, and the quick succession of one personage to another, call the mind forward without intermission from the first act to the last. But the power of delighting is derived principally from the frequent changes of the scene.

Its attraction seemed to him to be its rapid movement and varied incidents; today we might describe it as 'action packed'. But he then criticized the handling of the story because although the principal events of the play 'are described according to history', they are 'produced without any art of connexion or care of disposition'. He also deprecated Cleopatra's 'feminine arts' (those which 'distinguish' her, i.e., mark her out) because some are 'too low'.[8]

More positive reactions appear in the criticism of the Romantics (German and English), for whom the famous pair are a fine example of passionate love and the free spirit that puts the heart before the head. Coleridge applauded the 'happy valiancy of style' and the 'strength and vigour of maturity' that make it a 'formidable rival' to the Great Tragedies. He sees it as a companion and comparison to *Romeo and Juliet* in so far as it reflects 'the love of passion and appetite' as opposed to 'the love of affection and instinct' of the earlier work. Coleridge also acknowledges the wide range of ambiguity in Cleopatra. Her character is 'profound' and our feelings of the criminality of her passion (i.e., their illicit love) are 'lessened by our insight into its depth and energy'. He admits, 'The passion itself springs out of the habitual craving of a licentious nature, and [...] is supported and reinforced by voluntary stimulus and sought-for associations, instead of blossoming out of spontaneous emotion.'[9] Yet he asserts it is 'of all perhaps of Shakespeare's plays the most wonderful' due to the energy and style of the writing. The dialogue is undeniably very lively and the story moves on rapidly, unhampered by long speeches – apart from Enobarbus' famous description of the meeting at Tarsus. The language is strong with vivid images and constant sharp interchanges between the characters. This is partly because the historical narrative provides many clashes between the key figures and because the short scenes consistently rush the storyline onwards to new developments.

For Coleridge's contemporary, William Hazlitt, *Antony and Cleopatra* is 'a very noble play'. It is 'the finest of his historical plays' and 'though not in the first class of Shakespeare's productions, it stands next to them'. For him its strength is in making 'poetry the organ of history'. In other words, the power of the poetry brings history alive. The German critic Schlegel applauds Shakespeare's masterful handling of history and feels that the protagonists 'are most emphatically distinguished by lineament and colouring, and powerfully arrest the imagination'. He sees Antony as Hercules enchained by Omphale, 'sunk in luxurious enjoyments and ashamed of his own aberrations'.[10] Cleopatra's 'seductive arts' are openly shown; she is 'an ambiguous being made up of royal pride, female vanity, luxury, inconstancy, and true attachment'. Like them or loathe them, Antony and Cleopatra are interesting, irritating, confusing, to be pitied and to be condemned, but never dull.

Part I

THE INHERITED PAST

Chapter 1

THE HISTORICAL CONTEXT

The Roman Context

The Roman world at the time of the play was in transition. Five centuries before, the Romans had ousted the last king, Tarquin, and established the Republic. Its philosophical/ethical basis was the pursuit of virtue – personal and civic – honour, patriotism, moderation and dedication to the state. In practice, though the people were represented through their spokesmen (the tribunes), the government was largely a monopoly of the patrician families and was subject to intermittent coups by individuals who wanted to rule alone as autocrats. Julius Caesar was the most recent man to achieve sole rule (through victories in Gaul and immense popularity with the people and the army). He had been part of the First Triumvirate (with Crassus and Pompey) and had become sole ruler after the Civil War, which was essentially a power struggle between himself and Pompey, nicknamed 'the Great'. He had dictatorial powers but refused to see himself as a king (or so he said). A group of committed republicans murdered him to pre-empt any move by Caesar to annexe even greater power. In the resulting conflict Antony, a lieutenant, friend, admirer and protégé of Caesar, led reprisals that wiped out the conspirators. This Civil War ended at the Battle of Philippi. He had been seconded, not very effectively, by Octavius Caesar (adopted son of Julius Caesar).[1] They, with Lepidus, formed the Second Triumvirate – splitting the Roman *imperium* (power/state) into three. Antony ruled the East, Lepidus ruled Spain and North Africa, while all the West was Octavius' domain, apart from Sicily, which was occupied by Sextus Pompey (Pompey the Great's son). When Octavius, driven by ambition, self-interest and self-preservation, annexed total sole rule (as he does at the end of the play), he set up a principality, proclaimed himself emperor, renamed himself Augustus and a new era began. So the setting of the play (it covers a ten-year period from

40–30 BC) is the pivotal point at which Octavius is looking to find an excuse to take over individual control. This means that the personal life of Antony and Cleopatra is both the cause and the victim of a crucial political phase in Roman history. As always, Shakespeare uses history to provoke reflections about current concerns in government and shows how history is made by people who not only administer large states but have personal problems and private lives.

The English Context: An Overview

In 1603 Elizabeth I died and James VI of Scotland became James I of England. The play was probably written in 1606, so falls into the Jacobean period (after *Jacobus*, Latin for James). In the wider European literary and political contexts, the period is the waning of the High Renaissance. Historians today call it Early Modern because many features of it are recognizably modern while being early in the evolution that shaped our world.

The new king, ruling until 1625, was of the Scottish family the Stuarts. They were a dynastic disaster. None was an effective king, all were profligate in different ways. Rule, moderation, order and authority were of great concern to the English throughout this time and are key themes in *Antony and Cleopatra*.

James was a learned but flawed monarch. Antony too was well educated, had studied rhetoric in Athens and gradually penetrated the very heart of Roman power. From a privileged family, his contacts were the leading men in the Republic (foremost among them Julius Caesar). Antony was 'born to distinction and glory',[2] but his personality was tainted. Like so many courtiers surrounding James I, he was a spoiled darling of privilege. He was used to satisfying his desires and 'restraint was never a prominent feature in Antony's character'.[3] James had not been indulged as a child, but was surrounded by intrigue (personal and political), murder and mayhem, as was Antony. Sudden access to the wealth and power of England and its Crown was something he was unable to control and administer in a rational way. Surrounded by flatterers and deceivers – both his own countrymen and the English nobility – he was often misled and gave trust to untrustworthy self-seekers. His weakness sexually was not women but handsome and personable young men, but an audience would see similarities between him and Antony.

James shirked the routines of work involved in government, but was not as bad a ruler as Antony, for though he disliked contact with his people, drank heavily, was extravagant, impulsive, tactless, hectoring and bullying, constantly in debt, a hard line right-winger in religion who backed the repression of Catholics and Puritans, and in perpetual conflict with

Parliament, he did not lead his realm into a war lost through mismanagement and strategy based on the whims of a lover. He was dubbed 'the wisest fool in Christendom'.[4] The epithet captures the discrepancy between his writings on political theory and his practice as a lazy man only intermittently engaged with his role. London celebrated with bonfires when he succeeded peacefully. Apparent initial engagement with his regal duties generated a hope that quickly evaporated as his failings and inconsistencies emerged. *Antony and Cleopatra* is underpinned by concerns about authority and rule (or misrule) of self and others. Misrule of self is a theme running through all Shakespeare's plays. Military miscalculation, lack of personal restraint, political naiveté, dishonesty, flattery and scheming are themes running throughout *Antony and Cleopatra* from opening to close. The major characters are guilty of misrule of themselves and each transgresses in some way.

James's predecessor, Elizabeth I, a Tudor, much loved and respected, had been a strong ruler, indeed strong enough to suppress the addressing of many problems which by James's time had become irresolvable. At times a sharply incisive intellect drove her political decisions; at others, caprice and temper made her a dangerous and unreliable force, all the more feared because of her cruelty and absolutism. She, like Cleopatra, always knew where her best interests lay. The Tudors (Henry VII, Henry VIII, Edward VI, Mary I and Elizabeth I), ruling 1485–1603, though dysfunctional and brutally absolutist, successfully brought stability after the turmoil of the Wars of the Roses (though there were various short-lived rebellions against them). Questions of succession, the nature of rulers, the use and limits of monarchical power, the influence of court and the qualities of courtiers were matters that concerned people throughout the period, and are among the contexts of *Antony and Cleopatra*. Religion was the major conflict area,[5] with Dissenters fighting for freedom from tight central control by the new established church and Catholics trying to avoid threats to their worship and, in some cases, actively seeking to topple the Protestant monarch. The effects on society and individual morality of the wealth that the new capitalism and expansion of trade were creating also worried Jacobean writers. This new individualism, another context of the play, emerges in the ruthlessness of Caesar and the sycophants surrounding him.

Henry VIII's great achievement (and cause of trouble) was breaking with the Catholic Church of Rome and setting up an independent English church. This remained Catholic until the reforms of his son Edward VI aligned it with the Protestant movements on the Continent. This period of seismic change is called the English Reformation. There was some limited alliance with the Protestant Reformation led by Martin Luther, but in many ways the English went their own way. Monasteries and convents were dissolved and the infrastructure of Catholicism banished. Altars were stripped of ornaments (leaving only the cross and flanking candles and sometimes not even these), churches emptied of statues and relics and many murals whitewashed over. New church services and prayers were conducted in English rather than Latin. New English translations of the Bible began to appear and there was a Book of Common Prayer to be used in all parish churches. Holy shrines and saints' days were done away with as idols and superstitions. The vicar was to be the only intermediary between a person and God. After the nine-day reign of Lady Jane Grey and a brief fiery and bloody return to Catholicism under Mary I (1553–58), Elizabeth I succeeded and the bedding-in of the new church continued. The freedom of a reformed English religion, supposedly stripped back to its simple original faith, encouraged the rise of more extreme reformist Protestant sects (not always to the liking of the infant Established Church). These groups were called Non-conformists, Independents or Dissenters. They included Puritans, Calvinists and Presbyterians – all Protestant, but with doctrinal differences. Some eccentric sects grew up too, such as the Anabaptists, the Brownists and the Family of Love. Religion and the tensions between different sects is a persistent consideration at this time, but despite all the official changes, the essential beliefs in sin, virtue, salvation, the centrality of Christ and the ubiquity of the Devil (the idea that he was everywhere, looking to tempt man) were the same as they always had been, as were the beliefs that punishment and possible perdition followed sin and that the world was in decline and would shortly come to an end. Though the play is set in pre-Christian times, sin and virtue are present throughout the play for they are linked inextricably with Jacobean expectations of how a leader should behave.

The political discourse concerned with kingship is another persistent feature. Elizabeth I (adoringly nicknamed 'Gloriana' after her identification with a character in Spenser's *Faerie Queene*) ruled 1558–1603, a time long enough to establish her as an icon, particularly as she headed up strong opposition (and victory) against the Spanish. She was much loved by the masses, though individual courtiers had a less than positive experience of her erratic and difficult behaviour.

While external threats were repulsed, the Elizabethan-Jacobean period was one of unstoppable internal changes. These gradually altered the profile and mood of society.[6] Religion, commerce, growing industrialization, increase of manufacture, social relationships, kingship and rule were all in flux. One feature of the period was the unceasing rise in prices, particularly of food, bringing about a decline in the living standards of the poor, for wages did not rise. The rich and the rising middle class could cope with inflation, but the state of the poor deteriorated. Enclosure of arable land (very labour intensive) and its conversion to sheep farming (requiring less labour) raised unemployment among the 'lower orders' or 'baser sort', who constituted the largest proportion (80–85 per cent) of the four to five million population. Rising numbers of poor put greater burdens on Poor Relief in small, struggling rural communities, adding to the elite's fear of some monumental uprising of the disenchanted. Most of the population worked on the land, though increasing numbers were moving to the few existing cities. Later ages looked back on the Elizabethan era as a 'Golden Age' and talked of 'Merry England' – it was not, except for a small section of rich, privileged aristocrats. Also enjoying greater luxury and comfort were canny merchants making fortunes from trading in exotic goods from the 'New Worlds' of Asia and the Americas and those manufacturers making luxury goods for the aristocracy and the increasingly wealthy, acquisitive 'middling sort'. The emotional detachment of the governing classes from awareness of the state of the poor was a resonant feature of contemporary England. On Sunday 13 March 1603, the Puritan divine Richard Stock delivered a Lent sermon at the Pulpit Cross in St Paul's churchyard, commenting: 'I have lived here some few years, and every year I have heard an exceeding outcry of the poor that they are much oppressed of the rich of this city. [...] All or most charges are raised [...] wherein the burden is more heavy upon a mechanical or handicraft poor man than upon an alderman.'[7]

The Jacobean period was quickly perceived as declining from the high points of Elizabeth's time, with worsening of the continuing problems she had been unable or unwilling to rectify during her reign. Economic difficulties, poverty, social conflict, religious dissent and political tensions relating to the role and nature of monarchy and the role and authority of Parliament all remained unresolved. Charismatic, strong rulers like Elizabeth carry their followers with them, generating loyalty though often through an element of fear. Emerging problems are ignored or masked because the ruler prevents them being discussed and councillors are afraid to raise them. Elizabeth, for example, passed several laws that made it treason to even discuss who might succeed her. It is a tenable argument that Cleopatra's volatile wilfulness is not unlike Elizabeth's, while Antony's weakness, his readiness to respond to the latest speaker or to make policy according to the moment's expedience or Cleopatra's whim, is similar to James. A polity needs an active ruler who is engaged with the key problems and day-to-day petty matters of the state and responds according to careful reason, not knee-jerk stopgap needs. Antony's readiness to marry Octavia is a prime example of making impromptu policy to answer an immediate need without thinking of the consequences. Circumspection is a quality expected in a ruler. States need rulers who engage physically and sympathetically with the people, not reclusive scholars who shut themselves up in their libraries (Prospero, *The Tempest*), or governors who are reluctant to exercise punitive laws for fear of losing the people's love (Duke Vincentio, *Measure for Measure*) or who react with cruel autocratic anger when thwarted (King Lear and James I). Contemporaries would have condemned any man who declared:

> Let Rome in Tiber melt, and the wide arch
> Of the rang'd empire fall! Here is my space,
> Kingdoms are clay: our dungy earth alike
> Feeds beasts as man; the nobleness of life
> Is to do thus [...] [*Embracing*]. (I. i. 33–7)

This might be thought of simply as a hyperbolic assertion designed to please a demanding lover, but Antony actually shows such negligence. We never see him administering his huge realm, but hear of him giving away numerous parts of it. Dereliction of duty deserves the loss of privilege and power. Monarchical commitment and a readiness to seek advice were often debated in James's time. In his first speech to Parliament he claimed he was as a husband wedded to England as his bride. It was to be a union in which the husband would bully, boss, insult and generally repress his 'helpmeet'. He would issue a royal proclamation prohibiting the English from discussing 'causes of state'. James's flaws consisted in regular absence from court (most often for hunting), delegation of power, inconsistency and a dictatorial manner. In making decisions of state James relied too much on favourites as advisers, gave them too much power and tended to lecture and bully Parliament rather than consider its input. This high-handed approach encouraged his son to make similar mistakes and would contribute to the unavoidable move towards civil war.

Purposeful, considered central rule dwindled under James into rule by whim and capricious diktat. His court became more decadent and detached from the rest of the population than in his predecessor's time, not dissimilar to Antony's Alexandrian court. Commerce and manufacture expanded rapidly, triggering a rise in the middle class that provided and serviced the new trades and crafts. Attitudes to religion and church authority began developing into resistance, and science began slowly to displace old superstitions and belief in magic. Like all times of transition, the Jacobean period and the seventeenth century in general were exciting times for some but unsettling for most, profitable for a few but a struggle for the majority. As always, the rich found ways to become richer, and the poor became poorer. Gradually the poor found men to speak up for them in the corridors of power, in the villages of England and in the overcrowded streets of the cities. *Antony and Cleopatra* should not be seen as merely a representation of a relatively well-known episode in Roman history. It is a political play deviously masquerading as a love story and is pointedly relevant to its age.

It is also a typical Jacobean play – dark at times, cynical, satirical, violent and psychologically disturbing, hinting at deep character flaws and suspect motives. It is also much concerned with sin and punishment. Though the narrative is tied to the outer world and the business of rule as recorded in history, and though many in the audience already knew the outcome of the conflict with Caesar, the immediate interest is in the characterization of the hero and heroine (both as individuals and as a couple) and how their demise is brought about. The play explores their inner failings and their inner turmoil. The meetings of the triumvirs and the battles are just the screen on which the psychological complexities of Antony and Cleopatra are projected. The inner tragedies are what hold the audience. The grounds for tragedy are built as a potential in the first half, where we see the imperfect characters of the protagonists. Danger appears to have receded when Antony marries Octavia, but may simply have been postponed, as Enobarbus hints: 'He will to his Egyptian dish again' (II. vi. 128). His separation from her then accelerates the action towards his and Cleopatra's speedy downfall. Superficially their deaths are a victory for Caesar, but they are at the same time a triumph for the lovers in that they escape capture and public humiliation, cheating Caesar of his opportunity to exhibit his prizes. They are exalted by their deaths, while he is diminished by them. But at the point where Antony agrees to the marriage and Enobarbus foresees Antony's weakness as triggering open conflict, we have the exciting, suspenseful prospect of a tragedy waiting to happen. Antony soon disabuses any audience member who wonders if the union will avert conflict:

> I will to Egypt;
> And though I make this marriage for my peace,
> I' th' East my pleasure lies. (II. iii. 37–9)

It is foolish in the extreme. These are the actions of a man with a death wish. Antony, shortly after admitting he will reunite with Cleopatra, assures Caesar he need not doubt his fidelity. He knows he is lying, but thinks to outmanoeuvre Caesar; he is politically naive. Caesar, though young, is an experienced Machiavellian. In Jean Anouilh's tragedy *Antigone* the Chorus warns: 'The spring is wound up tight. It will uncoil of itself. [...] The least turn of the wrist will do the job. Anything will set it going [...] and the tragedy is on.'[8] Antony and Cleopatra's tragedy is waiting. Their personal sins, already having been committed, await punishment. The interest now lies in just what they will do to bring on their own downfall and how Shakespeare will stage it. The tragic machine waits throbbing. How horrific and destructive its path will be the audience can only partly imagine, if they already know their Plutarch.

Whether the first performance was to the mixed audience of the Globe or the more select, socially restricted clientele of Blackfriars or the court, the spectators would have found many echoes of the criticisms that were beginning to be made of the new monarch. The court's entertainments – particularly the many masques performed – its fashions, lifestyles and attitudes, indicate a ritualization and artificiality that were fast detaching it from life outside. The public rituals of monarchy are of their nature theatrical, but the day-to-day running of a state is founded in the dullness of bureaucratic minutiae. Antony and Cleopatra's life is one long debauch, a continuous round of drunken feasts and games. It consists of perpetual conspicuous consumption and the never-ending pursuit of novel entertainments to chase away boredom. The trick is to know where the make-believe ends and reality begins. Antony and Cleopatra seem not to know or are unwilling to find out. Their public personae, their narcissistic fantasies of being Isis and Osiris/Dionysus, Venus and Mars, are assimilated into their private lives. Each day is another performance, another self-dramatizing revel. James's court was not far different. Both Antony and Cleopatra display the human face of monarchy, a very human face – weak, vacillating, petty minded, vindictively using power to threaten and punish, and accessing all the pleasures power and wealth provide. It is a portrait in which a Jacobean audience would recognize many features of James I's court.

The new reign and new century were still much overshadowed by the past. Just as Antony's past (his marriage with Fulvia, his appropriation of Pompey's house, his uneasy relationship with Caesar, his own reprobate character, etc.) resonates in his present, so past events resonated in the heads of the audience, while a cluster of new problems were developing outside, in London, in the nation.

Chapter 2

THE ELIZABETHAN WORLD ORDER: FROM DIVINITY TO DUST

The orderliness of the universe reflected God's will, God's plan (as conceived by man). Strict hierarchy (everything having its place according to its importance in God's order) and organic harmony (everything being part of a whole and having a function to perform) were the overriding principles of the broad orthodox background to how the audience thought their universe was structured (cosmology), how they saw God and religion (theology), and how their place in the order of things was organized (sociology). The disorders and disharmonies upsetting roles and expectations in *Antony and Cleopatra* stem from Antony's dereliction of duty, giving rise to disruptions that act as enveloping emblematic metaphors of a world turned upside down. A series of images of reversal, subversion and destruction project a world cracking, sinking, melting, cleaving and overflowing – a world in flux. Such reversals of normal order were unsettling to an audience that lived with a strict etiquette of precedence and whose sense of social order was based upon a highly stratified positioning of everything. They believed disaster was inevitable whenever the order of nature was disrupted.

Everyone was fairly clear where they were in the universal order, the Great Chain of Being. There were three domains: Heaven, Earth and Hell.[1] God ruled all, was omnipotent (all-powerful) and omniscient (all-knowing). Man was inferior to God, Christ, the Holy Ghost, all the angels, apostles, saints, the Virgin Mary and all the blessed, but superior to all animals, birds, fish, plants and minerals. God ruled Heaven, kings (and princes, dukes, counts, etc.) ruled on earth, and fathers ruled families, like God at home. The chain stretched from God through all the hierarchies of existence to the very bottom in descending order of importance – from the divinity to dust – all interconnected as contributory parts of God's creation. The chain links were each a separate group of beings, creatures or objects, each connected to the one before and the one after, semi-separate, dependent but partly independent, both separate and part of something greater. Within each link there was a hierarchy. The human link contained three different ranks – 'the better sort' (monarchs, nobles, gentry), the 'middling sort' (merchants, shopkeepers, farmers) and the 'baser sort' or 'lower orders' (artisans, peasants, beggars). The word 'class' was not used then, but these ranks are equivalent to our upper, middle and lower classes.

Cosmology

Astronomically, medieval and Renaissance man thought of Creation, the cosmos, as an all-enveloping Godliness that incorporated Heaven, the human universe and Hell. The universe was thought of as a set of revolving transparent crystal spheres, one inside the other, and each containing a planet. It was a geocentric model, with the Earth in the middle encased in its sphere, enveloped by the Moon's sphere, then Mercury, Venus, the Sun, Mars, Jupiter and Saturn – like the rings of an onion.[2]

The Ptolemaic system

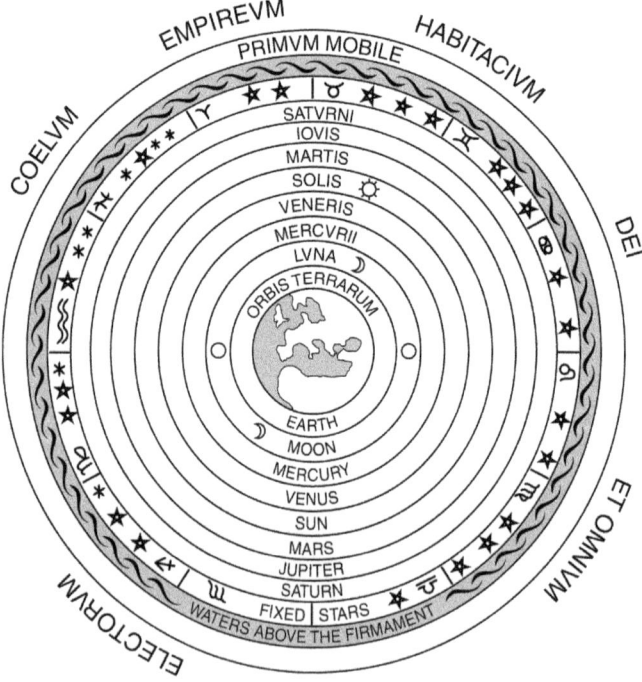

Adapted from engraving for Peter Apian's *Cosmographicus Liber* (*Book of the Universe*, Antwerp 1524). Enclosing the spheres is the 'COELUM EMPIREUM HABITACIUM DEI ET OMNIUM ELECTORUM' (The Empyrean sky, home of God and all the elect – i.e. those judged worthy of Heaven).

Each planet in its sphere circled the earth at different orbital angles and different speeds. The set of concentric crystal balls was imagined by some to hang from the lip of Heaven by a gold chain. After Saturn came the firmament or fixed stars (divided into 12 seasonal zodiac sectors). Outside this were 'the waters above the firmament' (Genesis 1:7). The tenth sphere, the *Primum Mobile* (First Mover), drove the spheres and then came the all-surrounding Empyrean, the domain that was all God's and all God (i.e., Heaven). Here he was accompanied by Christ, the Holy Spirit, the angels, the Virgin Mary, the saints and the blessed. This cosmological organization was the Ptolemaic system formulated by the second century AD Graeco-Egyptian astronomer/geographer Ptolemy (Claudius Ptolemaeus). In Tudor times his *Cosmographia* was still recommended by Sir Thomas Elyot for boys to learn about the spheres.[3]

A man could see the stars and sometimes some of the planets, but not beyond, his vision being blocked by the 'waters'. As the Empyrean, the destination for the virtuous saved, was thus made invisible, people needed a visualizable image. It was easier to imagine the blessed 'living' in a celestial city rather than existing vaguely and spiritually in the heavenly ether, so the idea grew of a fortified city with towers and gates made of different substances. At the Gate of Pearl, St Peter supposedly received each approaching soul, consulted his 'Book of Life', recording all the good and evil a person had done, and decided if the soul was worthy of entry. Medieval painters show the *Civitatis Dei* (City of God) as resembling the walled cities of Italy, France or Germany. Painters often simply depicted the city they knew.[4]

By Shakespeare's time the Ptolemaic system was beginning to be undermined. The great Copernican revolution, supported by Galileo, Kepler and others, put the sun at the heart of the universe. This idea entered the public domain with Copernicus' study *De Revolutionibus Orbium Coelestium* (*On the Revolutions of the Celestial Spheres*, 1542), but was only slowly accepted by scientists and took even longer to filter down to ordinary people. Dissemination was impeded by church repression and the difficulties of communication at the time. In 1603 Sir Christopher Heydon, displaying his knowledge of the new advances, declared: 'Whether (as Copernicus saith) the sun be the centre of the world, the astrologer careth not.'[5] This references the triple belief system in which most people lived: 1. Christian doctrine existing uneasily alongside, 2. the new astronomy and sciences, and 3. old semi-magical beliefs in the authenticity of astrology. Heliocentrism, opposed by the scepticism of some astronomers (like John Dee), was frighteningly repressed by dogmatic, authoritarian churches. The Catholic Church's Inquisition enforced conformity persuasively with thumbscrews, the rack and many other grisly tortures. The English church had its own courts to question and punish deviations from customary practice and belief; visitations within their diocese enabled bishops to keep vicars and congregations in line and serious infractions could be brought before the Star Chamber.[6] Torture was endemic in England too.

Other beliefs concerning the structure of our world were being transformed. Magellan's circumnavigation of the world without falling off the edge (1522), showed the flat earth theory was inaccurate. Drake's 1580 voyage brought this home more directly to British people when the Queen permitted an exhibition to publicize his discoveries. A map displayed at Whitehall Palace made the spherical world graphically clear. But how many people saw it? Shakespeare knew of the new development in thinking about the world's shape as evidenced by Puck's referring to putting 'a girdle round about the earth' (*A Midsummer Night's Dream*, 1595–96) and Lear's demand the gods 'strike flat the thick rotundity of the earth' (*King Lear*, 1606). To most people, unenlightened by new discoveries, Earth's roundness and the centrality of the sun were unimportant and perhaps still unknown. In an age when the nearest town was often as alien as the moon, 'New Worlds' were places of fantasy and nightmare, inhabited by unnatural beings like the cannibal *anthropophagi*, 'men whose heads/Do grow beneath their shoulders' (*Othello* I. iii. 144–5) and a whole bestiary of strange animals.[7] As long as the sun rose to grow and ripen corn and fruit and assist them in telling the time and the season, most people were indifferent. The centre of their universe was their village. The ordinary farmer would know the stars and some of the planets but thought of them as belonging to the mystical world of superstition, astrology, weather lore and magic rather than to the measurable world of science and astronomy.

The Great Chain of Being

There were thought to be three domains of existence: Heaven, Earth and Hell. Earthly creation was thought to be arranged in a set of hierarchical links that made the world order. Man was at the top, followed by animals, birds, fish, plants, minerals. Each stratum of existence was internally organized in order of importance. Humans were organized with monarchs at the top down through the ranks to beggars. Man, the pinnacle of God's animal creation, was not entirely perfect. Flawed by Original Sin, with animal weaknesses and negative passions, he was nevertheless part angel, endowed with soul, reason, language, intelligence and sensitivity. A human acting morally was an imitation of Christ. Choosing the left-hand way, the path of sin, he resembled the Devil. The conflict between these two aspects made man an angel with horns, but the tensions between virtue and passion, the perpetual *psychomachia*[8] of life, sparked the interest of literature.

The Great Chain of Being, a construct of human imagining, helped people from the early medieval period to the Renaissance picture how the universe was put together socially and how it worked physically. It was a general view still held by the majority of people in Shakespeare's time, though its physical structure was increasingly challenged by new astronomical research and by socio-economic changes. Most people still thought the universe geocentric (Earth-centred). The Renaissance is regarded as a time of change, new learning and new knowledge. Men were discovering new lands and new ways of thinking about God and society, but this only slowly affected everyday life. The iconoclastic, rationalist, free-thinking Renaissance Man, daringly breaking through barriers and questioning old orthodoxies, was an oddity often in conflict with the authorities. Such men were confined to small minority groups of progressive artist/scientists/intellectuals.[9] Seventeenth-century Everyman was conservative and backward-looking in his beliefs and daily lifestyle. If literate, he would have few books apart from a Bible, though religious pamphlets and many sorts of non-fiction and fiction books were becoming available.[10] He still went to the wise woman for semi-magical medical help, believed in divination, went to an astrologer to predict a suitable day for travelling or a suitable mate, and still believed the Chain of Being was constructed by God.

Hierarchically arranged, reflecting descending importance, usefulness and perfection, the chain was sometimes imagined instead as a ladder, a ladder of nature (*scala naturae*). The ladder image was agreeable to Christian thinkers because it suggested rising towards the divine (or descending towards perdition), as each person was supposed to do by a life of virtue that would cleanse away their earthly faults, purifying them as they metaphorically rose rung by rung to a holiness that prepared their soul for Heaven. Walter Hilton's *The Ladder of Perfection* (written between 1386 and 1396), reflects in its title the image of the step-by-step rise from sin to virtue, presented as a spiritual journey towards the peace given by Christ and the peace which was Christ. He is the perfection achieved in climbing the ladder, reached by denying the primacy of the 'anti-Trinity' of mind, reason and will, and trusting faith alone.[11] In the busy, corrupt world of London in1606, the same belief persisted among the godly sort. These were not just fervent Puritan zealots, but those ordinary folk who believed their Christian duty was to live the good life. The good life meant not the carnal life of fleshly pleasures, but the hard-working, devoted and devout life of the family man or woman, whose days were struggled through with the example of Christ as their perpetual model. It is important not to underplay the general piety of most people at this time. They listened regularly to preachers of different sorts and attended church regularly. The literate bought, borrowed, read or had read to them more and more of the religious pamphlets pouring off the presses. Printed pamphlet production accelerated from a trickle in 1600 to a flood by the Civil War.[12] Though they lived physically 'by the rule of the flesh', as St Augustine put it, they were dominated by 'the rule of the spirit'.[13] While many lived dedicated Christian lives, many others lived at various intermediate stages ranging from occasionally lapsing piety to a more sinful existence, less concerned with virtue than bodily pleasures, and shading down towards outright irreligion and criminality. This vast spectrum was much represented in the City Comedies of the 1600s and in the Revenge Tragedies of the 1580s to 1630s. Shakespeare's Problem Plays (*Troilus and Cressida*, 1601–02; *All's Well That Ends Well*, 1602–04; *Measure for Measure*, 1604), his late Romances (*Pericles*, 1608–09; *Cymbeline*, 1609–10; *The Winter's Tale*, 1610–11; *The Tempest*, 1611) and above all his tragedies are all concerned with the ethical complexities and ambiguities provoked by the tensions between flesh and spirit. *Antony and Cleopatra*, a tragedy of sorts, addresses questions of conduct in areas that were of great contemporary interest. The audience's responses will have largely been made within the Christian, Bible-based context that constituted everyone's background, but attached to it would be a century of theoretical writings about the nature of kingship.

Chain or ladder equally suggest unbroken interconnection between all the many phases of created existence between the Creator and dust. Originating in the pre-Christian philosophy of Plato and Aristotle, this idea of hierarchies reflects a Western obsession with taxonomy (classification). Medieval Christian theology assimilated the heavenly hierarchy to fit above the feudal system of human society and the descending levels of the rest of creation. Below earthly life (physically and morally) came the hierarchy of Hell, traditionally thought to be in the bowels of the earth. Dante (1321) placed it below Gehenna, the rubbish dump outside Jerusalem.[14] The orderliness of God's creation was so imbedded in people's minds that any disassembling it was like an attack on the foundations of life and faith. Order was part of everything and the maintenance of order was a form of worship, an acceptance of God as author of that order. Disorder or any threat to established hierarchy was like loosing the legions of Hell. Within each dominion – Heaven, Earth and Hell – there was a series of graduated structures. In Christian thought the domains of Heaven and Hell, equivalents of the classical world's Olympus (home of the ancient gods) and Hades (the underworld, the place of the dead), had their inhabitants ranked according to priority and power like the various types of earthly creation. All three realms had rulers and below them were ranks of diminishing power and diminishing virtue. This was 'a society obsessed with hierarchy'.[15]

Hierarchy of Heaven: God > Christ > the Holy Ghost > Seraphim > Cherubim > Thrones > Dominations > Principalities > Powers > Virtues > Archangels > Angels > the Virgin Mary > the disciples > the saints > the blessed (saved, elect, good souls admitted to Heaven after a virtuous life)[16]

Saints were still intermittently prayed to as intercessors for specific concerns in Protestant England. Though the Church disapproved, having banished such idolatry, it takes generations to change a mindset that has for centuries been integral to thought and belief.

Hierarchy of Earth: Man > animals > birds > fish > plants > rocks/minerals

Hierarchy of Hell: Devil/Lucifer/Satan > first hierarchy (Hell's 'nobility'): named devils like Beelzebub, Mephistophelis, Mammon, Belial, etc. > second hierarchy: demons > goblins > imps > incubi/succubi[17] > familiars

Familiars are spirits controlled by a witch/wizard and acting as an assistant. Often they are in animal form. A black cat is commonly thought to be the standard witch's demon familiar, but records include black frogs, dogs and toads. They could take human shape too. Seventeenth-century witch confessions regularly describe a good-looking, blond-haired young man, but with giveaway cloven hoofs. A familiar attached to a necromancer/witch was thought to be a malevolent servant/assistant imp/demon, a limb of Satan, sometimes even Satan himself. If it was benevolent and assisted a white wizard/cunning woman it was sometimes called a fairy. The latter could have mischievous tendencies, like Puck in *A Midsummer Night's Dream*. They could appear as three-dimensional forms or remain invisible.

Human society was arranged in three main ranks, degrees or orders: the 'better sort', the 'middling sort' and the 'lower orders' ('commoners' or 'baser sort'). It was thought those of highest rank were there by the grace of God and were therefore automatically more virtuous. They certainly thought themselves superior and were encouraged to think themselves better than those below them. This view was endorsed by a classical text they would have studied at university, Aristotle's *Nichomachean Ethics*. Among the conclusions in his closing section they would have found these views 'with regard to virtue':

> While [arguments] seem to have power to encourage and stimulate the generous-minded among our youth, and to make a character who is gently born, and a true lover of what is noble, ready to be possessed

by virtue, they are not able to encourage the *many* to nobility and goodness. For these do not by nature obey the sense of shame, but only fear, and do not abstain from bad acts because of their baseness but through fear of punishment.[18]

This ignores the fact that many elite men did wrong because they knew they could evade penalty by buying off the law, by family influence or by the psychological pressure they could put on the subordinate majority. By the Jacobean period, other views were voiced. Dante had defined nobility in terms of conduct and 'gentillesse', not rank.[19] Castiglione highlights this too when, during a discussion on what makes the best sort of courtier, he has Pallavicino remark that while some 'of the most noble blood, have been wicked in the extreme' there were 'many of humble birth, who, through their virtues, have won glory for their descendants'.[20] Conduct is the determinant of true nobility, not a family tree and fancy titles. It suited the better sort to think the lower orders naturally sinful, the middle ranks dour, pious money-grubbers. They somehow thought it justified their snobbery and bullying of such lesser mortals and did not see it as a slur upon their honour. In practice such attitudes persisted despite Humanism's attempts to introduce more enlightened thinking.

The three-tier medieval feudal system (those who fight, those who pray, those who work) was refined in the Renaissance. The remaining clergy ranks, 'those who pray', diminished by the Dissolution of the Monasteries, were assimilated into the upper ranks. 'Those who work' were split into 'the middling sort' and 'commoners'. The former included the important expanding new masses of bourgeois entrepreneurs (bankers, projectors [speculators], merchants, wealthy clothiers, industrial manufacturers, etc.) that had hardly existed before, but which were driving the astonishing explosion of culture and commerce that was the Renaissance. As money and investment spread through the arteries of European trading, so the bourgeoisie expanded. This rising class was to be *the* vital feature in Elizabethan-Jacobean social change, hugely increasing the numbers of the 'middling sort', creating confusion about whether powerful 'merchant princes' and 'captains of industry' belonged within the middling rank or among the better sort.[21] In Roman times the stratification was simpler. The 'better sort' or patricians had money, family history and power. They monopolized positions of power, governed, and provided the priests and the officer elite in the army. They liked to think of themselves as representing the core values of the Republic: the virtues of public service, of community before self, of courage and honour. (The truth was mostly rather different by the time of Octavius, as the huge wealth of Rome encouraged selfishness, decadence, luxury and chicanery.) Below but linked to them were the *equites*, men who could afford to buy and keep a horse. They were like the gentry but often were wealthy middle-class merchants and entrepreneurs. At the bottom was the mass, the mob, the plebeians. These were made up of the *cives* (citizens), freedmen (slaves who had been emancipated) and huge numbers of slaves (foreigners, usually prisoners of war). We see some of these in *Antony and Cleopatra*. The *cives* were mostly peasant labourers, small farmers, servants, artisans and the denizens of cities. The 'middling sort' was a narrow band of merchants, physicians, lawyers and shopkeepers. The plebeians appear in the play as ordinary soldiers, palace servants and the clown (countryman) who brings the asps to Cleopatra. The main characters are high-end, privileged and powerful people – men of family. This is a play about people of high degree and there is no one in it (not even Enobarbus) who is untarnished as to conduct. In this respect it is in keeping with all the dramas of Shakespeare's last works, in which the corruption of the governing ranks is exposed.[22]

In general terms, in Jacobean times, the old, simple world of the Middle Ages (unified in religion by Catholicism and unified socially by the feudal system) was morphing into dynamic new forms. Rising wealth created new types of employment and developing industries created new roles and services. The broad social stratifications were still the same, but within them the three levels were diversifying into complex new types, while social/political/commercial interactions were changing in destabilizing, disturbing ways with which many could not easily cope. These social changes destabilized traditional values. This conflict between the old world and the newly emergent one is reflected in *Antony and Cleopatra*. Caesar represents the coldly calculating, ruthless modern man reaching for power, while Antony is stuck in an older tradition of a politically inept, self-indulgent leisured class. Similar distinctions were evident in England and in the court. Distanced in time and culture, the story enabled Shakespeare to address contemporary problems without appearing to offend anyone. Even Enobarbus is compromised by the failure of the old values of virtue and loyalty. This failure is triggered by the deteriorating effect of contact with the East. That is not to say that the Roman Republic did not have its liars and yes-men, its political machinations and hypocrisies. The new, self-obsessed ruthlessness of some in James's court (like Robert Cecil and Sir Francis Bacon) is reflected in Caesar's calculating use of his sister to achieve what might be a politically useful alliance or a handy excuse for bringing conflict to a head. James's court is there too in the docile sycophants with moveable morals represented in Maecenas, Dolabella and Thidias. As Jonson did in his tragedy *Sejanus* (1603), Shakespeare uses the dangerous Roman world of greed, assassinations and power politics as a correlative for the English court. The state of official corruption was highlighted in the oration delivered to James on his arrival in the city. It demanded, 'No more shall bribes blind the eyes of the wise, nor gold be reputed the common measure of a man's worth.' The burden of monopolies, generating taxes that went into the pockets of the monopoly owner and not into the national revenue, was described as 'most odious and unjust' and sucking the marrow out of the life of the people. The legal profession too was indicted: 'Unconscionable lawyers and greedy officers shall no longer spin out the poor man's cause in length to his undoing and the delay of justice.' The speaker, Richard Stock, demanded benefices no longer be sold, the nobility be encouraged to shoulder their responsibilities to the poor, and placemen rebuked for their 'abuse [of] the authority of his Majesty to their private gain and greatness.'[23] Ironically, the spur to these pointed demands was the recent republication of James's own book on kingship.[24] Seven copies were published in Edinburgh for private circulation in 1598, but James had thousands reprinted in London on his accession. Each false step in Antony's slow-motion fall from power would trigger connections with the principles promulgated in James's book. The levity, luxurious spectacle and sexual decadence (of Charmian, Iras, Mardian, Alexas and the Alexandrian court), and the deceptions and half truths of Caesar's dealings with Pompey and Antony, would provoke echoes of Whitehall. The readiness of Mardian, Alexas and others to take advantage of the unwary, unthrifty wastefulness of Antony and Cleopatra reflects the warnings Richard Stock made. Delivered on behalf of the Sheriffs of London and Middlesex, the speech warns against those that 'mean to sell the king to his subjects at their owne price and [...] who perswaded him, that to shut himself up from the access of his people, is the meanes to augment his state.'[25]

Human Hierarchy: The Social Pyramid of Power

Each man was placed within different hierarchies relating to 1. society in general, 2. work and 3. family. It is usual to see human hierarchies as layered pyramids. This simple sociological model classifies according to priority, power and function. First you had a place in one of the three ranks in the social pyramid. Every rank had its internal hierarchy, its duties and its role to play. At work you were in another pyramid, where position depended on age, experience, seniority, qualification and success. Within the family pyramid an unmarried man was subordinate to his father and other male elders. Once married, he was still subordinate within his extended patrilineal family but ruled his own nuclear family – wife, children and servants.

For each of these social structures obedience to those above was paramount, resistance to change was the default attitude and threats to order were seen as blasphemy, defying God's arrangement. Those with most to lose were most

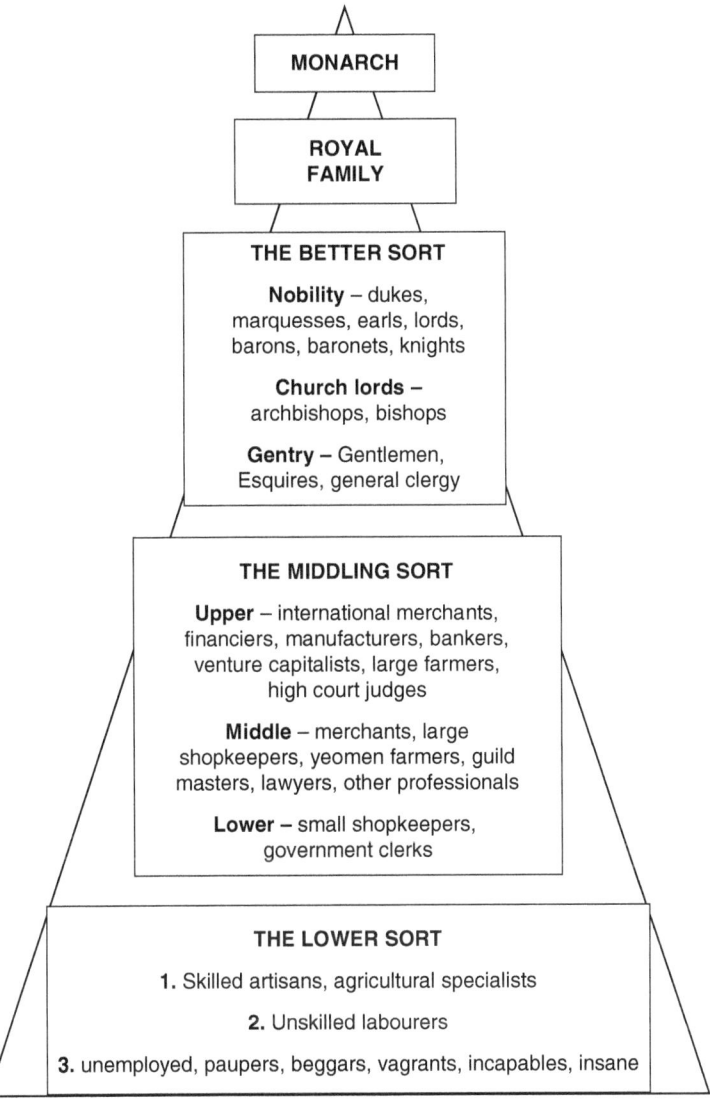

in favour of things staying the same and so in history and literature noblemen and kings promote order and hierarchy as ordained by God; it was not to be overthrown. Maintaining the status quo guaranteed the perpetuation of their power and privilege. The Bible, as so often, authorizes this view: 'Remember them that have the rule over you' (Hebrews 13:7) and the Commandment 'Honour thy father and thy mother'. Antony's conduct persistently raises the question of whether he is fit to rule. He subverts hierarchy at the very top of the pyramid. Betrayal (of family, country or liege lord) was not only a damnable sin but carried resonant overtones given recent history. Betraying your rank and the duties that came with it was equally dishonourable.

At the pyramid's pinnacle the ruler reflected God's dominance. The idea of Divine Right is founded on the belief that kings are chosen by God as his representatives on earth. The sermon preached at James's coronation by the Bishop of Winchester, asserted:

> God ordained the power of men over other men, & with manifest words authorized Rulers to take and keep their places. [...] Their authority is derived from GOD, resembling his image; Their dignitie is allowed of GOD [...]. They are the gods by Office, Ruling, Judging, and Punishing in Gods steede, & so deserving Gods name here on earth.[26]

This endows monarchs with immense psychological (or superstitious) influence. If you tell a superstitious people often enough that kings are semi-divine, they eventually come to believe it. As God's vice-regent a king could no more be questioned, tried, imprisoned or executed than you might think of questioning or dethroning God. James, like Antony at times, could become aggressively angry when opposed or ragingly jealous (as Antony does over Thidias in Act III, Scene xiii). James began increasingly to think of himself as a god in a manner disturbingly close to megalomaniac mental instability. The king's will was sufficient for anything to be done unquestioningly by willing courtiers. It was the magic password for absolute power, though increasingly James found his will thwarted, often because there was no money to execute it, but increasingly because Parliament opposed him. Here we encounter the uneasy tension between the divine aura attributed to kings and the daily experience of their human failings. Antony has generated the loyalty of some officers and legionaries, has a reputation among his men for courage, endurance and occasional generosity, but his recent foolish military tactics and dishonourable personal behaviour causes them to question his loyalty to them and to Rome. This forces some of them to desert him, isolating him, making him a figure with whom an audience may sympathize. He behaves sometimes as an egotistical autocrat, but more often as a rampaging bull or drunken buffoon who assumes his big character will simply drag everyone after him in amazed adoration. He does as he wishes (as long as it suits Cleopatra). The night before his final battle he celebrates with 'one more gaudy night'. Is this military wisdom? Even he acknowledges 'my fortunes have/Corrupted honest men' (IV. v. 16–17). Given the ritualistic, emotional reverence accorded to monarchs (and as triumvir Antony is like a king or emperor), customary obedience to hierarchical superiors and the range of arbitrary punishments James had shown himself willing to mete out to those who crossed him, the audience would probably see links between Antony and the king's sometimes harsh absolutism and undignified behaviour.

The better sort

Below the king came the royal family, the nobility and gentry. The descending ranks of the nobility (dukes, marquesses, earls, viscounts, barons, baronets and knights) were highly stratified, jealously preserving distinctions of precedence. This upper section included archbishops and bishops, men of immense power and wealth. The 'better sort', the 'quality', was the governing elite. What did they actually do? Some titled aristocrats were ministers, privy councillors, government officers, MPs, army or navy officers (when there was a war), or local magistrates.[27] Those with estates might manage them (though probably a steward did the day-to-day managing). They were essentially idle, a leisured class pursuing their own pleasures (hunting, gambling, drinking, whoring and lounging about at court), owning huge swathes of land, living off rents, a do-nothing aristocracy doing nothing – or not very much. Yet they had clear social duties as outlined in the Corporal and Spiritual Works of Mercy (see Chapter 4).

Part of the upper sort, but untitled, was the gentry – men eligible to be called esquires and gentlemen. They were ranked – upper, middle and lower – according to size of fortune, size of landholding, civic profile and ancientness of family title. Because many of the older generation of gentry families lived in the country they effectively ruled vast areas of the nation. As Sir Walter Raleigh put it, 'The gentry are the garrisons of good order throughout the realm.'[28] Increasingly there were younger men who never had an estate (or had lost it through debt) but who called themselves gentlemen on the grounds of having (or having had) some sort of independent means, university education, officer rank, skill with weapons, no need (or intention) to work for a living, gentry parents or a coat of arms. The City Comedies of Dekker, Middleton, Heywood and Jonson are filled with impoverished gentlemen, living on the edge of high society, scrounging meals and hustling for an heiress or favour at court.

The distinguishing material feature of the nobility and gentry was land ownership. Estates meant tenants (farmers and land workers) paying rents. Rent rolls provided the basic, unearned family income. Estates also meant farm produce and timber to be sold. Increasingly the landed nobility invested in speculative ventures in industrial manufacturing, commerce, in the natural resources on their land and in foreign venture capitalism. Many titled men held sinecure government posts (requiring little actual work), enabling them to sell other places to family members, friends and political contacts who formed an obligated clientage. This nepotism (giving jobs to relatives), once a sin, now accepted, added to the growing grievances about court and government corruption.[29] Wealth could be materially improved if the monarch gave or sold you a monopoly, giving you control of the taxes and other charges on a commodity or service, like imports of wine, tobacco, sugar or starch.[30] This provided further opportunities for selling posts within the infrastructure. The upper sort thought themselves superior in virtue, born with innate leadership abilities and better moral qualities than other ranks. *Probitas* (physical and moral courage) was believed to pass through the male bloodline (a reason for ensuring the legitimacy of your heir), giving each generation the qualities of prowess, honour and magnanimity. Noble in rank, supposedly noble, courageous and generous in nature, they thought themselves deserving of respect from all below them. They were the contemporary evolution of the medieval warrior class, now demilitarized and without apparent function. Many were fine and decent people, living on their estate and doing their social-moral duties. Many others were simply weak personalities, extravagant, in debt, idle, sexually decadent, syphilitics, drunks, fools, inveterate gamblers and incompetent estate managers, indifferent to their role as social exemplars and leaders. James did nothing to encourage reform. Antony is a Roman version of this aristocratic, privileged group, with access to power by birth and rank and a tendency to idleness and decadent conduct.

The discrepancies between the expected conduct of the upper ranks and how they actually behaved were regular targets for satire. Knowing how to behave and actually conducting themselves decorously, respectfully and modestly were two different matters. A similar problem had emerged in Rome. The sons of old families, often with no civic role, had access to money through a paternal allowance, inheritance or moneylenders, and were a sexually active, alcohol-fuelled, antisocial force thronging the city. The poets Horace and Juvenal, among others, satirized the decadent lifestyle of such young men. Antony had early shown a predilection for such roistering, a characteristic he continued to display in what should have been his maturity. Running after the latest fashion or innovation was a feature of Roman life as it was of Jacobean city life, fed by leisure and the expanding availability of luxury goods; huge fortunes were made in Rome as the empire expanded and in London as commerce and capitalism took hold. Decadent behaviour was encouraged too by the increasingly closed nature of the court as a separate world in a protected bubble. In Antony, a favourite of several men before Julius Caesar, the Jacobean audience would see the spoiled darlings of Whitehall like Sir Robert Carr, the first of a number of young men privileged by King James's special notice.

Contemporary plays are full of men claiming gentlemanly status but behaving badly. Drunken, roistering, lecherous misconduct highlights serious discrepancies between the expected behaviour of aristo-gentry men and their actual comportment.³¹ Inconsistently, bad behaviour often co-existed with oversensitivity to offences to their honour. Reacting to the slightest perceived insult to their conceived status and the respect they believed it deserved, the response was usually angry and violent. In an age when gentlemen habitually wore swords, the ready resort to arms was all too easy, especially when alcohol played its part in the constant outbreaks of street and tavern brawls and court incidents. This gives a topical context to the swaggering braggadocio of the Montagu/Capulet bravo boys of *Romeo and Juliet*. Jacobeans were obsessed with genealogy and proving the ancientness of their noble or gentry origins. Pride of rank was a sin if excessive. Many family trees, however, were fabricated, claiming descent from Norman knights, Saxon thegns, the pre-Roman Trojan roots claimed for the British nobility by pseudo-historians like Geoffrey of Monmouth, even from Old Testament kings. Suitable payment to the College of Heralds bought you an 'authenticated' coat of arms and genealogy. Audiences knew full well that young men of titled or gentry background often behaved like rowdy boors, and that some of them were currently watching the play – or probably ogling the female spectators. In the 1600 City Comedy *Eastward Ho!* Francis Quicksilver claims gentlemanly status because his mother was a gentlewoman and his father a senior Justice of the Peace. He feels it is beneath him to be apprenticed to a goldsmith, and spends his time drinking, whoring and scamming money out of other gallants.³² To him idleness, drunkenness, violence and carelessness over money are gentlemanly markers:

> Do nothing […]. Be idle […]. Wipe thy bum with testons [sixpences; approximately 5p], and make ducks and drakes with shillings [10p]. […] As I am a gentleman born, I'll be drunk, grow valiant, and beat thee.'³³

Golding, the industrious apprentice, scorns Quicksilver as 'a drunken whore-hunting rake-hell' (I. i. 125). Sexual licence was common in the elite. A 'rake-hell' was a troublemaker and alludes to the gang mentality and hooliganism of the many unsupervised, upper-class young men floating around London.

Despite the intense stratification of society, dividing lines between groups were becoming blurred by individual cases of social mobility, the proliferation of new knights, growing bourgeois wealth and the increasing complexity of society. People became obsessively fussy about precedence, about being treated according to their rank and preserving fine differences that made them feel superior. Ambition is a subset of pride or vanity, so overambition is seen as pushy, selfish and sinful. A little ambition was proper use of your God-given talents. However, to avoid the *hubris* of becoming too proud of advancement, you should humbly thank God for the good fortune of your rise, downplaying the extent and effect of your own efforts.

Political theorists and moral polemicists formulated programmes emphasizing the upper ranks' duty to serve the state and the people. Elyot's *The Boke Named the Governour* (1531) proposed careful education combining a reverence for virtue and a readiness to assume social responsibilities. This meant residing on your estate, leading the community, helping the poor, and establishing schools and alms houses, as enshrined in the Corporal and Spiritual Works of Mercy. These good works justified living comfortably off income derived from the labours of tenant farmers and tenant labourers. Rank and privilege were counterbalanced by a requirement to put something back into the community, but one of the features of the growing new individualism was that civic spirit and charitable work were discarded by elite young men. This was assisted by the growing tendency of the governing class to gravitate to London and become detached from their locality. A responsible role for the ruling classes, built upon a virtue-based humanist education, was promulgated by many writers throughout the decades leading to the Civil War, but the actual behaviour of many gentlemen conformed more to Viscount Conway's definition: 'We eat and drink and rise up to play and this is to live like a gentleman; for what is a gentleman but his pleasure?'[34] The pursuit of personal pleasures dulled the ability or willingness to make moral distinctions, if they threatened enjoyment. The audience witness nothing of Antony or Cleopatra administering justice or addressing social problems, only their excessive pursuit of pleasure.

The middling sort

The next layer down is the newly enlarged bourgeoisie or 'middling sort'. In the Middle Ages, the feudal system included them with 'those who work' (anyone earning a living – 90 per cent in medieval times). This group had comprised everyone from day labourers to the wealthiest merchant. By the Renaissance the rank split to differentiate between the manual labourer or artisan forming the baser sort and a commercial, entrepreneurial bourgeoisie, the middling sort. The country arrangement was village centred with the lord of the manor or a local gentleman (living in or near the village) governing and guarding his 'flock' of farmers and labourers like a shepherd guards and guides his sheep. The workers lived in or near the village, where the priest represented 'those who pray'. The professional 'middling sort' (lawyers, doctors, produce factors, clothiers, etc.) hardly existed in country areas, tending to cluster in towns, and were numerically an insignificant demographic nationally. By the Renaissance the pattern had changed.

With the growth of commerce and in the size and number of towns, the 'service' industries expanded and with them the numbers of the bourgeoisie. Although 80 per cent of the population was still rural – farmers and labourers – 15 per cent were now largely town-dwelling middle class. The remaining 5 per cent was the aristo-gentry which had absorbed the clergy, whose numbers were drastically cut by the Dissolution of the Monasteries. The upper ranks thought the middling sort were greedy, obsessed with making money, virtuous enough, but lacking taste, elegance and culture. They were mocked as 'cits' (citizens or city dwellers – i.e., not landowners), derided as social climbers whose wives and daughters were snobbish, fashion mad, empty-headed, and easy prey for lascivious, gold-digging courtiers. Some were like that, but many were educated, cultivated people, looking after their families (especially their children) better than many of the nobility. Most were hard working, eager to put a comfortable buffer between themselves and poverty, but modest in lifestyle and personal behaviour. They showed civic spirit, were pious and drove conservative church reform.

The rise of the middling sort was *the* big social change in Elizabethan-Jacobean England. Division into upper, middle and lower classifications distinguishes between, say, a very rich international merchant, the farmer of a thriving farm and a small shopkeeper. The upper echelons were merchant bankers, financiers, large-scale traders, major clothiers, wealthy manufacturers, leading lawyers and judges, and large-scale farmers – men of wealth and local (and increasingly national) power. The middle group would be comfortably wealthy merchants and masters of guild trades, living in cathedral cities and market towns. The lower 'middling sort' were small shopkeepers, small farmers who owned a little land, and growing numbers of low-paid metropolitan-based government clerks. What differentiated between the upper, middle and lower 'middling sort' was money. More money meant access to mayorships, masterships of guilds and alderman or councillor status. Money brought the capacity to invest in speculative enterprises and loan cash, thus becoming a sort of local banker or simply a moneylender. Usury (lending money at interest), a sin in medieval times, was acceptable by the seventeenth century, a natural development of the growing cash richness of the expanding commercial world. As the economy grew and fortunes were made and wasted, satire against moneylenders, money-amassing citizens and the debt-fuelled lifestyles of parasite gentlemen became regular features in contemporary plays.

The middle ranks looked up to the aristo-gentry and showed public respect. Privately they thought themselves morally better than the upper sort. Pious, hard working, earning their living, living moderately, paying their debts, establishing schools and hospitals, doing civic duties, and giving their children disciplined home lives, education and love, they saw the gentry and nobility as vain, idle, showy wastrels, parading in silks they did not pay for, gambling, drinking, acting promiscuously and demanding deference not always deserved. Yet, many merchants longed to rise and put on the outer show of gentlemanly status – a fine country house, a coach and horses, fashionable clothes and social power. 'The old English gentry were powerfully reinforced [...] by an influx from the professional and mercantile classes. Lawyers, government officials, and successful merchants bought land not only to better their social standing but also to increase their incomes.'[35] These social conflicts do not appear in *Antony and Cleopatra*. There was a merchant class in ancient Rome, but they do not appear in the play, which is essentially focused on the power struggles of privileged, ruling patricians.

As England became a more active trading nation the middle class expanded and became wealthier and more upwardly mobile. Those at the very top could be awarded or buy titles. They tended also, with this status rise, to move into the country, selling their business, cutting themselves off from the taint of trade or distancing themselves from it by hiring a manager. Legislation restricting bourgeois land ownership was increasingly ignored or circumvented. The bourgeoisie was unstoppable, buying estates, thinking themselves equal to the nobility; some even became nobility. Money power enabled such men to push out the cash-strapped yeoman farmer. Agricultural depression led to many of these freemen, who owned their own farm, selling up to opportunist incoming merchants-turned-landowners looking to add to their holdings. Small, independent farmers were also under pressure from some gentry augmenting their estate.[36] Another expanding bourgeois group was made up of top civil servants administering the proliferating departments of government. The three most prestigious power posts were those of Lord Treasurer, Lord Chancellor and the King's Secretary. These were political as well as royal household appointments. Below them was another internal pyramid of court power – the bureaucrats – reaching down to the lowliest 'base pen clerks'.[37] The most junior dreamed of catching the eye of a superior or a titled courtier and being promoted. Once in a higher place your future was made. Place was gained by patrimony, patronage or purchase. A poor clerk without family connections or money to help him advance had to find a patron. It was difficult to penetrate 'the grand efflorescence of nepotism' if you could not buy promotion or inherit a post from your father.[38] The court was awash with idle young men seeking opportunities for advancement. In *Eastward Ho!* the idle apprentice, Quicksilver, cast off by his irate master, declares, 'I'll to the Court, another manner of place for maintenance [...] than the silly City!' (II. ii. 54–5). Such bureaucrats and yes-men were part of the ruling hierarchy of Roman patricians, and the parasite, looking for advancement, was a stock figure of Roman comedy.

If your courtier-patron had some measure of power you were made. In the plots, counterplots and intrigues of the Jacobean court there are innumerable examples of servants ready to bear false witness, cheat, slander or kill to get on. An aspect of Antony's rule in the East was his reluctance to oversee the behaviour of his officials. Placeholders turning blind eyes to local injustice in return for cash payments gave his administration a bad name. Corrupt practices in Jacobean England are a common target in plays because James never bothered to reform them.

The lower orders

The mass of the population formed the broad base layer of the pyramid. Skilled artisans were at the top along with farm workers with a specialism (shepherds, horse men, cattle men, etc.). Apprentices, learning a trade or craft, would count themselves as being in the middle of the lower orders, but with diligence and industry aspired to move into guild membership and shop ownership, thus becoming bourgeois. Below was the mass of unskilled labourers, with the unemployed, paupers, beggars, vagrants, the insane and the incapable at the very bottom. Farm labourers were severely squeezed at this time. Many, like their urban counterparts, were unskilled and the work intermittent rather than permanent. They were hired by the day and vulnerable to weather and the seasonal nature of some work. Prices rose steeply throughout both Elizabeth's and James's reigns, but wages did not. Common land, where game could be caught, firewood gathered and vegetables cultivated, was being enclosed by greedy landowners. Thus, the opportunities to augment food and comfort were diminishing. This sector of society too was growing alarmingly, not because of a high birth rate but because the changing economy caused 'casualties' that fell out of working society into unemployment. The growing unemployed poor put pressure on local Poor Relief resources and represented a dangerous underclass with the potential for social unrest and riot. A 1597 law aimed at reducing poverty by local taxation that provided for assistance for the poor. It also allowed for the banishing of vagabonds to Newfoundland and the East and West Indies, but remiss or reluctant justices of the peace meant the law failed to reduce or repress the problem.[39] The bulk of Roman citizens were of this group.

The lower orders were thought by those above to be lazy, delinquent, ignorant, feckless and vicious (in the physically brutal and morally unsound senses). There was much truth in that, particularly among the growing numbers of urban poor, but there were many such among the 'better' sort too.

Some commoners were hard-working men and women living godly lives and bringing up families despite hardships. Those living in the countryside were particularly susceptible to rent rises, fluctuations in labour needs, prices of produce and winter feed for livestock, and changes in land usage brought about by local enclosure. A series of disastrous harvests in the 1590s exacerbated matters, bringing famine to many doors. Piety, thrift and frugality could not feed hungry children. Nor could hard work and decent living protect you from market shifts caused by the greed of others in higher ranks. The self-satisfied court and the negligent king knew well that outside the comfort of Whitehall beggars thronged the streets. There were about twelve thousand in London in 1600, plus eighteen thousand idle and 'masterless men'. Economic conditions would have added to that by 1606. Some were indolent fraudsters preferring begging or thieving to work, but many were genuine victims of hard times.[40] They were all the responsibility of those with wealth, rank and privilege. They were all morally and metaphorically (some literally) sons and daughters of the nobility. It was the job of the king and court to look after them; most did not. While the wealthy and powerful played out their power games, the poor were failing. Shakespeare, in another foray into Roman history, roundly criticized the detachment of the rich from the poor in the opening to *Coriolanus* (1607–09) where the privileged senator Menenius and the arrogant Martius clash with starving citizens of Rome:

> *1 Citizen*: We are accounted poor citizens, the patricians good. What authority surfeits on would relieve us. If they would yield us but the superfluity while it were wholesome, we might guess they relieved us humanely. But they think we are too dear. The leanness that afflicts us, the object of our misery, is as an inventory to particularize their abundance. (I. i. 13–19)[41]

If the governing orders expected quietist deference from those who know themselves to be the least of Christ's servants, and the poor were expected to be grateful for the protection of the rich and to behave in an orderly, controlled way, the privileged had a responsibility to aid the poor. They owed the disadvantaged a reciprocal duty. Social difference and tensions between the ranks do not feature as themes in *Antony and Cleopatra*. The servants and slaves are dumb cyphers in the background. The servant's brief comment about failing to do your duty (II. vii. 14–16) and the soldier advising Antony to fight by land (III. vii. 61–6) are the only critical voices from below, from the plebeians. All the rest are court servants and are part of the establishment. The misconduct of the governing class is, in any case, very comprehensively represented in action throughout. Antony's self-obsession would be identified as similar to that of the increasingly inward-looking Jacobean court. This relates to the duty of kingship, the Christian duty of charity, the concept that brothers (in Christ) and neighbours should take care of one another. Antony never achieves awareness of this dereliction on his part. Though Rome was not at this time Christianized, nevertheless the work of Seneca and Cicero had established a standard of expected civic service that was still valid in Jacobean times. In any case, an audience, probably of mixed social origins, would still have judged Antony's negligence negatively. Any man, whatever his rank, who preferred his appetites above his reason and duty would be harshly judged.

The Theory of the Humours

Hierarchy and harmony were thought to be part of the inner-body world as well as the outer macrocosm. The microcosm, the body, was feudally arranged: the head, like the king, ruled, the organs were the better sort, the limbs the working commoners. The alignment of stars, planets and the ascendant zodiac sign at the precise hour of your birth was believed to fix your fate and personality, enabling predictions to be made concerning your future fortune. From classical times until the end of the eighteenth century people believed that the body contained four fluids (humours) influencing personality, attitude and behaviour. While your astrological sign provided the broad characteristics of your personality, the proportions of the four humours determined your temperament more precisely. Whatever these proportions were at birth defined your healthy, normal state and your psychological type. The humours were: phlegm, yellow bile (choler), blood and black bile. Four temperaments were associated with the humours. The phlegmatic person was normally easy-going and stoical, remaining calm in crises and seeking rational solutions. Caesar exhibits something of this in his calm (cold?), calculating (ruthless?) analyses and careful planning. The choleric man was inclined to temper, was bossy, aggressive, ambitious and liked to take charge. The sanguine man (in whom blood predominated) tended to be positive, active, impulsive, pleasure-seeking, self-confident, sociable, open, friendly and warm-hearted. Antony has some aspects of this complexion, as does Cleopatra. Both also have some choleric characteristics. Those in whom black bile was dominant tended to be considerate of others but melancholic, negative, overly introverted and inclined towards pessimism about the imperfections of the world. Between these four cardinal types there were many permutations, explaining the huge variety of character types and the range of emotional phases to which an individual might be subject.[42] Illness was thought to be caused by an increase or decrease in one fluid and led to (and explained) mood changes.

The medical practices of bloodletting and purges were thought to rebalance the humours, getting rid of any excess of one humour, while certain foods or drinks redressed deficiencies. Some natural philosophers (scientists and rationalists) were beginning to question this theory, believing parental attitudes, early life experiences and education formed personality. Some physicians were beginning to ascribe other causes to illnesses, though today's knowledge of chemical imbalances causing maladies and mental aberrations shows the humours theory was not entirely wrong. Belief in these characteristics led to 'humour' stereotypes in literature that were sources of comedy (grumpy fathers, shrewish wives, romantic lovers, bloodthirsty soldiers, gold-mad misers, sex-mad widows, scheming villains, etc.). The character flaws of tragic heroes and villains fall easily into these broad categories as well.[43] There were those who rejected the astrological origins of personality and claimed they created their own destiny. *King Lear*'s Machiavellian individualist Edmund rejects the idea of the stars forming personality. Conceived 'under the dragon's tail' and born 'under Ursa Major' he would be expected to be 'rough and lecherous' (I. ii.), but his belief in himself as maker of his own destiny ('I should have been that I am, had the maidenliest star in the firmament twinkled at my bastardizing') was a minority view. This mix of astrology and humour theory is evident in what the Soothsayer says of Antony's spirit – that it is overpowered by Caesar's. Caesar is his nemesis and they are astrologically locked in enmity:

> [...] thy spirit
> Is all afraid to govern thee near him;
> But he away, 'tis noble. (II. iii. 27–9)

The Rest of Creation

Below humankind come the other animals – mammals, birds, fishes, insects, etc. – able to move, reproduce, experience appetites (e.g., hunger, thirst, heat, cold, sexual urges), with limited sensory responses, limited problem-solving intelligence, lacking capacity for a spiritual life, without ability to reason or make moral decisions and unaware of God. Animals were thought not to have souls, logic or language.

Animals were also ranged hierarchically though less precisely than humankind and often according to conflicting ideas about their nature. Some were highly regarded, while others were denigrated for what were thought to be their distasteful characteristics. The lion topped the animal world because of its imagined links to courage, nobility and kingship (reflected in the use of lions as royal heraldic emblems). Tigers were noted for ferocity. A mother tiger's protectiveness of her young is admired but tigers could also display an unreliable, savage aspect – a quality attributed to ruthless humans. Wolves and hyenas were lowly ranked because of their savage, predatory, scavenging nature. Apes and goats were thought particularly lustful. Reptiles were low in the hierarchy, snakes particularly being associated with evil, temptation and Original Sin in the Bible. Frogs, toads and bats had associations with witchcraft. Lowest of all were rats, mice and other vermin. Domesticated animals were ranked by usefulness. Dogs (guards and hunters), listed with the working creatures, could be highly prized and Elizabethan-Jacobean gentlemen endlessly discussed the qualities of their hunting dogs. Canine loyalty was highly regarded, but there were negatives – a fawning, flattering nature, greediness and readiness to follow anyone who fed them.[44] 'Whoreson dog' and 'cur' are common abusive epithets in plays. Antony talks of 'the hearts/That spanieled me at heels' (IV. xii. 20–21) when lamenting those who had followed him but switched loyalties. Animal imagery, a common feature of Shakespeare's language, is minimal in *Antony and Cleopatra*, though serpents (inevitably) and crocodiles play a part in the lexical profile. Snakes and poison are referenced over a dozen times.

Birds were highly thought of because of flight's association with air, thought to be a divine element along with fire. Birds of prey, used for the chase, were ranked according to their suitability to be linked with different social levels – an eagle for an emperor, gerfalcon for a king, peregrines for the nobility, goshawks for yeomen (small-scale landowning farmers), sparrowhawks for priests and kestrels for knaves (servants). After the birds of prey (including the owl, synonymous with wisdom) came the carrion eaters (vultures, crows, kites, etc.). As scavengers they were ranked lowly, like hyenas in the mammal hierarchy. Kites (many of which combed the rubbish tips in London) are always represented negatively, linked with the parasitical/scavenging behaviour of those sycophantic feeders hanging around the households of men of power.[45] The parasite (the yes-man toady, like Mosca in Jonson's classic play *Volpone* [1606] and Oswald in *King Lear*) was a familiar figure of scornful fun on stage, originating in Roman comedy and satirical poetry. A parasite was anyone attaching himself to a rich, powerful man in order to curry favour, to be rewarded for running errands (including pimping) and to flatter his master's self-esteem. At the very least he hoped to be invited to dinner, at most retained as a household member and personal assistant-cum-fixer. Mosca, the paragon of parasites, is so-called after the Latin for fly, since flies are lowly carrion eaters buzzing round anything rotting. Volpone is named after the Latin for fox, since he is both devious and cunning. Jonson names his fortune hunters after the allegorical animal figures of the medieval-Renaissance didactic fable – Voltore (a vulture-like advocate), Corbaccio (a raven-like miser) and Corvino (a crow-like merchant). Ravens and crows also have associations with witchcraft and evil, and are birds of ill omen. Below the scavengers came the worm- and insect-eating birds and then the seed eaters. Cockerels were renowned for their lustfulness, and peacocks were symbols of pride in Renaissance iconography. The nightingale, as a semi-divine heard presence, was long celebrated for its evocative, sweet song.

Abusive name calling occurs plentifully in Jacobean drama and involves animal/avian epithets that use the negative characteristics associated with these creatures. A few animal epithets are positive, but likening human behaviour with animals is mostly negative, a reminder that the animal side of man was sinful – lustful, brutal, devious, greedy and slothful. The worst type of connection involves monsters – unnatural, mythical, animal hybrids. The word applied to humans connotes anyone behaving outside the acceptable parameters of civilized conduct and signifies an extreme shift from what is regarded as decent, normal human form and behaviour to brutal, uncivilized manners and deformed appearance. Shakespeare introduces numerous savage, monstrous characters to his plays. In *The Tempest*, Caliban actually represents the savage, wild men Europeans were meeting as they explored the Americas. Some of the European characters in the play are devious, debased and monstrous too. Two of them call Caliban 'monster' and plan to show him as a sixpence-a-time curiosity. Antony warns Cleopatra that she will be shown off 'most monster-like' in Caesar's triumph (IV. xii. 36). The Roman Plays display a similarity to Renaissance culture in their mix of the barbaric and the civilized. Shakespeare offers the audience the chance to reassess their view of the Roman world by showing how like the European courts of his time it was – highly sophisticated and cultured, but brutal and decadent too. It is a collision of old and new philosophies that casts doubts on European culture. Characters, from supposedly civilized backgrounds, exhibit monstrous behaviour in play after play. In Shakespeare alone we find Richard III and his homicidal henchmen, Macbeth and his murderers, Iago, Edmund and the fratricidal Claudius. And there are all the sinister, bloodlusting psychopaths in the mass of Italy-based Revenge Tragedies.

The final groupings of animals were the fish, reptiles, amphibians, insects and sessiles (unmoving shellfish). Fish were ranked low, as water was thought to be a dull heavy element like earth. Reptiles, amphibians and insects were thought of as even lower, fleas and lice being seen as verminous like rats. Bees and ants were positively regarded for their industry and apparent social organization which suggested something approaching intelligence. This period valued any form of corporate, civic or community co-operation as a mark of moral engagement with civilized behaviour.[46]

Lower still, the plant world had only the ability to grow and reproduce. But it too had its hierarchy. Trees were at the top with the oak as the prime form – useful, because of its hardness, for ships and houses – associated with stability, rootedness, imperturbable fortitude and Englishness. A king was seen as a great oak, sheltering his people as the tree did birds and insects.[47] Antony, symbolizing his fall from prosperity, sees himself as a pine stripped of its bark (and thus dying), though he once 'overtopped them all' (IV. xii. 24). Shrubs and bushes came next, along with flowers. The rose was thought to be the most beautiful, associated with love and with the Virgin Mary (the rose without a thorn). The lily signified purity, chastity and death. There was a panoply of floral/herbal significations: pansies for thought, rosemary for remembrance and so on. Next came useful plants – corn crops and herbs with their medicinal and edible uses. Ferns, weeds, moss and fungus were such basic forms they often furnish pejorative metaphors for useless, troublesome, threatening humans. The rising middle class were sometimes described as 'so many early mushrooms, whose best growth sprang from a dunghill'.[48]

Even rocks and minerals, at the bottom of creation, were ranked by their values as gemstones, precious metals or their usefulness for building or yielding minerals. Many were thought to have magical/medical power. Pearls, much prized in the Renaissance (by Queen Elizabeth particularly) were long associated with purity. Diamonds had the power to increase love, emeralds helped resists magic charms and cool lust. Amethysts were believed to prevent you getting drunk, agates helped you interpret dreams. Among the metals gold was king, succeeded in descending order by silver, iron (and steel), bronze, copper and lead. Gold had particular power over the Renaissance imagination. It was the regal metal, used for crowns and sceptres, superior to silver and lowly lead. Gold also had its negative side as a symbol of man's greed. It is the means to suborn, seduce and corrupt. Its corrupting power is most forcibly and comically expressed in Jonson's *Volpone*, where, blasphemously, gold has become Volpone's god. Flamineo sharply describes this idolatrous blasphemy in Webster's *The White Devil* (1612):

> O gold, what a god art thou! And O man, what a devil art thou to be tempted by that cursed mineral [...]. There's nothing so holy but money will corrupt and putrify it. (III. iii. 21–8)

King Lear's reference to gold's power to corrupt justice is particularly pointed considering the persistent contemporary pleas to reform and purify public life and James's ignoring of complaints about venial judges.

> Plate sin with gold,
> And the strong lance of justice hurtless breaks;
> Arm it in rags, a pigmy's straw does pierce it. (*King Lear*, IV. vi.)

Gold became a Renaissance obsession. People longed for it, got it, then wanted more. Foolish speculators gave huge amounts of money and metal objects to alchemists experimenting to turn base metals into gold. Some seriously believed this possible; others saw its potential for lucrative scams. This avaricious dream became the subject of Jonson's powerful satire on human greed, *The Alchemist* (1610). The exploration of America was triggered by the belief that huge amounts of gold could be found there to rival the spoils brought home by the annual Spanish treasure fleet. Sir Walter Raleigh fantasized a South American kingdom – El Dorado – of limitless gold.[49] Gold thread woven into cloth, gold jewellery, gold plates and gold drinking goblets all showed off your pride in your wealth. Pride was a Deadly Sin, and display was a vanity associated with pride.

Among rocks marble was most prized (for sculpture and building), followed by granite, sandstone and limestone. Even lowly chalk and clay had their uses, though clay was connected metaphorically with man's mortality. Last of all are the particle forms – sand, gravel, soil and dust. Sand and gravel represented the precariousness of man's attempts to build a solid life. Earth was thought a dull, heavy element, appropriately typifying man's last state: 'earth to earth, ashes to ashes, dust to dust'.[50]

Order

Not only were humans ranked in an order reflecting how they were valued, but the preservation of that order was seen as a guarantee of social harmony. Orderliness reflected, therefore affirmed, God's ordering of the universe. Order and hierarchy are shown to be subverted in the opening scene by Antony's infatuation exceeding what is regarded as measured, rational control. A governor who had lost all sense of what was right, proper and decorous could not be relied upon. The audience would have felt uneasy at Philo's comment, for positions at court and in the world at large relied absolutely on preserving order, the status quo. Courtiers regularly bribed or blackmailed their way into their post. They and all sorts of officials had recently undergone the nervousness naturally accompanying a handover of power. The new king calmed anxieties by decreeing all posts held under Elizabeth I would continue in the hands of the current placeholder, but then (not the last time would he go back on his word) replaced with Scots all the gentlemen of his Bedchamber (responsible for organizing his bed linen, night clothes, day clothes and washing and toilet needs). These salaried posts gave the holders valuable access to the king. The increasingly elaborate ritualization of all aspects of the king's life, the daily theatre of monarchy, meant nobles and titled men doing menial tasks. Some enjoyed the honour, some found it degrading but necessary to maintain their influence. Sir Philip Gawdy describes the king's dinner served not by ordinary household servants but by titled courtiers:

> [The king] was serued wth great State. My Lo: of Southa [Southampton]: was caruer [carving the meat], my L. of Effingham Sewer, and my Lo: of Shrewsberry cup bearer, my poore selfe carried vp ij [2] dishes to his Ma[ties] [Majesty's] table.[51]

Courtiers struggled indecorously for these places, flattering, bribing and defaming rivals. James unsettled the order of things by rearranging the current tenancy of posts. The tense uneasiness and ever-watchfulness of the court was something the audience well understood. An unreliable, inconsistent king (or triumvir) was an omen of possible and probable disaster. The court was a precarious world; power and place struggles were everyday happenings. Loss of post meant shame, dishonour, loss of influence with the king, and loss of valuable patronage saleable to those wanting your help accessing the monarch. The dangerous fluidity of place and favour suggested that the running of the country was in unreliable hands – a feeling that began very quickly after James's succession and grew with the passing months. It meant that uncertainty was at the heart of things. Cleopatra's unreliable moods represented the fickleness of royal favour. Antony's mismanagement and the disassembling of power would have had uneasy political relevance for the audience, the feeling of a takeover of power, a new force, adding to the general mood of uneasiness in a society that already sensed the world was in decline. The Privy Council was expanded and among the new members were five Scots, two of whom were additionally given top legal and financial posts. New monarchs usually brought in favourites, but James gave unprecedented power to men regarded as foreigners. This Scottish usurpation generated grievances to add to others accumulating around the wholesale Scots incursion into London and Whitehall. Crucial in any court was who controlled access to the ruler. The Romans express a sense of xenophobic fear that Antony has been annexed by contact with Egypt (as indeed he has), that he is no longer loyal to Rome or its values and has allowed Egyptian ministers to wield power. The English, after only three years of James, felt the same. The Venetian ambassador, Giovanni Scaramelli, recounted how English courtiers complained:

> No Englishman, whatever his rank, can enter the Presence Chamber without being summoned, whereas the Scottish Lords have free entrée of the Privy Chamber, and more especially at the toilette; at which

time they discuss proposals which, after dinner are submitted to the Council, in so high and mighty a fashion that no one has the courage to oppose them.[52]

Gawdy complained that the king put Scots 'in all offices' and 'put out many English, meaning to make us all under the name of ancient Britons'.[53] James's blatant favouritism had the effect of uniting rival English courtiers and politicians. Scaramelli observed: 'The English, who were at first divided amongst themselves, begin now to make common cause against the Scots.'[54] This weakness of the king worsened when favourites began to emerge; the Villiers faction in particular gained huge influence and huge amounts of money. The instability of Antony's moods reflects the emotional swings James exhibited, from mawkish sentimentality to blistering anger. Montaigne's comment, 'No passion disturbs the soundness of our judgement as anger does',[55] echoes a theme schoolboys knew from studying Seneca's *De Ira* (*On Anger*). James was well established as an intemperate, irascible monarch liable to burst into rants and swearing if opposed. Hasty, ill-considered action and rash judgements are unwise. When the actor is a father the consequences can devastate lives; when he is a king the consequences are national; when he is leader of a third of the known world the consequences are global. In his essay 'Of Anger', Bacon quotes Seneca: 'Anger is like ruin, which breaks itself upon that it falls.'[56] Ephesians 4:26 warns, 'Be angry, but sin not', and Luke 21:19 exhorts, 'In your patience possess ye your souls.' Wrath is one of the Seven Deadly Sins, but Antony often loses control of himself, makes an outburst, then changes his mind swiftly after. Such fluctuations were considered unsuitable in rulers. There is disorderly variability at the heart of Antony's psychological make-up. The ruler who cannot keep order in his own life, in his own self, cannot long keep order in his state. As Antony's personal life falls apart so does his political control.

Orderliness is given its most famous and detailed definition in *Troilus and Cressida* (1602). Ulysses upbraids the bickering Greek leaders for neglecting the 'specialty of rule'. If the clarity of 'degree' is blurred the unworthy will appear no different from the meritorious. James himself blurred degree when, relieved at the welcome of his people as he progressed south, he made hundreds of unworthy knights.[57] The specialty of rule is founded on the traditional Aristotelian belief that some were born to rule, the rest to obey.[58] Ulysses points out that the whole universe follows an ordained rule:

The heavens themselves, the planets, and this centre,
Observe degree, priority, and place,
Insisture, course, proportion, season, form,
Office, and custom, in all line of order. (I. iii. 85–8)

If orderliness is disturbed:

> What plagues and what portents, what mutiny,
> What raging of the sea, shaking of the earth,
> Commotion in the winds. (I. iii. 96–8)

Disorder affects human society when rank is disrespected:

> O, when degree is shaked,
> Which is the ladder of all high designs,
> The enterprise is sick! How could communities,
> Degrees in schools, and brotherhoods in cities,
> Peaceful commerce from dividable shores,
> The primogenitive and due of birth,
> Prerogative of age, crowns, sceptres, laurels,
> But by degree, stand in authentic place? (I. iii. 101–8)

Order is the cement that bonds human society and Ulysses warns of the consequences of disassembling order:

> Take but degree away, untune that string,
> And hark what discord follows! each thing meets
> In mere oppugnancy: the bounded waters
> Should lift their bosoms higher than the shores,
> And make a sop of all this solid globe;
> Strength should be lord of imbecility,
> And the rude son should strike the father dead. (I. iii. 109–15)

Shakespeare was always concerned with order – nationally, socially, personally and spiritually. Rebellion, usurpation and collapse are political themes found in all his history plays (including the Roman ones). Disorder, excess and misrule figure too in his tragedies and comedies. Like many writers in the early 1600s, he was much preoccupied by political and social questions relating to how society should be run. Loss of 'degree' meant force would dominate society, justice would be lost, and illegitimate power, will and appetite ('an universal wolf') would rule. James warned his son, 'Beware yee wrest not the World to your owne appetite, as over many doe, making it like A Bell to sound as yee please to interpret.'[59] Ulysses uses images of natural order turned upside down, unnatural human behaviour and the dominance of sin. The Jacobeans were haunted by the fear of order being overturned. It had not just local social consequences, but threatened disaster throughout creation and the universe. It could bring the end of days, the Apocalypse, as predicted and threatened in Matthew's and Luke's gospels and in the Book of Revelation. The irony is that history shows repeatedly that what is natural for man is that order is broken, the strongest oppress the weak, the brutal take control and the ruthless rule. The need and desire to co-operate creates society and unites community, but such bonding is often weak when faced by strong men backed by pitiless, armed henchmen ready to shed blood to gain power. Shakespeare's history plays and tragedies show time after time how devious men gain power and how decency and virtue are slow to react. They also focus on ineffective rulers: Richard II, Henry VI, Othello, King Lear and Antony.

The seventeenth century was much concerned with political theory. Playwrights, especially Shakespeare, picked up on sixteenth-century interests in how society was best to be administered. Sir Thomas More's *Utopia* (1516) fantasized about an imaginary perfect state, Sir Thomas Elyot's *The Boke Named the Governour* (1531) proposed a curriculum for educating statesmen and leaders, and the various editions of *The Mirrour for Magistrates* (between 1559 and 1603) retold the exemplary stories of fallen governors. James contributed two theoretical conduct books on kingship: *The True Law of Free Monarchies* (1598) and *Basilikon Doron* (1598). Sadly, though typically, there was a discrepancy between his ideas and his actions. So too the theory of order, the desire for peace and harmony, was belied by the actualities of life. Order seemed continually under attack and the constant fear of disorder added to Jacobean angst. Rising crime figures in the 1600s contributed to the general gloomy sense of decline and decay.[60] As did incidents of family dissension, gruesome murders, increasing illegitimate births and increasing alcoholism. On 15 March 1604 James made a formal procession through the City to Westminster. At one of the seven highly ornamented gates set up for him to pass through, a Latin oration was delivered (among many sycophantic speeches). It spoke of 'this sixt age of the world […] *in the declyning age of our Kingdome*'.[61] These factors feed into those dramas which reflected the feeling of increased dishonesty, licentiousness, greed and brutality. The City Comedies are peopled by petty criminals, shysters, cozeners, cony catchers, usurers, legacy chasers, greedy merchants and braggart, penniless, heiress-hunting gentlemen. London itself emerges as the subject and often the setting of critical dramas in the 1590s. Though foreign cities (especially Italian) are often the setting (especially for Revenge Tragedies), they are only a mask; the virulent satire, the abuses and 'ragged follies' are transparently English and associated with London and the court. The increase in the crowded metropolitan population (200,000 in 1600, 575,000 in 1700)[62] provided a huge variety of human types and writers revelled in portraying the seedier characters, enjoying their vitality while deprecating their immorality and trickiness. Being constrained by historical facts, *Antony and Cleopatra* is less topically specific than *Measure for Measure* or *King Lear* and much less so than Jonson's comedies, but its overall mood still reflects those neurotic fears of collapse. It reflects too the interest in imperfect leadership evident in so many of Shakespeare's works. The message is that states will fall without monarchical excellence and vigilance and personal strength of character. Evil men are ever present, always looking to undermine order. In this play it is the 'hero' who undermines himself, while the audience watches helpless the unstoppable fall of his life and his polity.

The authoritarian orderly social structure was enforced in the geographical arrangements of the nation. Divided into a network of counties, each with a Sheriff or Lord Lieutenant, hierarchy imposed order on what might otherwise be, and sometimes was, a restless population. Below the Sheriff, a patchwork of estates owned by rich, titled, powerful men imposed local authority. Estates varied in size, but within reach (sometimes within the actual perimeter) of even the smallest would be villages, parishes and individual dwellings rented by families dependent on the landowner's good will. Grand nobles often owned huge estates in different parts of the country, each providing income from rents and farm produce.

Increasingly, though land gave status, its value was diminishing. Landowners were becoming entrepreneur-employers exploiting mineral deposits on their domains and other natural advantages like water, timber, rush for thatching and clay for bricks. Men of lesser title and less money, with smaller estates, would still have dependent tenants and a home farm to provision the family. The gentry might only own a house, maybe a fortified manor, and their land might be no more than a small acreage surrounding the house, but as part of the ruling class (magistrates, justices of the peace, chairmen of parish councils, etc.) they further imposed the values of their privileged elite. Hierarchy even penetrated parish churches, where the better sort had boxed-in family pews near the pulpit, the middling sort sat on benches and the poor stood at the back. The gentry monopolized parish councils through the so-called 'select vestry' that barred lower ranks from attending. Local politics was controlled by landed families and Parliament was 88 per cent upper orders and 12 per cent merchants and civic authorities. The top 5 per cent had the whole country under their nominal control. The few large cities – London, Bristol, Norwich and York – also had their networks of power, with aldermen, beadles, mayors and the wealthy liveried companies. Richard Stock's 1603 Lent sermon in St Paul's churchyard directly addressed the Mayor of London, the aldermen, nobility and privy councillors:

> You are magistrates for the good of them that are under you, not to oppress them for your own ease. I would speak to him who is chief of the city for this year. What is past cannot be remedied, but for the future, as far as lies in your power, prevent these things.[63]

'The wealthier sort feared sudden uproars and tumults, and the needy and loose persons desired them.'[64] The gentry largely resided in the country while titled men spent much of their time at court and Parliament. In a period of high produce prices and little profit to be made from agriculture by any except the great farmers, landowners raised rents, reducing further the profit margins of husbandmen holding leases from them and forcing many labourers into homeless unemployment. Increasingly, gentry heirs and younger sons drifted to the capital, forming a large, shifting population of troublesome young men, some hanging about the court seeking posts or heiresses. They saw London as a pleasure ground, removed from immediate parental disapproval. Drinking, whoring, gambling, fighting, theatregoing and chasing rich merchants' daughters, they were generally a nuisance. Though it was centuries before, this was how Antony had spent much of his youth.

Many titled families were founded by men who, coming to power under Henry VIII, bought or were given by the king church lands that came onto the market at the Reformation. These once-new families were now the old upper-rank families. A few titled dynasties could trace their ancestry to the Conquest. Most were of relatively recent authenticity, some paying the College of Heralds to manufacture fake genealogies that gave them more respectable and ancient descent.[65] This network of power and privilege was intended to keep the king's peace. It largely did so, despite outbursts of local unrest, but at the expense of the physical and political repression of the 'baser sort'. Generations of psychological pressure established a fear of the upper ranks, a belief that, like the king, they were part of God's order and opposing them was a grave blasphemy, pitting your puny, sinful self against the divinely ordained state of creation. The civil power was not the only repressive network controlling England. Hand in hand with government, often synonymous with it, the church attempted to guide conformity and forcibly dissuade dissent. In 1549 Thomas Cranmer, Archbishop of Canterbury, had re-enforced this in upbraiding rebels: 'Though the magistrates be evil and very tyrants against the commonwealth and enemies to Christ's religion, yet the subjects must obey in all worldly things.'[66] This encouragement to submit even to injustice was repeated in the 1571 *Book of Homilies* in the sermon 'Against Disobedience and Wilful Rebellion'.[67] Tyranny was a divine punishment against a sinful people who should not 'shake off that curse at their owne hand'. Identifying hierarchical deference with submission to God was part of seeing the social order as ordained by God. By making it an aspect of church doctrine the Anglican hierarchy aimed to curb rebellion, maintain power and enforce doctrinal uniformity. Rebellion was blasphemy. Social and religious submission to the established power structure, however unjust its actions, worked for the mass of fearful, superstitious people. But opposition was slowly rising.

Each English diocese had a bishop responsible for ensuring priests and congregations followed the Anglican form of worship. These dioceses totalled between nine and a half and ten thousand parishes, each (theoretically) with a priest and an average of 300 parishioners (450 in the less controllable, expanding cities). Pluralism (holding more than one living) was a growing practice whereby already rich vicars could augment their wealth or a poorly paid vicar could augment his stipend. Either way it was a corrupt practice. Non-resident priests employed curate substitutes so there was religious presence to oversee the social and spiritual state of the congregants. The priest, representing the church's might, was a figure to be respected, part of the ruling establishment, part of the control troika of magistrate, lord of the manor and priest. Often the lord of the manor was the magistrate, thus narrowing the power base. Part of the priestly aura of power was education. The ability to read and write gave priests special, magical status (though not all were highly literate). As mediators between this world and the next, they had immense psychological influence. Education enabled them to advise on moral and practical matters and their spiritual role made them privileged mentors in matters related to living the virtuous life. Not everyone in a village would necessarily defer to the priest. Some saw him as an arrogant snob, allied to the gentry, parading his learning, an outsider speaking an incomprehensible, elite language.[68] Some vicars were ineffective – drunk, ignorant and more interested in hunting. Closet Catholics and Dissenters would only pay lip service. Puritan dissidents were slowly increasing in number and increasingly vocally critical of the church. More worrying for the episcopal elite was the spread of vicars of Puritan sympathy. In the 1590s large numbers of progressive, radical-thinking young ordinands graduated from Cambridge University, adding yet another destabilizing factor to an age already undergoing disturbing changes. The principles absorbed from the lectures and writings of Cambridge don William Perkins inclined them to be less obsequious to their gentry parishioners and more mindful of the hardships of the poor, though some gentry families, sympathetic to reform, protected Puritan-minded vicars from church persecution. This was particularly evident in the 'Pilgrim Quadrilateral' and the Boston area of Lincolnshire in the years 1600–1610.[69]

Another burgeoning force undermining the establishment was the irreverent, radically minded university-trained playwrights. Vitriolic in criticizing purse-proud citizens, their ostentatious wives, the explosion of greed, the obsession with luxury, vanity and lust, the idle and incompetent aristocracy, and particularly those many ungentlemanly gentlemen buzzing like flies around the court, they also deplored the state of the lower orders. Many plays, set firmly in the contemporary city, are essentially morality based, harking back to medieval values. Shakespeare tended to avoid overt attacks on the establishment by setting his plays in other countries or in other periods. *Antony and Cleopatra*, though set before Christ, is not just a historical drama. It has relevance to 1606. The original audience would not be fooled into thinking the play was a romantic costume drama. They would see allusions to current issues embedded in the text. The economic and political system of England was firmly organized for the benefit of those who already had much. The audience would see that behind the games these 'great ones' play lie issues relating to the necessary limitations to the scope and style of autocracy. Antony, Cleopatra and Caesar are lessons for the 1600s about how the 'great' rule. The play is an exposé of human frailty and the consequences of dishonesty in public office and of putting the personal before the public.

King James expressed the principle that concern for 'the well-fare and peace of his people' identifies a king 'as their naturall father and kindly maister'. In 'subjecting his owne private affections and appetites to the weale and standing of his subjects' he shows himself better than the tyrannical king who 'thinketh his people ordained for him, a pray to his passions and inordinate appetites'.[70] James soon revealed himself as stand-offish to the 'baser sort' and obstinately pursued his own appetites. *Antony and Cleopatra* is a reminder that history should not be the plaything of those with power and that those in 'great place' are often as weak and foolish as those who have no name in the register of fame.

Detachment from people encourages desensitization, which leads to brutal attitudes to them. The leading trio of characters show little concern for the thousands that march to their command. Their rivalries bring death and disablement. Any courtiers in the audience should feel awkward observing the play, for it reminds the rich man of his duty to help the poor, to show God gratitude for being wealthy by not wasting his excess fortune on pointless extravagances, not indulging in war games as if they were a throw of the dice, but putting his riches to the good of the whole polity. The Bible is clear about this: 'For unto whomsoever much is given, of him shall be much required' (Luke 12:48). The middling and lower orders had to work to live; those with wealth and rank did not. However, the standard view was that 'none are less exempted from a calling than great men'.[71] The Bible story of Dives and Lazarus (Luke 16:19), a popular text for sermons, told how the rich Dives refused to pass the crumbs off his table to the poor Lazarus. Dives dies, goes to Hell and in his sufferings sees Lazarus among the elect. The rich and powerful had a duty to be fathers to their neighbours, shepherds to the flock around them. Brathwait put it starkly: 'The higher place the heavier the charge.'[72] Many privileged lords and ladies sent to the poor unwanted food from their own table, endowed alms houses and schools and did other acts of charity.

Many did nothing. Each new generation inheriting wealth needed reminding that charity

> […] should flow
> From every generous and noble spirit,
> To orphans and to widows.[73]

Thomas Dekker deplored those who, although 'they haue the fulnesse of welth to the brim, that it runs ouer, they scarce will suffer their poore Seruant to take up that which runs at waste'.[74] This selfishness was one form of the sin of cruelty he saw infesting London. The concept of *caritas* (love expressed through charitable acts), integral to medieval church teaching, was derived from canon law's delineation of the basic duty of the rich to assist the needy. It was taken up in Protestant thinking too. Compassion was a necessary virtue in a Christian and essential for those who had never experienced adversity or affliction. Antony, however, treats the world as his toy. The Jacobean governing classes had similarly detached themselves from the rest of society, living their own self-interested, selfish, narcissistic lives at court or isolated in their mansions on their estates. What a prick to the consciences of the pampered young men and women in the audience *Antony and Cleopatra* might have been – unless they only saw the protagonists as heroic, romantic victims and the play as a celebration of great love sacrificed to the demands of an ambitious politician. Would any be cheered (or even actually cheer) to see a great fool botch his suicide and have to be heaved aloft into Cleopatra's monument? And all because she sent a false message that she was dead. It is an absurd end, but in a sense appropriate for a man who had shown himself to be such a besotted fool. Very few of Shakespeare's kings and princes show themselves to be truly noble. Corrupt, ineffective, arrogant leadership was a feature of the time, figuring in many plays as in real life. The period is full of admonitions to kings and nobility. In 1609 the Earl of Northumberland wrote:

> There are certain works fit for every vocation; some for kings; some for noblemen; some for gentlemen; some for artificers; some for clowns [country people]; and some for beggars. […] If everyone play his part well, that is allotted him, the commonwealth will be happy; if not then it will be deformed.[75]

The Bible (e.g., Ezekiel, Proverbs, Ecclesiastes, Thessalonians and Timothy) strongly criticizes idleness and recommends employment, including kings and courtiers. They knew they had a job to do, a duty to perform. It was an injunction increasingly ignored. James did read state papers and attend councils, but only when it suited him; he might just as readily disappear suddenly on a hunting trip. His effectiveness diminished, bribery and favouritism became the norm and his court became increasingly idle and debauched in its pursuit of pleasure, increasingly corrupt and self-seeking in its administration of the realm.

Chapter 3

SIN, DEATH AND THE PRINCE OF DARKNESS

> Stand thou in rightwiseness and in dread, and make ready
> thy soul to temptation, for temptation is a man's life on the earth.[1]

An inescapable factor in every aspect of Jacobean life was the ever-present possibility of sin. Jacobeans were neurotically alert to the temptations surrounding them. People's sinfulness was the greatest threat to order. Conflicting Christian sects shared basic beliefs when it came to right and wrong: man was perpetually open to sin and temptation was all around him, the Devil was to be defied, and Christ was man's redeemer and the way to salvation. The religions may have differed homicidally about doctrine, but the moral bases of life were agreed. The Roman view of honourable and dishonourable conduct had many points of contact with Christian morality.

The Ten Commandments were the foundational start point for Christians:

The Ten Commandments (abridged from Exodus 20:19)

1. Thou shalt have no other gods before me.
2. Thou shalt not make unto thee any graven image.
3. Thou shalt not take the name of the Lord thy God in vain.
4. Remember the Sabbath day, to keep it holy.
5. Honour thy father and thy mother.
6. Thou shalt not kill.
7. Thou shalt not commit adultery.
8. Thou shalt not steal.
9. Thou shalt not bear false witness.
10. Thou shalt not covet […] any thing that is thy neighbour's.

They were paired inextricably with the Seven Deadly Sins to mark the way to avoid damnation and win salvation through godly living (the Seven Cardinal Virtues are discussed in Chapter 4):

The Seven Deadly Sins

1. **Pride** (arrogance, vanity, vainglory, *hubris*)
2. **Wrath** (anger, violence)
3. **Lust** (lechery, wantonness, lasciviousness)
4. **Envy** (covetousness)
5. **Greed** (avarice)
6. **Gluttony** (including drunkenness)
7. **Sloth** (laziness, despair)

Sin and Satan were as much a part of religious consciousness as the desire to emulate Jesus and live virtuously. The church's cultural monopoly meant even those indifferent to religion would acknowledge that faith was the common, underlying feature of life at all levels. The passing year was marked by religious events and each day was punctuated by aspects of faith. The parish church bell indicated the times of services, pious families gathered for morning and evening prayers, and individuals might well visit the church during the day too. Schoolboys had communal classroom prayers with their teacher. A master craftsman, his journeymen and apprentices might start the working day with prayers. The formal ceremonies of their guild involved prayers, readings and sermon-like addresses. Children were taught the Bible, learned texts, creeds, catechisms and prayers and would kneel by their bedside to ask for protection during the dangerous hours of darkness. The Lord's Prayer was central to ordinary belief, asking for daily bread, the forgiveness of trespasses and protection from temptation. Those of weak faith attended Sunday service rather than be fined in a church court.[2] Those not particularly pious in their everyday life had scriptural grounding as children and, like everyone else, would know how they were expected to behave as Christians, would be aware of biblical allusions, echoes and ethics in what their neighbours said and did, would observe how stage plays displayed, reinforced and debated the basic Christian values of society. The church was omnipresent. When you were born, married, committed adultery, defamed a neighbour, were rowdy, sharp-tongued or shrewish, or traded on Sunday, the church was there approving or wagging its finger. You lived in public, your sins were easily made public and your punishment would be public. Your misdemeanours would be spied out by constables, beadles, the watch, servants or neighbours and dealt with in the local church court. Anglicans were rarely left to solve a problem alone. Individual conscience was too weak to deal with matters of sin and morality without help. In times of national or personal stress many people turned to the consolations offered by being part of a communally held belief. When you were afraid of imminent disaster, the support of others was a coping mechanism; the church was a mental, spiritual and physical refuge.

All Shakespeare plays allude to or echo well-known biblical texts. *Measure for Measure* does so abundantly and despite its pagan setting the actions of the central characters (and other peripheral characters) in *Antony and Cleopatra* have an unspoken, indirect, implicit biblical context evoking Christian values, reactions and assessments. The second agent, after the author, in the mediation of a text was the reader or viewer, who provided a religious assessment. An audience of whatever mix of ranks could not watch a play without judging it within religious criteria. Christian values shadow the actions of *Antony and Cleopatra*. The text may lack direct allusion to Christian dogma, but Shakespeare knew his audience would make the connections. Every scene provokes a Christianity-focused judgement of what is said and done. The play buzzes with excess, pride, lust, lies, wrath, gluttony, envy and betrayal. Whatever the level of engagement with faith, Christian upbringing triggered a vigorous conscious or subconscious religious reaction to everything seen. Debauched libertines or audience members who had lost their religion still had vestigial memories of values learned as children. The Bible was the standard of all conduct. Responses might vary according to education, upbringing, experience of and attitude to the world, class, or political and religious allegiance, but there would be broad agreement, since all the viewers – from pit to top gallery – shared this common Bible-based background. The ways in which time after time the characters offend the Commandments or commit sins would be glaringly obvious to the audience. It is an absolutely fundamental aspect of the play, informing every other motif in it.

Life was seen as a journey, a pilgrim's progress. From birth people were to pursue virtue, shun sin, imitate Christ, keep the soul pure, and progress towards death, ready to pass through to the life everlasting. Life here was a transient state preparatory to the afterlife. In John Ford's late Revenge Tragedy *'Tis Pity She's a Whore* (c. 1629–31), when sexual sins and violent plots begin to gather and drive the drama, the character Richardetto states the basic situation of Christian existence: 'No life is blessèd but the way to heaven' (IV. ii. 21); he then encourages his niece to flee a vile world by entering a convent: 'Who dies a virgin lives a saint on earth' (IV. ii. 28). The virtuous life gained Christ's favour and a state of grace. No advantage in the fleshly, physical world was of any value if you lacked grace. Ford presents even good looks in a religious context:

> Beauty that clothes the outside of the face
> Is cursèd if it be not clothed with grace. (V. i. 12–13)

Antony and Cleopatra are not Christian, do not inhabit a value system that sees sinful life as punishable by death. But the Romans had a sense of virtue and grace. They called it honour and dignity. For all their vitality, charisma and spontaneity, the protagonists lack these qualities. They are merely hedonists seeking a constant succession of pleasures. Uncontrolled appetite was something the church feared and punished. Lust was the most common everyday sin, but any of the Seven Deadly (or Mortal) Sins could damn you eternally if unrepented. Antony is an adulterer and Cleopatra is complicit in fornication. Their children are therefore illegitimate. Shakespeare relied on his audience seeing the danger of unrestrained sexuality and the guiding restraint Christian morality offered.[3] The Romans too regarded highly (in theory) the quality of restraint. The emotional intemperance of the pair offended humanist ethics too. Calm and balance were valued, particularly among those who governed states and had judgements to make. Shakespeare could rely on his audience seeing how the royal pair reflected the conduct of pleasure-driven members of court behaving outside the moral framework of the time. His audience had enough biblical knowledge (even if their faith was weak) to put the actions and words before them into a moral context that reflected poorly on themselves and the Jacobean court and offended Roman and Christian virtues. The evil of appetite has overcome the circumspect, moderate requirements of their roles as civilized exemplars; this couple is unused to having ever to control their desires.

The pervasive religious atmosphere made identifying sin instinctive. Sin was the Devil's portal, giving access to your soul to damn you. The Devil was a very real entity to people, not a metaphor of evil, but a actual horned, cloven-hoofed, fork-tailed, sulphurous presence. Progressive thinkers tried to internalize the Devil as the evil in man, but most people believed he was a real creature. His earthly work, assisted by legions of demons, imps, goblins, incubi and succubi, was devoted to corrupting man and thwarting God's will. The Book of Revelation describes 'the great dragon' who 'was cast out, that old serpent, called the Devil and Satan, which deceiveth the whole world' (22:9). John's Gospel calls him 'the prince of this world' (22:31), and Corinthians 'god of this world' (4:4), suggesting that the fleshly world of greed, brutality, cheating and lust (ever present in the plays of the 1600s) is the Devil's domain. Paul's Epistle to the Ephesians (2:2–3) goes further, placing the Devil firmly in this world, embodied in the waywardness and violence of men. Seeing the Devil manifesting himself through human evil suggests how the audience might see Antony and Cleopatra, even though they were pagans. An audience would not judge them otherwise than on Christian lines. Camille Paglia sees the play as prioritizing the feminine values of Egypt against the militaristic, male standards of Rome, applauding love over politics.[4] This fails to recognize the play is only nominally Roman. The contemporary audience could not avoid judging actions and outcomes according to the seventeenth-century system of sin and virtue and beliefs about how governors should behave. For them the deaths are inevitable as a punishment. It is a play showing how evil is loosed when cultivated, civilized, sensitive and sympathetic behaviour is ignored. Castiglione highlights the problems of those 'who for all they were borne of noble bloud, yet have they been heaped full of vices'.[5] Dante, like the political theorists of the seventeenth century, defined nobility in terms of virtuous conduct, not rank. Antony's actions are ignoble; he is rightly defeated. Cleopatra is an unreliable schemer and it is right she too should be defeated. It is, however, typical of Shakespearean ambiguity that Caesar, though victorious over a maverick, naive fool, is represented as a relatively unsympathetic character, but it is the nature of the world that ruthless men gain power while weak men let them.

Viewers would see the piece as not simply a tale of love defeated by machination or as the world lost through imperfect leadership, but a *psychomachia*, an allegorical drama in which various emanations of evil are displayed in contrast to and in conflict with virtue. But the virtues are largely abstract (and certainly not embodied in Caesar). All three protagonists have virtues and weaknesses that have evil aspects. They are present as opposites to the follies enacted on the stage; it is history used to exemplify fate. The gods punish the *hubris* of Antony and Cleopatra and the instrument of their justice is Caesar. But Caesar's orderliness and concern for the integrity of the state are countered by his Machiavellian machinations. The couple's *hubris* consists in arrogantly assuming that their selfish pleasure-seeking and negligence of duty would go unpunished. Though not written in the style of the earlier morality plays, the subject and ethics are the same. The overlap of the Christian upbringing and the classical schooling of most educated men in Shakespeare's time is evident in the intermixing of Christian and Roman values and references to the gods and goddesses of pagan mythology. The play is thus supported by a framework, typically Renaissance and humanist, of interlocked classical and Christian ethics.

Vicars loved loosing their imaginations sermonizing about the workings of the Evil One and the torments of Hell awaiting unrepentant sinners. Creative writers too enjoyed the opportunities for fantasy descriptions offered by ideas of Hell, Sin, Death and the Devil. The awareness that sin is ever present, that life is a persistent battle between good and evil, that the lure of vice has to be constantly rejected, was reinforced by the witch trials that were common at the time. Witchcraft was another subject upon which King James delivered his opinions and his book *Demonologie* (1597) captures the contemporary mood of fear and suspicion. Many painted representations of demons and the Devil gave visual concreteness to people's fears. Hell and the sufferings of the damned were popular subjects. Hieronymus Bosch (1450–1516) graphically depicts the horrors of perdition in *The Last Judgement*. In late medieval times (responding perhaps to the holocaust of the Black Death) artists turned from depicting Christ in Majesty and took to decorating churches with scenes of the Last Judgement. Many (but not all) were scratched out or whitewashed over during the Reformation. It was an age when hanged bodies were routinely publicly displayed strung up in chains, 'heretics' were burnt at the stake, and Gunpowder Plotters had their entrails cut out and burned in front of them. The rack, thumbscrew and strappado were regularly used to extract information. Noses were slit and ears cropped for criticizing royalty or church, thieves were branded, and blasphemers had their tongue pulled out or a hole bored in it. Birching, blinding and being broken on the wheel were simply part of institutionalized cruelty. The gruesome acts portrayed in plays reflect a violent culture. Sin against the state, sin against God – the painful punishments were similar. These brutal punishments reflect the age and how people imagined the damned were tortured in Hell. Rome too was a culture founded on violence and the end of the Republic was marked by plots, assassinations and bodies floating in the Tiber. The atmosphere of uncertainty and disorder was akin to what the Jacobeans felt. The dangerous world of English politics is suitably paralleled in all the Roman Plays. It had echoes too for James I of the complex, devious and bloody machinations that surrounded his childhood. There is no evidence he saw the play, but it would perhaps have been reported to him and was perhaps a topic of temporary chatter around court.

The threat of damnation and eternal torture if you were an extreme sinner was a useful moral control device to frighten naughty children and a moral corrective for adults, but there were those who did not care about hellfire and damnation, and those who did not believe in Hell. Marlowe's Faustus declares that 'hell's a fable' (Scene v. 128). Despite Mephistophelis asserting 'this is hell, nor am I out of it' and 'where we are is hell', Faustus arrogantly laughs off the possibility:

> FAUSTUS: Think'st thou that Faustus is so fond to imagine
> That, after this life, there is any pain?
> Tush, these are trifles and mere old wives' tales.

> MEPHISTOPHELIS: But, Faustus, I am an instance to prove the contrary,
> For I am damn'd, and am now in hell.
> [...]
> FAUSTUS: How! now in hell!
> Nay, an this be hell, I'll willingly be damn'd here.
> (Scene v. 134–44)

People were beginning to question Hell's existence, claiming this life was our Hell. In *'Tis Pity*, the reckless Giovanni, a scholar like Faustus, thinks reasoned argument can demolish the idea of Hell, confidently announcing to his confessor:

> The hell you oft have prompted is nought else
> But slavish and fond superstitious fear,
> And I could prove it too. (V. iii. 19–21)

The friar replies, 'Thy blindness slays thee.' Most of the audience, if they thought about it, probably believed in both Heaven and Hell as places of reward and punishment in the afterlife. Most, except extreme libertines, believed sin was everywhere and virtue needed to be cultivated. This would not have prevented them sinning or encouraged living a particularly good life. Like most people they would probably experience guilt and fear, resolve to improve, then lapse into their normal 'not very bad but not very good' everyday lives. An affecting play might well prick their consciences – temporarily at least.

In *King Lear* the mad king makes a brief mention of Hell. Commenting on female lust he shifts from describing how from the waist down 'is all the fiend's' domain to recognizably describing the Christian idea of the Devil's kingdom:

> There's hell, there's darkness,
> There is the sulphurous pit – burning, scalding,
> Stench, consumption [...]. (IV. vi.)

In *'Tis Pity* the friar, trying to frighten Annabella into repentance for fornication and incest, describes Hell:

> There is a place [...] in a black and hollow vault,
> Where day is never seen. There shines no sun,
> But flaming horror of consuming fires,
> A lightless sulphur, choked with smoky fogs
> Of an infected darkness. In this place
> Dwell many thousand thousand sundry sorts

Of never-dying deaths: there damned souls
Roar without pity [...]. (III. vi. 8–16)

He continues to describe the punishments meted out for specific sins:

> There are gluttons fed
> With toads and adders; there is burning oil
> Poured down the drunkard's throat, the usurer
> Is forced to sup whole draughts of molten gold;
> There is the murderer forever stabbed,
> Yet can he never die; there lies the wanton
> On racks of burning steel, whiles in his soul
> He feels the torment of his raging lust. (III. vi. 16–23)

Sin and Death

The Prince of Darkness[6] was inexorably linked with temptation, reminders of what awaited after death and the very fact of death itself. Sin and Death are linked as a hellish duo in opposition to Christ and the Holy Spirit. The everyday world was a minefield for the morally unwary, full of devils waiting for any hint of ungodly, impure thought. Momentary lapses – a nasty comment, bitchy gossip, a bad-tempered, snappish reply, blasphemous expletives, temptations to gluttony, theft or the prickings of lust – were opportunities for 'the Enemy of Mankind'. I Peter 5:8 warned: 'Be sober, be vigilant; because your adversary the devil, as a roaring lion, walketh about, seeking whom he may devour.' Wary Christians prayed regularly for protection. Prayers at bedtime were especially important, calling on guardian angels as night security. A habit grew of eventide self-examination of your day, casting up your account of good and bad acts, making resolutions to improve, repenting and praying for salvation. It was end-of-the-day quiet time for assessing how well you had behaved that day and resolving to be better if need be. James recommended to Prince Henry:

> Remember ever once in the foure and twentie houres, either in the night, or when yee are at greatest quiet, to call yourself to account of all your last dayes actions, either wherein yee have committed things ye should not, or omitted the things yee should doe, either in your Christian or Kingly duty.[7]

A marginal note references I Corinthians 11:31: 'For if ye judge your selfe, ye shall not be judged.' Temptation to sin was everywhere and everyone knew 'the wages of sin is death' (Romans 6:23). You had to fight constantly to win the gift of eternal life through Jesus Christ. What made it more difficult was that you were born a sinner, with the susceptibility to sin already in you. This 'Original Sin' was the curse Adam and Eve's fall brought to mankind. Their disobedience meant that all successive generations were weakened by being open to temptation – a weakness played upon by omnipresent devils and much utilized by playwrights. This idea provoked a rich language of condemnation among moralists – pamphleteers or preachers – and a delight in describing the pains of Hell.

In the turbulent times when *Antony and Cleopatra* was written there was no shortage of targets named as the source of sin. Sin bred like disease in the growing capital. Disease itself was God's punishment for sin – not just the usual bodily sins of lust, gluttony and sloth, but pride in rank, the vanity of fashion, the greed of amassing a fortune. Society seemed falling apart; crime, alcoholism and illegitimacy were all rising,[8] and heresy and religious dissent were rife. Anglicans blamed Puritans, Puritans blamed Anglicans, everyone blamed the Catholics, the Pope (the Antichrist), the French, the Spanish, the court or the king.

Life was a battle to preserve your virtue and live like Christ, cleansing sin by prayer. Prayer would involve repentance and begging forgiveness ('Forgive us our trespasses ...'). An accumulation of unrepented sins, particularly grave ones, could damn you when you died, though repentance (even at the last minute) could save you. The terrified Faustus, about to be dragged down to Hell as payment of his side of the bargain with Satan, cries out:

> See, see where Christ's blood streams in the firmament!
> One drop would save my soul, half a drop. Ah, my Christ!
> Ah, rend not my heart for naming of my Christ!
> Yet will I call on him. (Scene xix. 146–9)

Death was never far away in those days of plague and illnesses easily brought on by a poor diet, unhealthy living conditions and ignorance of basic hygiene. Infections were a leveller making little distinction between rich or poor, though the better-off might be protected by superior food. The world was an insecure place, made more uncertain by persistent Puritan claims that epidemic diseases were punishment for tolerating Catholicism or changing church ritual, performing plays, not keeping the Sabbath holy, the sinfulness of the court or the sinfulness of everyone in general.[9] There was no escape. Poverty, illness and sudden disaster were constant anxieties people lived with. As Montaigne put it: 'We do not know where death awaits us: so let us wait for it everywhere.'[10] Starting and ending the day with family prayers was part of that protection/salvation process, behaving piously during the day was another. James I advised his son, 'Pray [...] God would give you grace so to live, as yee may everie houre of your life be readie for death.'[11] This life, though the gift of a bountiful God, was short and merely a preparation for the life eternal, spent in the torments of Hell or among the blessings of Heaven.

Increasingly in the seventeenth century small coteries of scientists and intellectuals questioned the authority and authenticity of the concepts of sin, damnation and salvation. Part of a growing rationalist movement, they encouraged cynicism, secularism and individualism. Questioning the existence of God, the centrality of Christ, the rights of kings, inhabiting the border between astrology/magic and astronomy/science, they were forerunners of the Enlightenment, but did not represent the beliefs of the majority. While Dollimore claims that Jacobean tragedies display man in an existential state, redeeming himself, unsupported by Providence,[12] a Jacobean audience would be rather more traditionalist, believing there was design and purpose in the workings of nature, that man was free to make devastating mistakes, but could find redemption. Raleigh asserted everything that happened was the 'secret will' of God, echoing the orthodox church view voiced by Bishop Cooper: 'Fortune is nothing but the hand of God.'[13] The idea that the individual was responsible for his own soul and for his personal relationship with God was refreshing and liberating, facilitating independence from a church mired in corruption and entangled in the establishment power structure. How did free will fit with the belief that all was part of God's plan? Machiavelli reconciled the two:

> I am not unaware that many have held and hold the opinion that events are controlled by fortune and by God in such a way that the prudence of men cannot modify them, indeed, that men have no influence whatsoever. Because of this, they would conclude that [...] one should submit to the rulings of chance. [...] Nonetheless, because free choice cannot be ruled out, I believe that it is probably true that fortune is the arbiter of half the things we do, leaving the other half or so to be controlled by ourselves.[14]

But individualism, emerging simultaneously with the capitalist practices of a profit-driven, go-getting, selfish commercial world, threatened old ideas of humble self-effacement and dedication to the community's good. This individualism prioritized your needs, discounted others, disconnected you from moral restraints and promoted a world where personal will and private appetite were the measure of actions, where villainy thrived and where Caesar, Cleopatra and Antony get their own way if not opposed strenuously.

Traditional morality demanded the bad be punished in fiction. In real life villains often got away with skulduggery and dishonesty. Machiavelli was demonized because his works 'openly and unfeignedly [...] describe what men do, and not what they ought to do'.[15] Discrepancies between moral expectation and actual behaviour shows that rule breakers succeed. Man's unique features – the virtues of charity, mercy, sympathy, intellectual ability and reason, and the emotional faculties of imagination and love – raised him above animals and closer to godlike status. But the pinnacle of God's earthly creation, part divine, part animal, was too easily tempted by fleshly failings. Mankind was God's second attempt after some of his first angelic creations rebelled with Satan. Because humans had bestial traits life was a constant battle between the animal promptings of appetite and passion and the angelic demands of reason and virtue. The exploration of that struggle between our baser and our better nature is the domain of literature. The Ten Commandments, the Seven Deadly Sins and the Seven Cardinal Virtues specifically address this need to fight the impulses towards lust, bloody acts, violence, theft, gluttony and sloth. The presence of these appetites gives *Antony and Cleopatra* its religious/ethical/political context. These conduct guidelines are implicit in all Elizabethan-Jacobean drama. Characters can be measured against them.

The list of sins, revised by Pope Gregory I in AD 590, was tabulated hierarchically by Dante in his influential poem *The Divine Comedy* (1321). Originating in Catholicism, these Mortal, Capital or Cardinal Sins were still relevant to the sin-conscious Anglican Protestants and dissenting sectarians of Shakespeare's time. They are cardinal because they were thought grave enough to require God to renew his grace to the sinner and for the sinner to show repentance before forgiveness could be shown. They are mortal or capital because they were serious enough to warrant death ('For the wages of sin is death'). God was thought able to strike down great sinners by sudden death or to use human agents. The Book of Proverbs lists as sins looking proud of yourself, lying, shedding innocent blood, having a heart ready to devise wickedness, a readiness to do mischief and stirring trouble. St Paul offers a longer list, any of which will lose you the kingdom of God: adultery, fornication, uncleanness, lasciviousness, idolatry, witchcraft, hatred, variance, emulation, wrath, strife, sedition, heresy, envy, murder, drunkenness, revelling 'and such like' (Galatians 5:19–21). Fornication was sex between couples not married to each other. The principle was that sex should not take place at all unless permitted by the sacrament of marriage. Some would see Antony as rightly punished for his double adultery. Roman attitudes to adultery varied as to how seriously it was regarded and the punishments meted out. It was grounds for divorce and might be also punished by confiscation of goods or return of half a woman's dowry. It was seen as a slur against family honour and could lead to bloodshed. A Roman double standard applied in so far as it was only considered adultery if the woman was married. A married man having sex with an unmarried woman was not considered an adulterer. It is unlikely anyone in the audience would have judged Antony according to ancient custom. To the Jacobeans adultery was not just a civic crime but a moral and religious one, originating in lust, the commonest of sins. The Seventh Commandment forbade adultery. The passion and the love (if it is love) of the two characters would not have been regarded as an excuse. James's court was a hotbed of promiscuity, condemned by many. He did nothing to curb or punish it, yet adultery was the leading criminal offence tried in courts. There are many other negative behaviours and vices regarded as sinful, though less serious. These are called venial sins. Committing them would not lead to you losing the grace of God, thus you could still be cleansed and saved, with effort on your part. Some audience members might have laughed at Charmian's lewd jokes at the expense of Mardian the eunuch, but others would condemn her, for ribaldry and loose conversation were sinful. Hypocrisy, another venial sin, is evident too, as are vanity and ostentation in the luxurious displays of the protagonists. Menas is guilty of contemplating murder (just thinking of it was a sin) and Pompey is guilty of wishing it had been carried out.

The idea of Hell as a fiery pit below the Earth is formalized by Dante in *Inferno* (Hell), the first part of *The Divine Comedy*.[16] Each sin was tabulated and allocated its sector. The lower Dante goes in his visit to the nine circles of Hell, the worse the sins committed by the damned he meets. In 'Upper Hell' are those guilty of incontinence, failings effected by those constant enemies of mankind, the appetites. These mainly personal failings, tied closely to the Seven Deadly Sins, are in descending order; the lustful, gluttonous, hoarders and spendthrifts, wrathful and suicides. In 'Nether Hell' – getting closer to Satan at the bottom of the pit – are sinners who committed planned transgressions – fraud or acts of malice. In descending order they are: panders and seducers (pimps and fornicators), flatterers, simoniacs (those who sold church offices), sorcerers, barrators (those abusing the legal system to profit by groundless cases or false claims), hypocrites, thieves, those encouraging fraud, sowers of discord, falsifiers and traitors (to kindred, country, guests, their lord, etc.). These broad definitions comprise a number of sins against the community and against probity in public office. Many of them are present in *Antony and Cleopatra* and the audience would easily identify them.

Pride was the first sin, committed by the Devil in thinking so well of himself he rebelled against God to replace him. As Lucifer ('the bright one'), he was God's favourite angel, but becoming ambitious, thinking that although God favoured him above the other angels he deserved even better and higher status, he rebelled, was defeated and was cast out of Heaven. He and his co-conspirators fell through the ether into Hell, a fiery pit full of sulphur and smoke, specially created by God. Vanity is a form of pride. At a venial level it is conceit about your physical looks, clothes or status. Both Antony and his consort have overly high self-esteem, an overblown perception of their own worth that leads them to neglect everyday matters, to neglect running their state. The arrogance of thinking yourself better than others, something special, is a small vanity until it becomes active disregard and bad treatment of others, behaving as if you were above the common courtesies. At a personal level Antony and his Egyptian 'strumpet' perpetually parade themselves as grand personae – Isis, Dionysus, etc. – even greater than they actually are. It is sheer arrogance (*hubris*) to masquerade as gods and goddesses; where is humility, where is moderation? Antony is out of control and behaves as if he could do no wrong, betrays his responsibilities to Lepidus and Caesar, and shows no remorse, but avoids an immediate outright split by claiming he is sorry and they misunderstood him. He had been feasting the night before and the messenger arrived when he was the worse for wear (wanting 'of what [he] was i' the morning' [II. ii. 77]). Vanity related to appearance and fashion is raised in Enobarbus's famous description of the queen's arrival at Tarsus on her barge. She loves to create settings in which to show herself off and have an effect, even staging her own death theatrically. Any reference to clothing as moral distraction would be relevant to a peacock court audience whose wasteful extravagance on clothes was infamous and where individuals dressed in their finest to go to the theatre. Orazio Busino (chaplain to the Venetian Embassy), generalizing about London playgoers, described them as 'people devoted to pleasure, who, for the most part, dress grandly and colourfully, so that they appear, if possible, more than princes, or rather *they appear actors*' [emphasis added].[17] Pride is the besetting sin of those with power, privilege, rank and wealth (like some in the audience). The Bible required such people to disregard their advantages and be humbly ready to serve those whom it was their duty to help. A king is most likely to be proud, but overweening self-regard was rife among courtiers too.

Wrath ranged from any tiny moment of anger flaring and soon dying away, through escalating losses of temper to the irrational rage that becomes violence against another. This is relevant to those men in the audience ready to fall out and fight. Men (not just gentlemen) wore swords, carried concealed daggers and were prepared to use them. With too much wine tempers frayed easily – over cards, dice, women or a word taken the wrong way. The Day of Judgement was known as the *Dies Irae* (Day of Wrath, a term used in the Anglican Communion). It was the day when God's ultimate wrath would be shown. Irascibility (a tendency to lose one's temper) is a sin liable to occur in any rank of society, but particularly among hot-headed young men. Those of rank and wealth were most susceptible to it, believing themselves superior to others and ready to defend any perceived slur against their honour. Noticeably, both Antony and Cleopatra display petty yet extreme wrath and physical violence against servants as a displacement of their anger and jealousy over other matters. This would be regarded as very unbecoming in a monarch, though a common characteristic with King James and Queen Elizabeth before him.

Lust was a universal sin, felt by both sexes, all ranks and most ages. St Augustine regarded the 'disease of lust' as persistently intrusive and the most destructive of the appetites.[18] Necessary for the continuation of the species, the human sex drive was difficult to control and greatly concerned all churches. The sin of fornication was defined as any prohibited sex, meaning outside marriage – sex between two unmarried adults was forbidden. Sex with someone other than your husband or wife was both fornication and adultery. The intention to conceive a child was the only justification for intercourse within marriage. Sex for pleasure alone was lust and fornication. Lust comprised all unclean thoughts and unclean acts, including unnatural ones like bestiality, incest and homosexuality (condemned in Romans 1:26). Masturbation, rape and sexual thoughts were all lust. A perceived growing libidinousness in society, with an increase in unwanted pregnancies in all ranks, worried preachers and playwrights alike. 'In political libels, lampoons, satires, and other forms of writing and action, upper-class immorality is almost inevitably the object of sharp disapproval, reflecting the growing grip of Protestant attitudes to sin, social order, and divine vengeance.'[19]

The church's attitudes to sexuality centred on two problem areas: women as the source of sin (particularly the belief that women were by nature more lascivious than men) and the central principle that appetites made men more like animals than angels and needed to be controlled or suppressed. The Christian ascetic tradition required avoiding all excess – simple food, simple clothes and a focus on the spiritual rather than the carnal. Every Deadly Sin was a form of appetite developed to excess. In *'Tis Pity* calm reason is recommended to a jealous, vengeful husband: 'Sir you must be ruled by your reason and not by your fury: that were unhuman and beastly' (IV. iii. 83–5). Unruly appetites (of different sorts) were a recurrent theme in drama. Very slowly, marriage was established as a means of controlling and channelling lust. While theoretically chastity was regarded as preferable for full spiritual perfection to be achieved, it was gradually conceded that marriage was the second best course if you could not effectively control your sexual impulses.[20] Marrying was preferable to promiscuity, but even within wedlock lust had to be restrained. Lust was a major topic for admonition in sermons and religious writing.

Men and women even sat separately in church. The Puritans, though in favour of marriage, had considerable difficulty with the whole area of sexuality.

Criticism of rampant lust is recurrent in plays of the 1600s. *Measure for Measure, Hamlet, Othello* and *Troilus and Cressida* all express concern about female sexuality. Sexuality has a part to play in *Antony and Cleopatra*, in the public passion/lust shown by the two protagonists. This had a topical context considering the moral reformation drive of both church and legal authorities against brothels, whores and prenuptial sex even between betrothed couples. A little show of affection would be acceptable between a king and his queen in public, but the overblown gestures of physical attraction and displays of other emotions are unbecoming. It is a blurring of the private with the public. Decorum, dignity and gravity were prized qualities for public figures. James I signally lacked them, both in physical appearance and in manner. Antony shows these qualities rarely and Cleopatra perhaps only in her last moments.

Envy or covetousness is jealous desire for what others have, a form of mental theft and discontent with the lot God gave you. It is not clear whether Caesar envies the free-spirited, open-hearted Antony, but there is clearly a personality clash. They are two different types who under any circumstances would be antipathetic to each other. Rivals they certainly are: one as the adopted son of Julius Caesar, the other as the favourite protégé. Though strictly they are not siblings, there is something of sibling rivalry in their dislike of each other. The history plays address this in relation to inept kingship and the question of succession. Sibling rivalry is doubly present in *As You Like It* with Orlando and his brother, and the exiled Duke and his brother. *Hamlet* focuses on Hamlet Senior and Claudius. In *Much Ado About Nothing* there are Don Pedro and his bastard brother Don John. These all involve deceit, cheating, attempts to oust the hated rival, an actual murder of one brother by another (*Hamlet*), and a war between siblings (*Much Ado*). In *Richard III* the Duke of Gloucester is deeply envious of his handsome, golden, successful brother, Edward IV. In *The Taming of the Shrew* an older sister is jealous of the younger because she is father's pet. In *King Lear* the long-held grievances of childhood surface in the jealousies of the king's three daughters and the conflict between a legitimate and illegitimate brother. It is deeply disturbing to see how little love can exist within a family, or how testing times can open cracks rather than strengthen bonds. In different ways, and to different degrees, Shakespeare reworks envy as an unsettling, potentially destructive aspect of family relationships. The early Chronicle Play *Gorboduc* (1571) goes back to a period of British prehistory, focusing on the rivalry of two brothers who are given half the kingdom by their father, Gorboduc, who is resigning from power. The plot pivots on sibling rivalry and succession.

The Mary Tudor/Elizabeth relationship had had its uneasy jealousies. The Mary Queen of Scots/Elizabeth cousin rivalry bedevilled English politics until the former was executed for yet another plot against the queen. Also pertinent is the support for Arbella Stuart as a more authentic claimant to the throne of James I. Plots, envious siblings and succession rivalries were all part of the ambient politics of the period. In *Antony and Cleopatra*, even the marriage alliance is insufficient to avert the inevitable clash of two forces that cannot co-exist. One must destroy the other or be destroyed. Had Antony been able to control his appetite for Cleopatra he might have made the Octavia union work, but he had neither the political sophistication nor the will to do it. The image of him being foreseen as returning to 'his Egyptian dish' evokes a tragic inevitability about his failure to remain with Octavia.

Greed and **gluttony** are sins of physical excess. Avarice (greed), excessive desire for material goods or wealth, is the miser's sin – hoarding for its own sake. It is the sin of the money maker – the financier/speculator/entrepreneur – accumulating more than he needs. It is the sin of both Antony and Cleopatra. Both are congenitally incapable of moderation. They are addicted to excess, greedy for each other and greedy for more of everything. From a religious standpoint it is the sin of the man who does not 'shake the superflux' to the needy, a theme much discussed in the increasingly hard times of the 1590s and 1600s.[21] Gluttony is a bodily excess, largely applied to overindulgence in food and drink. It was believed that 'enough is as good as a feast'; if you had eaten and drunk in moderation, sufficient for the body's needs, anything more was unnecessary indulgence. The leftovers should be given to the old and the poor – the Dives and Lazarus story again, a story reminding the rich and comfortably-off to do their duty to the community. It was part of the harmony of society, payment for deference, putting back into the community. We hear nothing of Antony and Cleopatra having a social conscience. There is Antony's generosity and nobility in sending Enobarbus's treasure and belongings after him when he deserts, but most of the large gestures he makes are for the aggrandisement of his own public persona. There is not only material excess (i.e., immoderate waste). Antony and Cleopatra are guilty of emotional excess.

Excess was a moral pivotal point; any form of it was a sin. The early church was built upon moderation, asceticism, fast days, a lack of material possessions – the simple life. It failed to live up to that ideal, becoming a monolithic edifice of accumulated wealth, land, power, corruption and self-indulgence. Its decadence and worldliness triggered various reformist heresies violently suppressed in the name of preserving the faith, but actually defending Catholicism's monopoly hold over the people of Europe. The theoretical basis was moderation and simplicity. Ancient Greece's Apollonian religion had a tradition of controlled moderation. 'Nothing in excess' was inscribed on Apollo's temple in Delphi and the concept persisted. A late fourteenth-century proverb says, 'There is measure in all things.' St Augustine wisely remarked, 'To some, total abstinence is easier than perfect moderation.'[22] The Puritans revitalized the traditions of asceticism, leading to them being seen as killjoys, but excess was a moral danger marker. In tragedy (classical and Elizabethan-Jacobean), once a character behaves with excess in one aspect of their life, disaster is unavoidable. Excess is fundamental to comedy: Sir Toby's persistent drunkenness, Malvolio's social aspirations, or Orsino's obsession with Olivia (just to take examples from *Twelfth Night*). Any form of obsessive/excessive behaviour is open to mockery. Excess triggers tragedy; it is a key feature of Antony and Cleopatra's lives.

Virtuous, rational living was thought to be its own reward. Moderation, abstinence, chastity, renouncement and avoidance were all ways to concentrate your devotion to God and virtue, but not much practised at court. The principle of moderation was integral to Christian belief from its beginnings. The simple life of John the Baptist, Jesus, the hermits of the Thebaid Desert and many saints prioritized spiritual cleansing over the demands of the body. Regular fasting and frugal living were practices that were continued in Protestant England among the godly. Extravagant banquets are always a marker of court decadence in any age. Periods of contemplation and prayer were encouraged, as was the rejection of luxury. Excessive, ostentatious displays of your spirituality were sinful too. The aim was to put the corrupting influence of this world into perspective; diminishing its power over you gave you time to focus on the next world, but balance had to be kept. It was acceptable to work hard, enjoy your family, be an active, useful member of your community *and* take pleasure moderately in the good things of this world. Shakespeare is always subtextually smuggling in warnings for the audience. The court – an ostentatious, drunken, promiscuous, gambling-obsessed, garrulous, debt-ridden lot, mostly living away from home, thus neglecting their families and their local social duty – needed more instruction than most. Given the sometimes noisy, inattentive, food-munching, giggling, gossiping nature of audiences, we can only hope that those watching *Antony and Cleopatra* were receptive to the lessons taught.

Sloth is another sort of excess – an overdeveloped laziness, not just disinclination to work, but a psychological/spiritual state of not bothering. Your duty to God was to work hard at your trade and at being virtuous. Many didactic stories and plays illustrate the spiritual and material rewards of industry. A popular motif compared two apprentices – one hard-working, who gets on well in his trade and gains his master's daughter, the other idle, who falls into bad habits and ends up in prison for debt. This is demonstrated in

Eastward Ho! (1605). Industry meant more than working at your livelihood, it meant being a committed, active Christian, helping the community and actively working at guarding and improving your own spiritual state. The Latin word for sloth, *acedia* (or *accidia*), also applies to spiritual slothfulness or despair, the state in which you lose belief that God cares for and watches over you. It was a state akin to melancholy or depression.

Antony's neglect of duty, his selfish preference for his own inclinations, is a form of sloth, a sin he occasionally regrets and is eager to absolve, but does not have the will or strength of character to persevere in. It is perhaps a sort of intellectual pride that leads him to see the daily routine of government as beneath him. The parade of sins would be easily spotted and an audience of the time would be of the mindset to interpret the drama before them in the light of these moral waymarkers.

Chapter 4

THE SEVEN CARDINAL VIRTUES

If the Seven Deadly Sins were the warning signs for avoiding damnation, the Seven Cardinal Virtues were waymarkers to salvation. The Seven Deadly Sins all had obvious opposites (pride/humility, wrath/calm forbearance, lust/abstinence or moderation, covetousness/generosity, greed/charity, gluttony/moderation, sloth/active engagement), but there was also an official list of virtues, some of which appeared as opposites to the sins, some of which related to broader matters of faith.

The Seven Cardinal Virtues

1. ***Temperance*** (abstinence, moderation)
2. ***Prudence*** (providence, foresight, circumspection, consideration, wise conduct)
3. ***Justice*** (justice, equity, fair judgement)
4. ***Fortitude*** (strength under pressure)
5. ***Faith*** (piety, duty to and belief in God)
6. ***Hope*** (hope of salvation)
7. ***Charity*** (love of, benevolence to, others)

A godly life won a heavenly crown. If life was a journey, each person a pilgrim on the highway, then conduct determined destination. Virtue's path was hard – steep, thorny, stony, winding and tiring, The way for the carnal man of weak character, Mr Worldly Wiseman, was easy – a 'primrose path', as Macbeth puts it – but it lead to an 'everlasting bonfire' and 'sulphurous pit'. Because *Antony and Cleopatra* is a tragedy the virtues are less prominent than the vices but they are there as shadows behind the characters as they act foolishly or do wrong. Evil and folly are more theatrically intriguing, holding our attention because they are horrible, fascinating and exciting. But in watching and assessing, the spectator's mind would identify automatically the virtues that are not enacted as each incident of wrong passes before their eyes. The sins provoke questions that hold our attention – will Antony break the 'strong Egyptian fetters' or lose himself 'in dotage'? (I. ii. 122–3). Will we see a definitive act that proves Cleopatra really does love Antony? For those who do not know the story or only an outline of it, the quick pace, the rapidly changing scenes and the intricacies of move and countermove will fascinate. As will the mounting mistakes. For those who know the outcome, the interest lies in how the writer portrays the ineluctable move towards catastrophe and how he portrays the protagonists. There is a horrible helplessness in watching Antony make move after move that only entangles him further in a net of fate from which there is no escape. This adds a tinge of pathos to his triumphant celebration of the battle he has won. He, of course, does not know his fate, while the hypnotized audience, privy to Caesar's machinations and knowing the history, watch spellbound by the horror of two victims struggling to win through yet only moving closer and closer to their awful destiny.

The centrality of virtue to living the good life was not only recognized in Christian thought. Classical writings extolled virtue, particularly Plato's Socratic dialogue *Protagoras*, Aristotle's *Ethics*, Cicero's *De Officiis* (*On Duty* or *Obligation*), and Seneca's *De Ira* (*On Anger*) and *De Clementia* (*On Mercy*). Each listed those qualities required to live the good (i.e., virtuous and wise) life. Plato names wisdom, courage, justice, kindness, circumspection and holiness as essential components of excellence. Aristotle identifies courage, temperance, liberality, magnanimity, proper ambition, patience, truthfulness, friendliness, modesty and righteous indignation. Cicero was studied at school as a model of the Latin style, elegant but direct. In an age when one's first public duty was to others and not to selfish individual desires, *De Officiis* became the *exemplum* of good citizenship. Studied at university as an essential guide to moral behaviour and public conduct for young men who might become active in national arenas, it advised how to discern false flattery from wise counsel, something of which Antony is unaware, especially as he often flatters himself. Self-deception is a feature of the tragic hero, leading to the moment of realization (*anagnorisis*) of the mistakes they have made. The classical virtues evolved into the four Christian virtues (temperance, prudence, justice and fortitude). Antony noticeably lacks temperance and prudence.

These classical qualities evolved into the four virtues of Christian thinking (temperance, prudence, justice and fortitude), then extended to seven with Paul's first letter to the Corinthians (13:13): 'And now abideth faith, hope, charity, these three: but the greatest of these is charity'. In his Epistle to the Galatians (5:22–3), Paul also says, 'The fruit of the Spirit is love, joy, peace, longsuffering, gentleness, goodness, faith, meekness, temperance.' Such characteristics are part of the moral excellence that constitutes a person's virtue. The Christian fathers St Ambrose, St Augustine and St Thomas Aquinas (*Summa Theologica*, II. i. 61), reacting to and refining St Paul, detailed what became the seven key characteristics of the pious Christian and incorporated them into the main body of church teaching. By the Renaissance (with its love of classical writings) they had become an amalgamation of classical and Christian virtues and proliferated into a huge mentoring literature aimed at any sort of leader or governor. For King James, temperance was not only an opposite to gluttony but meant moderation in all things, particularly in the exercise of justice, power and controlling anger – not something he actually followed himself, being an intemperate drinker, given to immoderate anger when thwarted, and often inconsistent, unjust and capricious in using his power. To Sir Thomas Elyot, self-control and emotional balance were crucial qualities in someone with the immense potential for punishment available to a king.

Along with prudence or circumspection, moderation was fundamental to kingly rule. In defining the ideal courtier, Castiglione has Count Ludovico Canossa specifically pick out 'prudence, goodness, fortitude and temperance of soul' as essential to a man of 'honour and integrity'.[1] Within the fiction of the play we see Antony as immoderate in physical excesses, immoderate in his emotions, and unjust in his treatment of Thidias and in his illegal appropriation of Pompey's house.[2] Not jumping to conclusions but carefully considering options and outcomes is a vital skill for any civic leader whose actions and judgements have widespread consequences. We do not know if the king saw the play, but he would presumably approve a piece displaying the consequences of negligent kingship. If he saw his own failings in the past and present weaknesses of Antony he may have felt awkward – all the more embarrassing since he had proclaimed the virtues required of a prince in 'A King's Duty in His Office', the central second part of *Basilikon Doron* (thousands were in circulation). Watching any recent Shakespeare play he ought to have squirmed in his royal seat, recognizing the virtues transgressed on stage as his own failings and those of his court. Patience, perseverance, courage (the bravery to do the right thing and to face evil), fairness (justice for all who deserve it), tolerance, honesty, respect for others, kindness, generosity and forgiveness are not much in evidence in *Antony and Cleopatra*. Their opposites, however – pride, intemperance, gluttony, greed, sexual licence, envy, indulgence, irreverence, dishonour, murder, violence, deceit, levity and undignified behaviour – present too.

The dark cynicism in plays from 1600 onwards reflects a sense of spiritual and moral decline. For an age believing everyone was a sinner to a greater or lesser degree, the corruption of man was a given. Pessimism about individual probity (personal goodness, honesty and openness) extended into the wider workings of society and government. Individuals from all ranks were thought to be corrupt in different ways, but the supposed leaders of society – the titled governing elite, the expected exemplars of good practice – were persistently shown to be selfish, indifferent and morally bankrupt. Due to the religious aspect of Elizabethan-Jacobean ethics, the Deadly Sins inevitably parade through the drama of the period, satisfying the demand for tension in the conflict between sin and virtue.

Three other moral schemas had become part of the thinking about how men should behave towards each other. All officially disappeared at the Reformation, but were still in people's heads and hearts, becoming absorbed into Protestant thinking, particularly in relation to social responsibilities:

The Seven Corporal Works of Mercy

1. To tend the sick
2. To feed the hungry
3. To give drink to the thirsty
4. To clothe the naked
5. To harbour the stranger
6. To minister to prisoners
7. To bury the dead

The Seven Spiritual Works of Mercy

1. To convert the sinner
2. To instruct the ignorant
3. To counsel those in doubt
4. To comfort those in sorrow
5. To bear wrongs patiently
6. To forgive injuries
7. To pray for the living and the dead

The Seven Gifts of the Holy Ghost

1. Counsel
2. Fear of the Lord
3. Fortitude
4. Piety
5. Understanding
6. Wisdom
7. Knowledge

These are the positives by which the characters would be judged by the contemporary audience, in which case Antony and Cleopatra's conduct would not score highly.

Chapter 5

KINGSHIP

Savage and relentless anger is unbecoming in a king. (Seneca, 'On Mercy', 193)

Now what shall I say about the courtiers? For the most part they are the most obsequious, servile, stupid and worthless creatures, and yet they're bent on appearing foremost in everything. (Erasmus, *Praise of Folly*, 176)

The aim of the courtier is to make his prince virtuous. (Castiglione, *The Book of the Courtier*, 320)

They do abuse the king that flatter him:
For flattery is the bellows blows up sin. (*Pericles*, I. ii. 39–40)

Antony and Cleopatra are 'prince' figures – he as triumvir and representative of Rome, she as queen of Egypt. Egypt was not technically a client state or vassal at this time, but an ally, an autonomous state, albeit protected by Roman arms. In effect, however, Rome was overlord of a very valuable state that was in the process of becoming a client province. The corn of Egypt and its other sources of riches were the lures for annexation. After Caesar's defeat of Antony and Cleopatra, Rome became ruler of the country and its wealth. Officially, at the beginning of the play, Antony is ruler of all the Eastern kingdoms but as they are mostly independent, he is in effect their supervisor. His role is to patrol their borders, keep the peace, ensure that taxes are paid and maintain the loyalty of the region towards Rome. Judaea was the only kingdom that Antony had come to terms with. Many of the others (even Cleopatra's Egypt) were of doubtful loyalty, some even supporting the Brutus–Cassius coalition during the Civil War. It is his dilatoriness in dealing with this that is one of the underlying grievances Caesar had against his co-triumvir. Antony's opponents in the senate persistently drew attention to his dallying in Alexandria, spending time (adulterously) with the queen. Historians of the time, while adverting to the wide political dereliction of Antony, also began to focus on the drama of the couple's affair and on the rumours of debauchery and excess. It is this that Shakespeare foregrounds in the opening stages of the play for it most effectively highlights their failure as leaders. It also had recognizable similarities to the growing extravagance of the Jacobean court. Later the love element becomes an auxiliary to the power struggle.

Whatever their actual title, anyone who ruled a state was generically defined as prince, governor or magistrate. As 'prince' figures the protagonists must be measured by the various criteria applied to rulers. There is no aura of loftiness and dignity about them. They are peremptory, impatient about having their orders obeyed, impulsive in pursuit of pleasure, and dilatory in dealing with the larger matters for which they hold their title, privileges and wealth. The education and conduct of princes much concerned moralists and political theorists throughout the Renaissance. James I's two books on monarchy written before he came to the English throne were followed by two more: *An Apologie* [explanation] *for the Oath of Allegiance* (1608) and *A Premonition to All Most Mightie Monarchs* (1609). His persistent failure to marry personal behaviour and monarchical role in conformity with his own well-publicized principles resonates throughout the play. The matter of government (of people, of self) common to Shakespeare's work, seems to be a particular feature of most of the works produced after James's accession. In a sense Antony is an absentee ruler, never seen or heard of dealing with business. The same goes for Cleopatra. Goldsworthy comments, 'There is no actual evidence to suggest her concerns went any further than ensuring a steady flow of taxation into her own hands, to cement her hold on power.'[1] Absorbed in their private dramas, they seem to have little time for governing.

Kingship is inevitably an explicit theme in the history plays. Audiences seemed insatiable for dramas revisiting the English past, displaying the fortunes of heroes and villains, plotters arrested and executed, monarchs succeeding or failing. The stories of Henry V, King John, Richard II and Richard III were popular subjects that Shakespeare would later rework in his own way. The fall of kings was endlessly fascinating, and the history genre remained popular at the Swan and Rose theatres even into the 1600s,[2] when other venues and writers, doubtful and discontented about the running of public affairs and the direction in which society seemed to be going, turned to topical satire to voice their anxieties. Reading or watching the many Chronicle Plays infesting the stage leads inevitably to the conclusion that although kings are theoretically honoured as God's vice-regents on Earth, in practice history shows them as persistently opposed, plotted against, harried from battle to battle, disrespected, often violently removed from the throne and violently disposed of. Given the developing political climate and the interest in political theory it is unsurprising that history drama seemed to raise more and more questions about the legitimacy and effectiveness of monarchical rule. It is brought vibrantly to the fore in *Antony and Cleopatra*, with the decline and further fall of both 'prince' figures. Antony had already earned a reputation for poor administrative skills. He was always more interested in the financial possibilities of his posts than the public duties they required of him. Goldsworthy claims that Antony was complicit in corruption by his officials (a feature of James's rule): 'Hostile sources characterize this whole period as one of indulgence, loose control that allowed unscrupulous followers to abuse their position, arbitrary decisions and squeezing the provincials for money.'[3] He made a prime mistake as a governor – putting his own ends before his duty.

Good rulers can be undermined by evil men if they are not vigilant and do not know the world. Bad kings have nasty ends, being shown as unworthy of their role, either on personal or political grounds. Weak kings, however virtuous, can be misled by devious lords and be vulnerable to flattery if they cannot discern honesty from attractive-sounding lies. Antony has undermined himself and played into the hands of an opportunist woman. Cleopatra was canny and never stopped playing politics. She could not afford to. Her situation had been precarious all her life. The Ptolemies were an ambitious, ruthless family, always focused on what was best for them and always afraid of assassination, whether it came from the court or within their own family. Cleopatra was naturally always on the alert for what served her needs best. A Roman general with a weakness for women served her purposes well. He and his soldiers could keep her safe and on the throne and she had the means to attract and keep him; at 28 she was a witty, intelligent, confident woman of experience in the world, not without looks (some said she was beautiful, despite the 'tawny front' comment). She is certainly more alluring and sophisticated than Octavia. It is part of Antony's self-delusion to believe she loves him. Perhaps she does. The text is ambiguous. Sometimes she thinks so: 'Did I ever love Caesar so?' (referring to her affair with Julius Caesar). Antony is caught between two strategists. Charismatic rulers generated powerful displays of patriotic loyalty and provoked a similar response in audiences when their stories were dramatized, but by the end of Elizabeth's life a general cynicism seemed to attach to real leaders (nobles and monarch) and transferred into the presentation of leaders on stage. Antony does not have the advantage of being a known English figure like Henry V. He has, for those of the audience who had any knowledge of his life, a reputation as a womanizer whose greatest conquest (if it was he who conquered her and not she who conquered him) was the great love of his life – Cleopatra. A strong leader's decline provokes consideration of failings that would otherwise have been diplomatically ignored while the ruler's strength was feared. Queen Elizabeth's death precipitated many long-repressed anxieties. The Chronicle Plays crowding the early public stage reflected not just an interest in rethinking the nation's past, they sublimated contemporary anxieties about stability, masked and made palatable by dead personae and long-gone events. The inexorable approach of the end of the century released many superstitious fears of the Apocalypse and gloomy anticipation of the new era. These fears transferred into negative representations of magistrate figures. Jonson's *Sejanus* and the numerous Revenge Tragedies do not portray leaders as divine or their courts and advisers as anything other than basely human, grasping and unscrupulous. Roman history and recent Italian city-state politics afforded a useful means of dealing with current English concerns under the mask of foreign settings.

The question of government is not confined to the history plays, it is present too in the four Great Tragedies, focusing on the qualities that may enable proper or improper governorship of self or *polis*.[4] Be that *polis* a household, a city or a nation, the control of emotions, appetites and vices (and the consequences of not doing so) is always at the heart of Shakespearean drama. With restrictions on what aspects of contemporary life could be presented and portrayal of the monarch prohibited, indirection was the only means. Satire on authority and power, the corruption of courtiers and the ruling infrastructure in general would have been of interest to a king who had contributed to the literature relating to the education of a prince, as long as he did not suspect he was a secondary, unacknowledged target. Any play with a tainted ruler so distinctly at its centre inevitably provokes questions about the current real-life ruler. Nothing is treasonably definite, but there are lots of little prompts that call King James to mind. His personal manner in conducting the court was certainly open to criticism, as was his variable administration of the government. Antony's end is a distanced warning.

Preparation for Rule

Tudor conceptions of preparation for rule were dominated by Sir Thomas Elyot's *The Boke Named the Governour* (1531). But there are other influences. Elyot's book echoes much of the thinking and conclusions arrived at in Castiglione, but then they shared a long tradition of works acting as *speculum principis* (a mirror for princes), defining the personality and conduct required to make a good ruler.[5] Castiglione moves from defining what makes the ideal courtier and court lady to a fourth and final book that situates the courtier as counsellor to a prince. Elyot asserts the need of 'one souerayne gouernour [...] in a publike weale', but acknowledges the need for councillors and a nationwide group of 'inferior governours called magistratis'.[6] It reflects poorly on Antony's personality that Ventidius, successfully fighting the Parthians in Antony's name, comments:

> I could do more to do Antonius good,
> But 'twould offend him, and in his offence
> Should my performance perish. (III. i. 25–7)

It is no way to encourage good performance of duties if deputies are afraid of rulers' petty jealousy if they do too well.

The basis for rule at any level is the proper upbringing of 'the chylde of a gentilman which is to have auctorite in the publike weale'. Elyot discusses lengthily the curriculum for this education because 'gentyllmen in this present time be not equall in doctrine to th'ancient noble men', due to 'the pride, avarice, and negligence of parentes', snobbery and a lack of teachers. Elyot complains that gentlemen believe 'it is a notable reproche to be well lerned'. The better sort of families paid high wages for skilled cooks or falconers, but not for a tutor to educate their child and inculcate virtue. Fate or the gods made Antony a ruler. It was his duty to the gods, to the *polis* of Rome, his fate, to rule.

The qualities needed by any man who was to govern at any level were prudence, industry, circumspection and modesty. Antony lacks all these. Monarchs required comeliness in language and gesture, dignity in deportment and behaviour, a demeanour of honour and sobriety, affability, mercifulness, placability, humanity, benevolence and liberality, well-selected friends, sharp discernment of the 'diversity of flatterers', a sense of justice, personal fortitude and 'the faire vertu pacience'. Some of these qualities Antony does possess, but his great flaw (his *hamartia*) is that he has become what he essentially always had the potential to be – a carnal man, driven by the need to satisfy the cravings of the moment. He has not the rational calm and self-control Cicero demanded of men who have privilege and rule. He is a fire always ready to ignite. With his impulsive fleshly manner comes a reluctance to engage in the drudgery of administration. Much of Cicero's *De Officiis* works as a running counter-commentary to Antony's conduct.[7] In Jacobean terms he is a libertine, but a dangerous one, for he has power and duties to perform. Neglecting the latter has dire consequences. He has allowed lust and gluttony to become excessive and therefore a danger and a sin. Plutarch is a source for stories of over-lavish wasteful banquets. Maecenas enquires whether it was true that for 12 people a breakfast of eight wild boars was provided. Enobarbus declares that was nothing to the 'much more monstrous matter of feast' on other occasions. This may sound like playful bragging, mocking

Maecenas's curiosity and tale bearing, but it is confirmed by Plutarch. The overindulgence in food and drink morphs into a metaphor of Antony's infatuation for Cleopatra. She becomes an exotic food to which Antony is addicted. Enobarbus refers to Cleopatra as Antony's 'Egyptian dish' and speaks of how at the supper on the Cydnus (described as a 'feast') Antony stared at her beauty as if he wanted to eat her (II. ii. 234, 235) and how he is now addicted to her: 'She makes hungry/Where most she satisfies' (II. ii. 247–8). This suggests that what we have here is a sexual obsession that has been given an acceptable label and called love. Food imagery is commonly used in Elizabethan-Jacobean poetry as metaphors of love and lust. It is a not uncommon experience that a temporary sexual attraction is given the name of love, is perhaps genuinely believed to be love, and then passes. Here, however, the obsession has not passed. Whether it is true love or lust mistaken for love is one of the play's rich ambiguities. Food and drink imagery occurs regularly in the play and takes on a moral dimension for it refers always to excessive consumption. This denotes decadence and sinfulness. Like King James arriving in England, Antony seems to have been carried away by the wealth to which he had access in Egypt. The ready compliance of his sexual partner has added to the attraction of the East.

Elyot sees obstinacy as 'a familiare vice' among men with power and recommends a set of virtues for controlling passion: abstinence, continence, temperance, moderation, sobriety, sapience (wisdom) and understanding. These requirements, echoing the Seven Virtues and the Works of Mercy, are demanding – and Antony lacks them. Privilege, power and the money that comes with them bring responsibilities, and responsibilities mean sacrifice. He has what Elyot calls 'the exposition of maiestie': he generates loyalty and love and has presence. Part of the pity the audience feels for Antony is that he loses that loyalty and becomes a sad, isolated, broken and hopeless man. The ability to inspire loyalty in subjects is crucial to rule. It was one Elizabeth had pre-eminently and James did not. Elizabeth, for all her faults, was adored and allowed her subjects to approach her. James, though he enjoyed their enthusiastic welcome of him to the throne, had little sympathy for his new people, was sarcastic about them, and kept them at bay whenever possible. As long as he kept giving – titles, posts, presents, etc. – his courtiers were loyal (to their own interests). The same self-serving is evident in the men surrounding Caesar. The flattery of yes-men is one of the greatest corruptors of court life throughout history and a disruption to proper government.

It is the governor's role to keep just harmony between the 'comunaltie' ('the base and vulgare') and those with honour and dignities (titles and responsibilities). Maintaining order is vital. The 'discrepance of degrees' (differences of ranks) is part of 'the incomprehensible maiestie of God'.

'Take away ordre [...] what shulde then remayne? [...] Chaos [...] perpeyuall conflicte [...] vniuersall dissolution.' This has an ideological affinity with Ulysses's degree speech in *Troilus and Cressida*. Elyot asserts that the hierarchies of Heaven are reflected on Earth – the elements have their 'spheris' and men do not all have the same gifts from God. Potters cannot dispense justice, ploughmen and carters 'shall make but an feble answere to an ambassadour'. Antony is a privileged, spoiled rich boy who had the means, by virtue of birth rank, to access consulship, senatorial status and other posts of power. He was not suitable to such elevation, but achieved it merely on account of rank and contacts. The same corrupt monopoly existed in Whitehall and would hamper English government until the nineteenth century. Central to the situation, as viewed by most orthodox Englishmen in 1606, is that Antony subverted normative views on what type of man was suitable to govern. Cicero had laid out in detail the virtues governors needed. Antony did not fit this template and it is no surprise that the two men became inveterate enemies. Cicero's two *Philippics* against Antony laid out his many failings. The lovers were attacked for their debts and lifestyle and Cicero's two critical pamphlets condemned Antony's character, accusing him of extravagance, promiscuity, ostentation, luxurious living and forgery. In revenge, Antony argued vehemently for Cicero's execution for an alleged role in the plot against Julius Caesar. When this was eventually achieved he allegedly had sent to him the head and the hand that wrote the pamphlets. They arrived during a dinner party. Antony laughed and exulted at his opponent's demise. Fulvia allegedly jabbed her hairpin in Cicero's eyes. This grotesque act of petty spite indicates that the triumvir was not of such a noble heart as he liked others to think. Antony shows similar vindictiveness when he has Thidias whipped for kissing Cleopatra's hand. This is not noble behaviour either. Magnanimity and mercy are prized qualities in a ruler. This impious act of revenge adds to Antony's growing *hubris*, setting him up for the gods to bring down.

Key to Elyot's curriculum for men destined to authority is that their early years be lived in a milieu of virtue, that the language and behaviour of mothers, nurses and maids be irreproachable. At the age of 7 boys should be removed from 'the company of women' and tutored by 'an auncient & worshipfull man' with grave demeanour, gentle manners and impeccable morality. Then began a classics course that would develop their rhetorical skills, improve their Latin and perfect the fluency and accuracy of their English. Elyot includes physical exercise in his regimen, recommending hunting, hawking, dancing, wrestling, running, swimming and weapons training – in moderation. This is standard Renaissance elite male education.[8] Elyot deplores the tendency of noble families to halt their children's education at 14 and 'sufre them to live in idelnes'.[9]

He believes education is a lifelong process and essential for the production of governors if they are to resemble Plato's philosopher-king. Antony received the standard education for Roman patricians, but for all that was still a deeply flawed, weak-willed character – incapable of restraining his appetites, determined to have his own way and brutal when thwarted. James had deprecated the tyrannical distortion of the state to suit the monarch, but tried to do exactly that himself. Antony displays unsuitable characteristics, some different from James, some similar. He appears to have been 'trayned in the way of vertue' as Elyot recommended, but his moral sense remained untrained, indulging in all the usual high-end lures of gluttony, avarice, lechery, swearing and gambling.

Elyot exhorts young men to 'lerne wisdom & fal nat [do not fall into sin]' and abide by Christian precepts of behaviour, for 'from god only procedeth all honour' and God 'shal examine your dedes & serch your thoughts'. Since no one man can know all that is happening in a realm, a king needs reliable deputies to act as his eyes, ears, hands and legs. The body image was often invoked. The nation was 'the body politic', the head was the monarch, the major organs the nobility, and the hands, legs and muscles were the labouring part of society. All had a job to do and if one part did not work properly the whole became less effective. Such subsidiary governors (courtiers, councillors/counsellors, etc.) should be men 'superiour in condition or haviour [and] vertue'. Elyot demands they have 'their owne reuenues certeine, wherby they have competent substance to lyve without taking rewardes: it is likely that they wyll not be so desirous of lucre'. This defence against bribery had disappeared by James's time. Jobbery, corruption and greed were standard at court as they appear to be in Rome. Two generations of luxurious living and extravagance left many high-end families financially embarrassed. An unseemly scrabble for lucrative posts, lobbying for monopolies and a readiness to accept bribes was one way to help recoup family fortunes. Another was a profitable marriage. In the sixteenth century, marriage for mainly monetary reasons stood at 20 per cent among titled families, rising to 38 per cent by 1660.[10] At the very top of the upper ranks (including royalty) political reasons also operated in marriage alliances. Antony's foolish agreement to marry Octavia is a means to keep peace between himself and Caesar, but Antony has not the moral strength to honour a bond he should not have made in the first place, sleepwalking into disaster by agreeing to marriage so easily.

A King's View of His Office

Antony's misrule and fall are contextualized by James I's contribution to conduct literature on the role and nature of kingship. *Basilikon Doron*, an advice book to James's son, Henry, Prince of Wales, is structured in three parts: 'Of a

King's Christian Duty towards God', 'Of a King's Duty in His Office', and 'Of a King's Behaviour in Indifferent Things' ('indifferent' meaning matters relating to leisure time). The first section about a king's duty to follow the tenets of Christianity strongly establishes the idea of a king as God's representative. This becomes a running motif throughout. Many ideas parallel Elyot and there are verbal echoes of his work. Marginal notes indicate how much the book owes to Plato's *Republic* and Cicero's seminal *De Officiis*, the common source for books on the perpetual need to remind the governing ranks what their function in society was. Though the Christian elements do not technically relate to the pre-Christian setting of the play, there is common ground marked by the allusions to Plato and Cicero. This activates the classical approach to virtue that has, as we have already discussed, considerable overlap with seventeenth-century ideas on correct conduct.

The key interests of *Basilikon Doron* in relation to *Antony and Cleopatra* are threefold: 1. establishing the criteria for measuring Antony against the idealized monarch presented in the *Basilikon*, 2. as an ironic reflection of the discrepancy between James's theory and practice, 3. as a topical- satirical mirror reflecting how the Jacobean court failed to live up to its monarch's precepts. The characters' conduct and the portrait of humanity emerging reflect some of the critical remarks made by James.

The book begins with an abstract of the 'Argument' in sonnet form:

> GOD giues not Kings the stile of Gods in vaine,
> For on his throne his sceptre doe they swey:
> And as their subjects ought them to obey,
> So Kings should feare and serue their God againe.
> If then ye would enjoy a happy raigne,
> Obserue the statutes of your heauenly King,
> And from his Law, make all your Lawes to spring:
> Since his Lieutenant here ye should remaine,
> Reward the iust, be steadfast, true, and plaine,
> Represse the proud, maintaining aye the right,
> Walk always so, as euer in his sight,
> Who guards the godly, plaguing the prophane:
> And so ye shall in Princely vertue shine,
> Resembling right your mightie King Diuine.

Overlapping the belief that kingship was divinely sanctioned with the image of God's 'lieutenant here', the king almost becomes divine. Few Jacobeans questioned that rule should be monarchical or doubted that the continuing English system should have a one-person government, but increasingly they questioned kingship's divinity, the relationship between ruler and ruled and what should be the limits to princely authority. It is often assumed divine right was universally accepted; it was and was not. More and more voices questioned the manner of kingship as exercised by Elizabeth and James.[11] The unthinking masses accepted that the king – a distant figure of power and awe – was like a god on Earth. Largely they were voiceless, but others spoke for traditional beliefs. Robert Filmer formalized these in *Patriarcha*. Written in the 1620s (published posthumously in 1680), it summarizes the accumulated ideology of divine right. Filmer believes the model monarchical state is founded on the idea of familial patriarchy and asserts Adamic dominion established by God (in Genesis) as the origin of patriarchy and kingship. As fathers rule the domestic *polis*, so kings rule the state. Elizabeth's death foregrounded discussions increasingly focused on the complex concept of divine right and how kings should govern. The justificatory line of argument was that God made Adam lord of all creation, with dominion over his wife, family and the fruits of the Earth. The male therefore had divine sanction for his rule. Kings had similar incontrovertible, unopposable rule. Disagreement was a sin against God, against nature. Thus bulwarked against opposition, monarchy and patriarchy became firmly embedded in society and their power developed. Kings had absolute power over life and property, could have people executed or pardoned, declare war, make peace, levy taxes, regulate trade, charter markets, issue licenses for manufacture, legitimize bastards or send people to the Tower. Their will was law and the law bent to their will. Regal proclamations were made with the mantra 'Le roi le veult' (The king wills it). Laws were only passed if the king similarly authenticated them. He nominated government officers, bishops, judges and peers. His power was absolute, his favour vital. James declared of kings that 'even by God himself they are called gods'.[12] One might ask how he knew this. No one did ask – to his face.

Antony too lived in an era where patricians had immense autocratic power and the potential to abuse it. A brutal age will always feature hirelings ready to commit (for a price) extralegal activities of all sorts. The whipping of Thidias indicates how violent Antony could become and how ready servants were to obey. He advises Thidias:

> If that thy father live, let him repent
> Thou was not made his daughter. (III. xiii. 139–40)

This implies that Antony could have had him castrated. Emasculated himself, he strikes out harshly, perhaps to reassert the power he feels he has lost in submission to Cleopatra. He scorns Thidias as a feed servant ('a fellow that will take rewards' [III. xiii. 128]) and defiantly tells the man to recount his treatment to Caesar; if he 'mislike' Antony's words and actions he can take revenge on the former slave Hipparchus (who deserted to Caesar's side) and 'whip or hang or torture' him (III. xiii. 155). This callous and demeaning disregard for mere servants indicates what Antony is really like. On a formal level it is a major insult to Caesar to abuse his messenger. Heralds, diplomats, servants or messengers working for another ruler were by mutual agreement and custom treated with honour, however disagreeable the information they carried.

The first book of *Basilikon Doron* opens with an orthodox declaration that immediately places Antony in the wrong:

> He cannot bee thought worthie to rule and commaund others, that cannot rule [...] his owne proper affections and unreasonable appetites, so can he not be thought worthie to governe a Christian People [that] feareth not and loveth not the Divine Majestie. Neither can [...] his Government succeed well with him [...] as coming from a filthie spring, if his person be unsanctified. (1)

Punishment was the prerogative of the gods and Antony is risking their retribution. James stresses the need for kingly piety and a life lived according to the demands of Christianity (as an example to his court and people): virtue, self-control, respect for and obedience to scripture, conscience and faith ('the Golden chaine that linketh the Faithfull Soule to Christ' [9]). The series of guiding precepts are as follows: 'Wrest not the World to your owne appetite' (4), 'The summe of the Law is the Tenne Commandements' (6), 'Wisely [...] discerne [...] betwixt the expres Commaundment and Will of God in his Word and the invention and ordinance of Man' (15), and 'Kythe [show] more by your deedes than by your wordes the love of Vertue and hatred of Vice' (16). Antony should be a role model to his people through his personal virtues. Public profile built through public appearance was an important aspect of Elizabeth's image. It was not effectively projected by James – or by Antony, who seems to think that grand displays or drunken games in the streets are sufficient.

The second book, 'A King's Duty in His Office', links the lesson of being a good Christian to the prince's second calling: being a good king. This office is discharged through 'justice and equitie [fairness]', achieved by 'establishing and executing good lawes' and 'by your behaviour in your own person, and with your servants, to teach your people by your example: for people are naturally inclined to counterfaite (like Apes) their Princes manners' (17–18). None of this reflects well on Antony or Cleopatra. Hopping 'forty paces through the public street' (II. ii. 239) is hardly likely to encourage respect. It may be high-spirited but lacks decorum. To us it may appear an expression of her unique charisma. Not to the Jacobeans. Enobarbus's conclusion that 'she did make defect perfection' (II. ii. 241) suggests a tainted definition of perfection and the idea that 'age cannot wither her' suggests she is as old as human corruption. Priests who would bless her 'when she is riggish' (I. ii. 250) merely reinforces the sense of the corrupted values of Egypt. Dignity was important to the public persona in Jacobean times, and yet James rarely displayed it. Antony reeling in the streets at noon, being pushed and shoved by 'knaves that smell of sweat' (I. iv. 21) is hardly dignified either.

To James a true king is 'ordained for his people', while a tyrant 'thinketh his people ordained for him, a pray to his passions and inordinate appetites' (18). A good king 'employeth all his studie and paines, to procure and maintain [...] the well-fare and peace of his people [...] as their naturall father and kindly maister [...], subjecting his owne private affections and appetites to the weale and standing of his subjects' (18–19). Antony is no father to his subjects. He passes power and land to his children but neglects the Egyptian state. He is neither a Roman nor an Egyptian and is thus relieved of the need to feel responsibility for his people. A prey to his passions, neglecting the 'weale and standing' of his subjects, he has the true voluptuary's freedom from all commitments other than to his own desires. He is not a tyrant (and both Roman and Renaissance history provide plenty of examples) but simply disengaged from his role. He enjoys the spectacle and public/court aspect of power, for they project and pamper his ego. Goldsworthy asserts, 'He paraded his power in a way that was both blatant and vulgar, giving the impression of enjoying himself in luxurious debauchery instead of labouring diligently.'[13] Considering his long-term career, 'he showed some skill as a politician and administrator, but had only limited ability as a soldier', and his rise 'owed little to conspicuous talent and far more to good connections, luck and the ardent desire for power, position and wealth'.[14]

James warns that new laws are always needed to deal with 'new rising corruptions' (20) and that 'a Parliament is the honourablest and highest judgement [...] as being the Kings heade Courte' (21). He constantly called Parliament when he needed money but regularly left the country in the charge of his Privy Council while he gallivanted off hunting for days on end. James did not deal with the old or new corruptions that surrounded him, did not settle the country 'by the severitie of justice' (22), but left in place the endemic institutional corruption. He did not 'embrace the quarrel of the poore and distressed' (26), neither did he live up to the precept that you should 'governe your subjects, by knowing what vices they are naturally most inclined to, as a good Physician' (27). It is easy to see why such demanding duties as James outlines did not appeal to Antony's libertine preferences. Antony suggests to Cleopatra: 'Tonight we'll wander through the streets and note/The qualities of people' (I. i 54–5). It sounds like another night-time entertainment rather than a genuine desire to gauge the mood and character of their subjects. Diligent, wise rulers listen to advice from different sources, weigh it up and make careful decisions. Antony admits to Cleopatra his 'purposes' 'are, or cease,/As you shall give th'advice' (I. iii. 68–9). While it is wise to take advice, it is unwise to make 'peace or war/As thou affects' (I. iii. 71–2) when that means according to the whim of one person (especially an unreliable hysteric). This has greater significance to a Jacobean audience as a serious subversion and reversal of orthodox gender roles. Rome is the power in Egypt, Cleopatra is a client, Antony is Rome's representative – and he gives away his power. If Cleopatra is the great love of his life and genuinely loves him, she is at the same time the gods' instrument of punishment for his neglect and *hubris*.

Both fictional and real ruler bear responsibility for their failure to deal with the social necessities of their states. It is probable James simply found the English situation too complex and deeply ingrained, gave up trying to reform either court or country on the lines of *Basilikon* and, hypnotized by the immense disposable income the Crown gave him, stopped bothering to be a good king and enjoyed the ritual, the status and the luxury. How like Antony. The failure to see that privilege, power and luxury come with responsibilities would lead James's son into civil war. Antony manages that himself. James never got to grips with any of the underlying social problems, seemingly letting the nobility act as they pleased, despite his admonitions in *Basilikon* about repressing pride and supporting the poor. James advises taming arrogant nobles: a governor must 'teache' them 'to keepe [the] lawes as precisely as the meanest' (34). Echoing Elyot he advises, 'Acquaint your selfe [...] with all the honest men of your Barrones and Gentlemen' (34) for 'vertue followeth oftest noble blood' (35) and such men 'must be your armes and executers of your lawes' (35). This expresses the common belief that the nobility are born innately virtuous. This view, promulgated by the nobility, ignores both Original Sin, the common belief that all men are born with a sinful tendency, and the daily evidence of aristo-gentry misconduct. The Romans, without the psychological baggage of Original Sin, knew all too well how power corrupts and how those born to power were by and large no better human beings than the plebeian mob.

James's recommendation to 'bee well acquainted with the nature and humours of all your subjects' and 'once in the yeare [...] visit the principall parts of the country' (40) was not something he did and clearly Antony had no 'meet and greet the people' policy. He gave his orders and expected them to be carried out, while he continued revelling. After reading Polydore Vergil's *Anglica Historia*[15] James agrees that a king's actions determine his country's fate, borne out by the outcome of Antony and Cleopatra's actions. The image of a 'filthie spring' polluting the stream (a ruler's corruption corrupting the country) occurs frequently in contemporary drama. Antony has corrupted good government by being disengaged. Robert Burton makes the point that 'their Love brought themselves and all Egypt into extreme and miserable calamities, the end of her is as bitter as worm-wood, and as sharp as a two-edged sword'.[16] The gap between precept and practice is made wider and more ironic in James's discussion of a prince and his court as exemplars:

> It is not enough to a good King, by the sceptre of good lawes well excute to governe, and by force of armes to protect his people; if he joyne not therewith his virtuous life in his owne person, and in the person of his Court and companie: by good example alluring his subjects to the love of vertue, and hatred of vice. [...] All people are naturally inclined to followe their Princes example [...] let your owne life be a law-book and a mirrour to your people. (45)

This was to be achieved 'in the governement of your Court and followers' and

> in having your minde decked and enriched so with all virtuous qualities, that there-with ye may worthilie rule your people. For it is not enough that yr [sic] have and retaine [...] within your selfe never so many good qualities and virtues, except ye imploy them, and set them on worke, for the weale of them that are committed to your charge. (45)

Care was crucial when appointing public officers who had responsibility for 'the weale of your people' (50). They should be men 'of knowne wisdome, honestie, and good conference [...], free of all factions and partialities: but specially free of that filthy vice of Flattery, the pest of all Princes' (51). James recommends: 'Commaund a hartly and brotherly love among them that serve you. [...] Maintaine peace in your Court, banish envie, cherish modestie, banish deboshed insolence, foster humility, and represse pride' (53–4). Brotherly love, modesty, banished insolence, repressed pride – the opposite of Antony's government (and Whitehall), in which suspicion, dissension, envy, debauchery and arrogance are common. Drama and tragedy lie in the ensuing confusion, mistakes, scheming and collapse.

As regards personal kingly virtues, James echoes many of Elyot's recommendations. Antony may be measured against these qualities. A prince should follow the four cardinal virtues with 'temperance, Queene of all the rest' (62). Elyot and James's synonym for temperance is 'moderation'. A king needs 'wise moderation [...] first commanding your selfe [...] in all your affections and passions, [...] even in your most virtuous actions, [so you] make ever moderation to bee the chief ruler' (63). If civility, education and cultured behaviour are to be part of social–civic interaction, moderation is vital in assisting the repression of those aspects of man's nature that are disruptive to the moral profile of a state. Antony is too drunk with his own fabricated image as a Herculean personality/celebrity to ever behave with moderation, and too weak to reform. After temperance comes justice, 'the greatest vertue, that properly belongeth to a Kings office [...]. Use Justice [...] with such moderation as it turne not in Tyrannie' (63).[17] Antony's behaviour looks like mental tyranny – peremptory, overly strict and inflexible. He has yet to learn that mercy and forgiveness may achieve much. Orthodox paternalist belief, both in Rome and England, favoured firm authoritarianism – within the law and according to ethical principles. James specifies 'Clemencie, Magnanimitie, Liberalitie, Constancie, Humilitie, and all other Princely vertues' (64) as essential. Another recommendation is to 'haunt your Sessions [court hearings], and spie carefullie their proceedings' (67). James advocates 'reading of authenticke histories and Chronicles [...], applying the by-past things to the present estate' (69), yet he learned nothing from history, seeming swamped by the complexity of English society's problems and the unmoveable corruption of a court and government he could never fully control.

Those who went to see the play for its history and passionate love story were also given a display of power politics and folly at the highest level. It would not take much effort to see its relevance to James and his Whitehall entourage. The second book of *Basilikon Doron* finishes with a series of pertinent precepts: 'Embrace true Magnanimitie [...], thinking your offender not worthie your wrath, empyring over your owne passion, and triumphing in the commanding your selfe to forgive' (71). James implores the reader to 'foster true Humility [...], banishing pride' (71), and to 'exercise true Wisedome; in discerning wisely betwixt true and false reports' (74), reminiscent of Montaigne's comments on the misuse of words. Montaigne deplored the art of fine speaking as 'deceiving not our eyes but our judgement, bastardizing and corrupting things in their very essence' so that feelings are 'inflated with rich and magnificent words'.[18] Antony trained as an orator in Athens, learning the flamboyant Eastern style rather than the clear, direct Roman manner. He and Cleopatra both use language in overblown, dramatic ways. All emotions are expressed at a high-octane level, so the trivial is indistinguishable from the grave. This casts doubt upon the sincerity of their feelings. James's final dictum resonates with the ironies of his and Antony's failings:

> Consider that God is the author of all vertue, having imprinted in men's mindes by the very light of nature, the love of all morall virtues. [...] Preasse then to shine as farre before your people, in all vertue and honestie; as in greatnesse of ranke [...] as by their hearing of your lawes, both their eyes and their eares, may leade [...] them to the love of vertue, and hatred of vice. (75)

Antony signally fails to lead, teach or guide his people; he leads them into war, teaches them debauchery and political mishandling, and guides them into annexation by Rome.

Antony and King James

Antony is not a fictionalized representation of James I. However, an exploration of the consequences of neglecting absolute power's responsibilities, contrasted with autocracy mal-administered by erratic whims and fancies, nevertheless throws up subtle similarities for the audience to identify. Antony's failings are never specifically and definitively allied to James's. On the surface they are very different. Overt identification of fictional ruler with real ruler would not be allowed. All plays were licensed by the Revels Office and registered at the Stationers' Office only once the government officials were sure the work contained nothing treasonable or heretical. The meaning of treason was elastically expanded to mean any criticism of the monarch. Direct representation of or critical reference to a reigning monarch was prohibited and would be removed from the script. Authors could face imprisonment and James had already shown readiness to do that.[19] A marginal note in *Basilikon Doron* ('Witnesse the experience of the late house of Gowrie' [47]) alludes to the 1600 plot by the Earl of Gowrie to kidnap James.[20] In 1604 the King's Men rehearsed a new play, *The Tragedy of the Gowrie*, for the court Christmas celebrations. Politically sensitive, it necessitated an actor playing the king, and represented an incident from his life. The play was suppressed.[21] Shakespeare, however, knew how to cloak his concerns by indirection, smuggling in themes and presenting them in such a way as to not appear overtly critical of particular persons. As one of the leading King's Men he could ill afford to upset his employer. Other political plays about the misrule of state, but less sensitive because they were not blatantly personal, were *Measure for Measure* (performed at court 26 December 1604) and *King Lear* (performed at court

26 December 1606). Satire of flawed leadership and the corrupt ruling classes is evident in all the last plays. The other Roman Plays, sourced from Plutarch and set in Rome, are distanced from the local situation but reflect on intrigues and corruption in politics and weak governance. *Measure for Measure* is set in Vienna, *Lear* in pagan times, *Macbeth* in the relatively recent past (but showing the restoration of a legitimate line from which James was descended), *Timon of Athens* in Athens, *Cymbeline* in pre-Christian Britain, *The Winter's Tale* in Sicily and Bohemia, and *The Tempest* on a Mediterranean island. Whatever the locational or periodic indirection, the themes were resonantly contemporary.

At the same time, Antony *is* James, but so obliquely as to be impossible for government censors to pin down definitively. Any ruler on stage invited automatic mental comparison. The critique of styles of rule aims at provoking thought and a possible adjustment of values. It effects this indirectly. Ancient history, a rampantly heterosexual affair – nothing treasonable there. But there is enough reference to rulers, parasites and politics to make his audience think about current court behaviour. Shakespeare's defence would be: 'If you think I am talking about today or anyone particular you have seen parallels I didn't intend.'

James looked a very promising replacement as ruler of England: experienced as king of Scotland, something of a philosopher-king, author of books on witchcraft and smoking in addition to two kingship studies. *The True Law of Free Monarchies* (1598) gives a clear statement of his belief in divine right absolutism, but its subtitle 'Or the Reciprocal and Mutual Duty Betwixt a Free King and His Natural Subjects' suggests belief too in rule involving a contract between king and people. There is an unresolved contradiction here. A contractual relationship suggests that the two sides agree to organize government through discussion and compromise. James's actual style of rule, once in power, betrayed him as a wilful absolutist. *The True Law* (1598) demonstrates (illogically and by closed arguments) that kings derived power from God, that their authority was 'the true pattern of divinity' and, like God's, kingly authority was part of the laws of nature and the customs of the realm. Some already supported the contract idea, tying people and ruler together in a liaison of mutual responsibilities and authority. James's practice took less notice of the customs of his realm than of his own will and needs. Quoting the Book of Samuel he asserted that all subjects' property was the king's to use as he chose. This was not well received by the Commons, whom he lectured on the subject, for they were all men of property. The great obstacle was the traditional claim that as God's deputy no one could judge him but God. Putting him above the law, blocking any suggestion that he could ever be judged by his people, diametrically opposed the view of his one-time tutor George Buchanan. Buchanan's *De Jure Regni apud Scotos Dialogus* (*Dialogue on the Rule of Kings in Scotland*, 1579) made an important contribution to the contractarian debate, proposing that royal power originates from the agreement of the people, that kings hold power only as long as they conform to the terms by which power was given them by the people, and that a people may resist, depose and punish a king who breaks his contract by becoming tyrannical.[22] James's belief in his divine mission was well established by his accession but endorsed by fawning verses, flattering speeches and obsequious courtiers. During his 1604 procession through the city he received an address at the Fenchurch Street gate in which a character, Theosophia (Divine Wisdom), announced '*Per me reges regnant*' (By me do all kings govern).[23] It would not be long before people would doubt James's will was identical to God's. Antony behaves at times like a god, but more often and more dangerously like a man who believes he can act as he likes without fear of retribution. This *hubris* brings him down. Increasingly desperate, he becomes increasingly foolish; his death, and the incidents leading to it, are farcical. The final act without him shifts focus to Cleopatra's reaction to Caesar. Antony's absence, with an act to go, casts doubt on how tragic he is as a central figure.

The Herculean persona Antony projects is not a fictionalization of James (physically, Herculean was the last characteristic one would ascribe to James), but they shared some similarities of character. Inviting identification with Antony are James's bullying manner; his determination to have his own way on matters ranging from the highly political or religious to the most trivially personal; his conviction that he was always right because 1. he was more learned than anyone else, and 2. because he was a god on Earth; and his deviation in every respect from Ciceronian and Elyotesque ideas of the ideal prince. The good prince was expected to be an example, expected to aim at the bettering of his people. He should cleanse himself of appetites and passions: those 'disturbances experienced by [...] intemperate souls [...] afflicted [...] by the stupor of ignorance, and [...] by the turmoil caused by their blind and perverse desires'.[24] James was prone to fixations that distracted him from his administrative duties. His academic commitment to serious polemic writing did not particularly divert his energies, but he did have an intellectual snobbery that revelled in displaying his knowledge. This particularly related to his tendency to lecture on doctrinal matters and give mandatory directions to his overly compliant bishops. James pressurized leading judges, especially when they upheld appeals against the High Commission of the Church. The need to always be right suggests insecurity, possibly resulting from his disjointed family life in his formative years. Antony too has a fixation that distracts him from business and an arrogance that makes him feel he is entitled to behave as he likes. He too drank too much, was always in debt, accessed state money for personal use, and could be vindictively brutal.

Chapter 6

PATRIARCHY, FAMILY AUTHORITY AND GENDER RELATIONSHIPS

> Yet will not I forget what I should be
> And what I am, a husband: in that name
> Is hid divinity. (*'Tis Pity She's a Whore*, IV. iii. 135–7)

The matter of gender relationships is full of ambiguities, prejudices, contradictions and inconsistencies, from both sides. Two features are definite: theoretically men ruled, and women often subverted male domination. Custom, doctrine and law made fathers heads of families. God ruled creation, kings ruled nations, fathers ruled families. God punished sin, kings punished earthly crime, and a man could beat his wife, his children and his servants. Custom recommended moderation in corporal punishment, advocating its avoidance if possible, but its support in law meant it could happen. Beating causing bodily harm was not allowed. No doubt there were abusive and violent men who caused serious injury, but they were protected by an all-male legal system. A husband was an authoritarian figure whose word was law and the law supported men. Patriarchy ruled.

St Paul authorized male dominance in the New Testament, *the* primary conduct book: 'Wives, submit yourselves unto your own husbands, as unto the Lord. For the husband is the head of the wife, even as Christ is the head of the church.'[1] Supposedly, husbands were dominant and wives subordinate in all things – in legal status, physical strength, intelligence and virtue. In reality petticoat power was exerted in many ways. The sexual aspect of female strength is forefronted in *Antony and Cleopatra*, with the queen subverting normative expectations.

Patriarchy originates in Genesis when God makes man first, gives Adam dominion over all animals, then makes Eve out of Adam's rib and gives him rule over her. She is designed as 'an help meet' (Genesis 2:18) – a companion and assistant. When Adam is tempted by Eve to eat the apple God upbraids him for listening to his wife and acting according to her encouragement rather than God's command against eating the forbidden fruit. This story, written by men, endorsing male superiority and rule, an extension of the hierarchy of the chain of creation, reflects how society was organized and was re-enforced by a misogynistic Catholic Church deeply suspicious of women. To the fallen Eve God says: 'I will greatly multiply thy sorrow [...]. In sorrow thou shalt bring forth children: and thy desire shall be to thy husband, and he shall rule over thee.'[2] Thus the pains of childbirth are annexed as punishment for Eve's sin and misogyny given divine authority. The seventeenth century saw female inferiority as pre-dating the Fall. Made after Adam, Eve was always secondary, so were all women secondary. The poet-satirist George Wither summed this up: 'The woman for the man was made/And not the man for her.'[3]

Advising his son about marriage, James I quoted Genesis 2:23 (where Adam claims Eve is 'bone of my bone, and flesh of my flesh'), commenting on the institution as 'the greatest earthly felicite or miserie, that can come to a man, according as it pleaseth God to blesse or cursse the same'.[4] Within the timeframe of *Antony and Cleopatra*, it is worth considering how much felicity or misery Antony derives from his association with Cleopatra. Misery predominates. James's advice is largely orthodox. He tells Henry to 'marrie one [...] of your own Religion; her ranke and other qualities being agreeable to your estate'.[5] There is awareness of the partnership aspect of marriage, but it is patriarchally slanted:

> Treate her as your owne flesh, commaund her as her Lord, cherish her as your helper, rule her as your pupil, and please her in all things reasonable [...]. Ye are the head, as she is your body: [...] your office to commaund, [...] hers to obey; but yet with such a sweete harmonie, as shee should be as readie to obey, as yee to commaunde [...]. Suffer her never to medle with the politick government of the common-weale, but hold her at the Oeconomick rule of the house; [...] yet all to be subject to your direction: keepe carefullie good and chaste companie about her; for women are the frailest sexe.[6]

Publicly, it was a man's world. Regardless of theory, whatever the biblical and legal support, the reality varied greatly. In defining gender roles and attitudes it is always important to remember, whatever the stereotypes, in practice matters could be different and women subverted patriarchy in many ways and in a variety of arenas.

The long-established medieval position on women still persisted, but there had been changes. Orthodoxy saw women as the origin of sin, the source of temptation, taking its authority from the Bible. Paul told wives to submit to their husbands and keep silent in church (Colossians 3:18). In I Timothy (2:8–12) he wrote: 'I will therefore that the men pray [...]. Let the women learn in silence with all subjection. I permit not a woman to teach, neither to usurp authority over the man, but to be in silence.' The Bible's good women, the Virgin Mary and an array of female saints, were outweighed by evil women in scripture, in history and in the diatribes of the church fathers.[7] Biased selection of biased texts built up formidable prejudice against women. Tertullian (AD c. 160–c. 225) saw them as 'the devil's gateway'.[8] St John Chrysostom (AD c. 347–407) exclaimed: 'How often do we, from beholding a woman, suffer a thousand evils; [...] entertaining an inordinate desire, and experiencing anguish for many days [...]. The beauty of woman is the greatest snare.'[9] Clement of Alexandria (AD c.150–c. 215) went further: 'Every woman should be ashamed that she is a woman' for they are 'the confusion of men, an insatiable animal [...], an eternal ruin'.[10] Male mistrust of female sexuality underlies much of the patriarchal system. It was a factor in the intermittent waves of witch trials and executions. The *Malleus Maleficarum* (*The Hammer of Witches*, 1496) declared, 'All witchcraft comes from carnal lust, which in women is insatiable.'[11] Women are commonly accused of sex with the Devil in accounts of witches' covens and other black mass rituals.

Women's main role was keeping the house and largely keeping to the house. Countrywomen helped in the fields at crucial times like harvesting, but many of their tasks were home based – cooking, feeding poultry, tending vegetable gardens, cleaning and making clothes. A shopkeeper's wife or daughter might help behind the counter, but saleable products (pastry, clothes, crafted items, etc.) were made by men (apprentices, journeymen and masters) and shop assistants were mainly men. Women were barred from the professions, public life and higher education. The standard view was that women were intellectually feeble, unreliable, irrational, shrewish, gossips, spendthrifts, bad tempered, endlessly demanding, and if given rein would monopolize any public/social meeting. A stock image in medieval comic writing was that while the man worked and the servants kept the house, the wife gossiped with friends, entertained her lover or gallivanted around wasting money shopping. This view persisted. It was generally believed women were overemotional and easily overheated sexually. Belief in the insatiability of the female sex drive reflected male insecurity and a man's uncertainty whether the child he was bringing up was indeed his own – fears related to questions of inheritance and keeping the family bloodline pure. It explains the obsession with the chastity of daughters and wives. A tainted daughter shamed the family, had little value in the marriage market and remained a drain on family finances. A wife who was 'loose i' the hilts' degraded the husband's public reputation and honour, wounded his personal esteem, cast doubt on his children's legitimacy, and made him the butt of jokes about cuckolds and horns.[12] Proverbs 12:4 put it thus: 'A virtuous woman is a crown to her husband: but she that maketh ashamed is as rottenness in his bones.'

Patriarchy's dominance explains why so many men had such low opinions of women, treating them unsympathetically and as sex objects. Such views are voiced frequently among the rakish male characters crowding Elizabethan-Jacobean comedies, though Hamlet and Iago are misogynistic too. This loose-living, loose-tongued, bawdy, joking brotherhood stretches from Lucio (*Measure for Measure*, 1604) through Willmore (Aphra Behn's *The Rover*, 1677) to innumerable libertines in later drama and novels. A counterbalancing tradition offers the *gentils domna* (gentle lady) of Courtly Love, the beautiful but virtuous woman whose example civilizes brutish men. Castiglione endorses this view. He describes the court of Urbino, presided over by Duchess Elizabetta Gonzaga, in command of all, endowing 'everyone else with her own discernment and goodness' and how she 'tempered us all to her own character and quality'.[13] She has the self-effacing quiet of the confident but restrained woman, not the silence of the repressed and downtrodden creature. Cleopatra is nothing like this – always talking, giving orders, changing her mind, teasing, hectoring and playing games. But then she is a queen, and has spent many years fighting for survival, using men as and when she needed them. She relied on Antony and the military presence of his legions to maintain her power. In Rome poets criticized her tainted character and reputation and satirized the situation whereby a Roman general and triumvir and his soldiers were ruled by her. Cleopatra was a strong character; she had subtly manoeuvred herself into political alliances that helped her survive and retain independence in a volatile Near East, amid the dangers of her own court and the changing fortunes of the Roman Civil Wars that preceded and followed Julius Caesar's death. In a male-dominated world where Roman women were allowed no public role and only influenced the political state of affairs from behind the scenes as wives (or mothers) of leading male figures, Cleopatra retained power as an independent woman and queen influencing the progress of things. Current feminist criticism, of course, sees her as a strong woman doing what is needful to survive in a male world. That includes some dubious behaviour – like the false message of her death which she would have known had a good chance of triggering Antony's suicide and making her own compromise with Caesar easier. Antony was not only an attractive man, but a man with immense power (and some women find male power an attraction in itself). He was therefore an agreeable, expedient lover who would help her maintain power until he became an obstacle. Cleopatra would disturb many in the audience. She subverts normality; she overturns God's order.

So, we have a unique situation; two strong personalities, male and female, both of huge importance politically. Patriarchy and the realities of politics theoretically make Antony the leading figure. The reality, responding to Cleopatra's character, is that she reverses the orthodox gender relationship. Antony largely accepts this. A Jacobean audience (the male part at least) would disapprove. Antony is a woman-led man, emasculated, his role as ruler put aside to satisfy the demands of his lover. He is uxorious, as Adam had been, and is too excessively ready to prioritize his woman's wishes above his other responsibilities. A man who can declare of his 'wrangling queen' that 'everything becomes' her (I. i. 50) is declaring his complete enslavement to her. He is suggesting that whatever she does (good or bad), everything in her character is still attractive. He is besotted. Philo suggests that sometimes 'he is not Antony' and 'comes too short of that great property/Which still should go with Antony' (I. i. 58–9). He has lost his sense of what is rational and balanced when he asserts, 'The nobleness of life/Is to do thus' (I. i. 37–8) and kisses Cleopatra. Furthermore, he has lost the power in the relationship. One person should not have the monopoly in any personal relationship, but from a Jacobean orthodox viewpoint if one person were to have the balance of power in their favour that person should be the man. Antony's submissive role is distasteful, laughable and disgusting from a Jacobean male perspective. Philo is right to warn Demetrius:

> Take but good note, and you shall see in him
> The triple pillar of the world transformed
> Into a strumpet's fool. (I. i. 12–13)

This announces to the audience that the play is a classic study of a man of rank and importance shackled by his attraction to a woman. The tragic machine is already ticking over.

The 1571 *Second Book of Homilies* (XVIII, 'Of the State of Matrimony') declared woman 'a weak creature, prone to all weak affections and dispositions of the mind', indicating that the Anglican Church was essentially little different from Rome. Greater respect for women, though still wary, emerged among the Puritans, who demanded abstinence from both men and women, but Puritanism was a minority sect. Theatre commonly reverted to stock types of female for their comic or dramatic value. The garrulous nurse in *Romeo and Juliet*, the witty but overwhelming Beatrice in *Much Ado About Nothing*, and the scheming, unscrupulous Lady Macbeth all follow stereotypical lines. Another stock character from drama, the widow – either rampantly free or easily victimized – reflects the standard view of predatory female sexuality and echoes anxieties about overhasty second marriage for women. Dynastic and financial concerns are involved. Family fortunes could quickly be lost to a predatory second husband and the children of the first union disposed of or simply sent to a faraway estate and neglected. The 'merry widow' was not just a comic figure. *Hamlet* and *The Duchess of Malfi* present tragic examples of the difficulties second marriage could bring. In practice second marriages were common among both sexes and all classes. Moralists admitted that humankind was inordinately lustful, but since most were male they tended to be more tolerant of male libidinousness and more critical of female failings. Neither the wildfire spread of syphilis nor the widespread ecclesiastical condemnation of intercourse outside marriage as a Deadly Sin for both sexes curbed the natural lustfulness of either. With the blatant hypocrisy, chauvinism and prejudice that each sex brings to stereotyping the other, there was, on the male side, a double standard in accepting young men fornicating indiscriminately and regarding possession of a mistress as a sign of manhood, while demanding chaste behaviour among women. And then there is Cleopatra. Sexually experienced, a self-dramatizing woman who knew how to get what she wanted, she is like an old actress, always creating dramas, always making herself the centre of attention, she is an amalgam of all the standard misogyny men believed about women.

The orthodox husband–wife relationship is defined in Shakespeare's early 'sex war' comedy *The Taming of the Shrew* (1593–94).[14] Petruchio, seeking a wife in order to refill his coffers (as many of both sexes did), announces to the assembled wedding guests:

> I will be master of what is mine own.
> She is my goods, my chattels: she is my house,
> My household stuff, my field, my barn,
> My horse, my ox, my ass, my anything. (III. ii. 229–32)

At the end of the play, Kate supposedly defines the theoretically submissive role of the wife:

> Thy husband is thy lord, thy life, thy keeper,
> Thy head, thy sovereign – one that cares for thee,
> And for thy maintenance commits his body
> To painful labour both by sea and land,
> To watch the night in storms, the day in cold,
> Whilst thou li'st warm at home, secure and safe. (V. ii. 146–51)

She sees wifely 'love, fair looks, and true obedience' as a duty like that 'the subject owes the prince' and deprecates the rebellious wife seeking 'rule, supremacy, and sway'. Is this sincere or has she, like women before and since, discovered she can get all she wants by appearing submissive while secretly gaining control of the household and of husband? This is the comic discrepancy inherent in the gender relationship. Man plays the master and to all intents and purposes is so publicly, while the woman pulls his strings behind the scenes.

Manipulation, deviousness, sheer bloody-mindedness and simple evil (their weapons of mass subversion in the sex war) were attributed to women in the social comedies of the 1600s. While female tenderness and sensitivity are acknowledged, misogyny is accurate in its definitions too. In Middleton's *A Mad World My Masters* a country gentleman, surreally named Penitent Brothel, admits the superior acumen of the courtesan Frank (Frances) Gullman and associates it with inventive, devious female resourcefulness:

> The wit of man wanes and decreases soon,
> But women's wit is ever at full moon. (III. ii. 159–60)

and

> When plots are e'en past hope and hang their head,
> Set with a woman's hand, they thrive and spread. (III. ii. 246–7)

The aptly named Gullman ('man fooler'),[15] lures into marriage Follywit, the heir of Sir Bounteous Plenty. Shakespeare's comic heroines (e.g., Beatrice, Rosalind, Viola and Portia) are similarly clever, inventive, scheming and resourceful women. Their virtue prevents them intending or doing evil, but they are irrepressibly wilful. Lady Macbeth and Goneril and Regan in *King Lear* are prime examples of devious women whose ruthless and destructive ambitions Shakespeare had recently explored. Cleopatra, never without a ploy to get what she wants, seems to be another negative study of womanhood.

In the real world theory and practice diverge and diversify into a variety of relationships. Every marriage was unique – some paralleled the orthodox model, in some the woman ruled unopposed, in most a compromise was negotiated or appropriated. There were happy marriages, arranged or not. In the upper and middle ranks many men and women married for fiscal or dynastic reasons. This did not always make for easy relationships, but neither did it preclude love, companionship and happiness. A slow shift evolved marriage into a partnership of physical and spiritual companions. Lord Montagu advised his son, 'In your marriage looke after goodness rather than goodes.'[16] Traditionally men sought love and sexual relief outside marriage. This was the negative aspect of arranged marriages where there was no initial attraction and none developed afterwards. The Earl of Northumberland advised his son: 'As you must love, love a mistress for her flesh and a wife for her virtues.'[17] Some women took lovers (though less openly), others sublimated their emotional needs through running estates and raising children, while their husbands attended court or Parliament, joined the army or spent their time in usual male activities – hunting, gambling, drinking, theatregoing, whoring, etc. Many marriages were based on separate lives, but many thrived on the love and respect that formed the new companionate marriage. Puritan pamphlet/sermon input to the marriage debate promoted the development of the helpmeet/companion element.[18] The tetchy, touchy, exciting yet irritating Cleopatra would be acceptable (just about) in a private relationship. But this is not a private couple. They are always on the public stage and their disagreements, misunderstandings and manipulations have international consequences.

A play marking the emergence of the strong, independent woman is Fletcher's *The Woman's Prize, or The Tamer Tamed* (1610). Taking Shakespeare's Petruchio, the shrew tamer, Fletcher has him tamed (or humanized) by his second wife, Maria, who outwits the standard chauvinistic male. No longer 'gentle' or 'tame,' her 'new soul' is

> Made of a north wind, nothing but tempest,
> And like a tempest shall it make all ruins
> Till I have run my will out. (I. ii. 77–9)

Her sister advises her to abandon her plans and accept her expected sexual destiny. Maria is implacable:

> To bed? No, Livia, there be comets yet hang
> Prodigious over that yet. There is a fellow [Petruchio]
> Must yet before I know that heat – ne'er start wench –
> Be made a man, for yet he is a monster;
> Here must his head be [...]. (I. ii. 101–5)

No stage direction indicates where she points – to herself (as his head), her breast (where his head must rest lovingly), or under her foot? She is being transgressive, though expressing something of the rebalancing of the gender roles of the time. Her cousin Bianca contextualizes Maria's stand:

> All the several wrongs
> Done by imperious husbands to their wives

These thousand years and upwards strengthen thee!
Thou hast a brave cause. (I. ii. 122–5)

Maria's apparent goal is equality in marriage, declaring:

[...] That childish woman
That lives a prisoner to her husband's pleasure
Has lost her making and becomes a beast
Created for his use, not fellowship. (I. ii. 137–40)

This play contributes to the lively late sixteenth-/early seventeenth-century debate about just what women were like and what their place in society should be. Opinion was mounting against arranged marriages forced for dynastic and material reasons (characteristic of royal and aristocratic unions) where there was no attraction or love. Arranged royal marriages were traditionally a façade only, sometimes fruitful, sometimes not, often becoming a union of separateness masked by ritual and splendour. Thomas Becon, in his *Golden Boke of Christen Matrimonie* (1542), describes couples trapped unhappily in arranged/forced marriages cursing 'their parents even unto the pit of hell for coupling them together', though there were also many who coped or even found happiness. Dekker asks gentlefolk who are so careful matching their coach horses, why 'will you be carelesse in coupling your children?'[19] The political union of Octavia and Antony is agreed to by Antony in a moment of thoughtlessness dominated by the desire to avoid open fracture between himself and Octavius Caesar. She is not the sort of woman to hold Antony (though in reality they had children), but she will be the unwitting, unwilling catalyst for their rupture. Gender politics underpin the play, with Fulvia and Octavia, two legitimate wives with very different personalities, and Cleopatra, the mistress with whom Antony is most happy and to whom he is most suitably drawn. In this respect they are an ideal partnership, but, given the political state of affairs, she is his fate, his destruction.

Though women were beginning to record their lives in private journals and letters, few are represented in print. Gender issues are mostly addressed through male dramatists. One feminine view is *The Memorandum of Martha Moulsworth, Widow* (1632), which offers a touching verse account of her life and three happy marriages.[20] A loving father brought her up 'in godlie pietie' and 'in modest chearfullnes & sad sobrietie'. Unusually, for her sex and rank (rural gentry), she was taught Latin, but lamented 'Two universities we have of men/O that we had but one of women then!' (lines 33–4).[21] Martha married at 21 (quite late), was widowed after five years, mourned a year, then remarried. Ten years later she was widowed again. After nearly four years she married for the third time. Of this last relationship she writes:

> The third I tooke a lovely man, & kind
> such comlines in age we seldom find
> [...]
> was never man so Buxome to his wife
> with him I led an easie darlings life
> I had my will in house, in purse in Store
> what would a women old or yong have more? (Lines 57–68)

She declares she loved all her partners, was very happy with them and enjoyed domestic responsibility: 'I had my will in house, in purse, in store'. She completes her autobiography with a neat and witty couplet in keeping with her sense of satisfaction in marriage:

> the Virgins life is gold, as Clarks us tell
> the Widowes silvar, I love silvar well. (Lines 109–10)

There is insufficient evidence to form a distinct pattern or profile showing how widespread such education for girls was or how common such happiness was in marriage.[22] Martha is a positive example of a woman living in the provinces. Her education makes her an exception. Reading, writing and enjoyment of literature was largely confined to small groups of gentlewomen housed with an aristocratic mistress whom they served. Martha is not unique, but the bulk of women (and men) had little learning. How much love they found within arranged unions is impossible to tell.

If work, running the estate or living a life of pleasure was a man's life, family tended to be the major part of the female sphere, along with overseeing the household economy (though a wife was responsible to her husband for expenditure in both areas). Traditionally women were thought more naturally inclined to be loving and nurturing, while many fathers were distant, even when at home. King James warned his son that when he had 'succession' (children) he should 'bee carefull for their virtuous education: love them as yee ought', but 'contayning them ever in a reverent love and feare of you'. As regards inheritance:

> Make your eldest sonne *Isaac*, leaving him all your kingdoms; and provide the rest with private possessions. Otherwaies by dividing your kingdoms, ye shall leave the seede of division and discorde among your posteritie: as befell to this Ile, by the division and assignment thereof, to the three sonnes of *Brutus*, *Locrine*, *Albanact*, and *Camber*.[23]

Some mothers too were distant (especially court ladies), so that noble offspring were often reared by nurses and maids. Fathers tended to be strict, concerned to discipline children to conform to society's expectations of their gender role and attitudes. Formality and ritual deference were more common among the elite. In their parents' presence children stood in silence, speaking only when spoken to. In very strict aristocratic families they knelt. Even a citizen's children asked father's permission and blessing before beginning any undertaking – a journey, going to university, leaving home to marry, leaving the table, going to bed, etc. Addressing father or mother could be very formal – using their title or calling them 'Sir' and 'Madam'. Similar formality could apply between husband and wife. That said, in many families there was affectionate informality.

Humility was not merely a device for keeping children and women quietly deferential. It was valued in men too. Overwhelming garrulousness was unacceptable whatever the sex or age. Knowing when to give your opinion and how to give it least offensively and most courteously was a social skill prized among courtly people. Cleopatra persistently displays the aggressive verbal independence of some of Shakespeare's female characters. But she goes a step further and may well lose audience sympathy for she plays games to trick and trap Antony. She shows the insecurity of an inexperienced teenage girl, yet has the pushy confidence of a woman secure in the knowledge that she controls her man.

Legal and biblical authority made man the head of the woman and the family. His wife's money and property became his, his claim to custody of the children took precedence and theoretically he had the final say in all things. In practice many different arrangements were negotiated by individual couples. Some married women owned estates separately from their husbands and had the use of the income from them. Some women were independent, bossy termagants.[24] Some were docile shadows. Some efficiently ran households with the power of decision over menus, furnishings, hiring and firing servants and educating the younger children. There was an immense range of different male familial profiles too, from the ultra-chauvinist, strict patriarch, through the liberal, kindly, affectionate, caring father, to the weak or indifferent non-entity.

There was considerable debate about how fathers should behave to their children and how best children should be brought up. Montaigne and Bacon have much to say on the subject. Largely, fathers were stern, distant and formal, partly because high infant/teenage mortality discouraged too close and affectionate a relationship developing, partly because strict fathers were thought better teachers of respect and discipline than mothers, who were thought too lax.[25] Fathers reflected the loving sternness of God. Children were thought to be like wild creatures needing taming and training if they were to be self-disciplined in later life and cope with the customs and practices of a highly stratified, ritual-conscious, traditionalist society. The entrenched suspicions men had of female irrationality, unreliability and emotional instability transferred into their attitude towards a mother's relationships with her children. In elite families boys were removed from female control at age 7, breeched and put under a tutor until ready to be sent away to complete their education.

Affective family relations did exist as did companionate marriages. Not all was male chauvinism or female submission, not all marriages were perpetual conflict. Many widows were bequeathed estates and businesses and managed them very effectively and remarried. There were many more of these than one might think since men tended to marry later than women and die earlier. The dangers of childbirth meant there were many widowers looking for young wives – for breeding an heir or mothering children of the first marriage. It was not unusual or unexpected for a woman to remarry. In business a widow commonly married one of the journeymen or a senior apprentice. A journeyman was a skilled worker who had completed his seven-year apprenticeship. Not yet master of his craft, he was sufficiently skilled and experienced for it to be a practical union keeping the business going and money coming in. His youthful energy might be welcome in other areas too. Among elite families marriage and family relationships were often thought of not as loving support networks developing within a sheltered environment, but as units of child production that would enable the family title, status, money and property to be kept together and handed on. It is a chilling fact that one-third of marriages did not last longer than 15 years. Remarriage was common, often swiftly following the funeral. These dynastic concerns seem inhumanly disagreeable to modern minds, but in an age when death was a constantly imminent possibility such severe considerations were crucial at every level of society where property (however minor) was held. At stake might be the tenure of thousands of acres and a place at court, a commercial enterprise or simply the hedging tools of a farm labourer and the lease on his cottage. Apart from biblical authority for patriarchy there were practical reasons for it. Among the aristo-gentry, remembering the violent precariousness of the Wars of the Roses, men bred large families hoping at least one male would survive. This required a wife who was fertile and would be based at home in order to rear the offspring. Stone puts it thus:

> Among the landed classes in pre-Reformation England [the] objectives of family planning were the continuity of the male line, the preservation intact of the inherited property, and the acquisition of further property or useful political alliances.[26]

Such objectives persisted in the seventeenth century.

Feminist historians and literary critics have drawn attention to the marginalized role and restricted potential of women throughout the ages.[27] This useful counterbalance to the male-dominated view of history and sociology has simultaneously overemphasized the negative aspects of male domination and underemphasized the forms of covert petticoat power. The behind-the-scenes and in-the-bedroom influence of women at court is an acknowledged but underexplored factor. Because women had no official political role, it has been assumed they had no power, yet literature shows their incitement and complicity in tragic and comic plots and history is increasingly revealing the influence they wielded in political, social and personal arenas. The most material sign of male dominance was his appropriation of his wife's property and money to do with as he wished, though sometimes family wealth could be held combined and administered jointly. Where the husband was a cash-strapped, debt-ridden, thriftless wastrel (whether eldest son or a younger) this led to the dowry being swallowed up, laying grounds for resentment and tension. Liberal and less chauvinistic men often left their wife's money and property in her hands.[28] Less publicized was the jointure arranged by parents and lawyers. This was an agreed annuity payable if the husband predeceased his wife and could represent a considerable and crippling sum if paid over a long period.[29] Women heir hunters would unashamedly access a husband's wealth, title and status. Debts accrued by a wife were legally payable by the husband and extravagant female spending, a traditional feature of satire, is frequently referenced in Jacobean drama and particularly targeted at women of the better sort and citizens' wives. Materially and emotionally every arranged union had two potential victims. Men could be hunted for their wealth and trapped unhappily in an arranged marriage. The patriarch kept family property intact through primogeniture, but may himself have been forced into marriage. The family money was, as always, a distasteful but vital matter. Younger offspring had to be found appropriate partners. Sons were particularly problematic, tending to drift into similarly cash-short homosocial groups in London, unsupervised, uncivilized and antisocial. They were increasingly pushed into high-status professions – the church, law, government service, the army, etc. – but often dropped out. Many high-status young women remained unmarried but without a vocation, without the chance to work other than at relatively unsatisfying domestic and social accomplishments (sewing, embroidery, music, etc.). Some upper-rank gentlewomen serving an aristocratic lady had leisure time for reading, thinking, writing and consensual discourse.[30] These cultured coteries tended to be located in the more splendid country mansions. Those daughters who did marry, even if they wed a rich man, had to be provided with a dowry. This could represent a cripplingly difficult sum to find.

While parental wishes, influenced by financial, hierarchical or political interests, were dominant in choosing a partner, increasingly the child's consent was sought. This approach was particularly evident in the wealthy upper-middle ranks. If a child did not like and was not attracted to a possible partner, that could end negotiations In *'Tis Pity She's a Whore* a fellow citizen seeks Florio's daughter as wife for his booby fop of a nephew. Florio tells him:

> My care is how to match her to her liking:
> I would not have her marry wealth, but love;
> And if she like your nephew, let him have her. (I. iii. 10–12)

Ironically, this liberal approach is voiced while Annabella is in bed with her chosen lover – her brother.[31] Drama presents many different conflicts over courtship and marriage because it offers excitement and more plot possibilities than demure agreement. Largely, however, in real life, parents commonly chose a suitor or bride when they saw there was already attraction. In the case of a candidate picked by the parents but unknown to the prospective bride/groom, proposed by the suitor/bride's family or self-presented by a free bachelor, the son/daughter's response was still taken into consideration. But if a candidate was strongly preferred by the parents on material grounds and rejected by the son or daughter, then parental pressure and patriarchal weight (threats of disinheritance and other punishments) would be applied. Marriage without parental consent was illegal, putting the archetypal romantic lovers, Romeo and Juliet, outside the law. King Lear, in his anger, disposes of Cordelia to the lowest bidder without her say. Prospero (*The Tempest*), a more caring father, approves of the mutual attraction between his daughter and future son-in-law. Antony, in agreeing to marry Octavia, is neither circumspect (on his own behalf) nor caring (on Octavia's).

Though the odds might appear against it and feminist critics have highlighted the injustice to the female of arranged marriage, there is evidence of loving marriages and happy families 'long before the eighteenth century'.[32] Studies show that 'patriarchal authority applied in theory to this period, but could be modified in practice, by illustrating the range of experiences of married couples in which much depended upon factors such as the personality and relative status of the husband and wife'.[33] More importantly, counterbalancing the idea of women being completely dominated: 'Far from being passive subordinates, some women developed strategies to modify or resist patriarchal authority, including marshalling support through friends, neighbours and kin to circumvent their putative subordination to their husbands.'[34]

Patriarchy and a Woman's Place

Deep-seated institutional misogyny persisted through the 1600s. Though the Catholic Church held no sway in England, its ideas had bitten deep into the male psyche, and suspicion of women was endemic in masculine thinking. The Church of Rome, systemically anti-female in its doctrines, saw women's secondary role as part of God's plan. The Church of England was more of the mind that men and women should respect one another, that husbands and wives should work in harmony, but was clear that ultimately the man was in charge. Women, as Eve's descendants, were thought more inclined to sin. Men too were sinners but a neat argument mitigated that 'though an husband in regard of evil qualities may carry the image of the devil, yet in regard to his place and office, he beareth the image of God'.[35]

No one statement or view can be universally true of the complexities of male–female relationships, but in general a woman's place was subordinate to the males within her family and social sphere. There were, of course, a number of strong-minded women who would not be dominated within their family or in any situation. Women did have some status: a mother had authority over her children (in the father's absence); a housewife had authority over her servants (in the master's absence); the wife of a guild master, a titled lady or a shop owner's wife was superior to anyone of an inferior station (male or female), but within her own rank was secondary to any adult male, even to a son of age if he had inherited from a dead father and was head of the family. Respect for her as a woman, as mother and as dowager (widow of a titled/propertied man) would partially mitigate his authority. However, irrepressible women dominated these situations. It is clear in *King Lear* that the king's daughters are very much his property. As father and king he disposes of them as he sees fit. But once free of him, with his power diminished to a level where only affection might work in his favour, the two older daughters display a barbaric cruelty transgressing custom and civilized behaviour.

The subordination of women was part of an unfair hierarchical system within a social structure that designated a place for everyone and in which most people (men included) were subordinate to someone. It was unjust but most of the social and legal structure was unfairly organized in favour of the rich over the poor and men over women.

In 1558, the year of Elizabeth I's succession, the most strident statement of female inferiority was made by the Scottish radical Protestant John Knox from his exile in Geneva:

> To promote a woman to bear rule, superiority, dominion or empire above any realm, nation or city is repugnant to nature, contumely to God, a thing most contrarious to his revealed will and approved ordinance, and finally it is the subversion of good order, of all equity and justice.[36]

Knox's views resonate with the fear that transgressing social, familial or gender order would herald anarchy and collapse. Even Montaigne, usually liberal and fair, expresses this orthodox view of females:

> Women should have no mastery over men save only the natural one of motherhood [...]. It is dangerous to leave the superintendence of our succession to the judgement of our wives and to their choice between our sons, which over and over again is iniquitous and fantastic. For those unruly tastes and physical cravings which they experience during pregnancy are ever-present in their souls.[37]

This fails to take account of the general tendency of women to: 1. oppose by a variety of means all attempts by males to repress them, and 2. achieve some independence for themselves by negotiation, by clandestine action or by default. Every relationship is different from every other. Some women failed to win any area of domination. Some ruled every area of family life, some a limited area. Some said 'Yes, dear', 'No, dear' and then secretly did what they wished. Some men could not be bothered about household matters or child rearing, so the wife/mother ruled by default. Some women gained rule of estates or businesses through their husband's decease, but largely Heaven's hierarchy persisted on Earth and religion backed it. Thus, 'By marriage, the husband and wife became one person in law – and that person was the husband.'[38]

Just where women were placed in day-to-day reality is problematic. The bulk of ordinary people were voiceless. Women provide even less evidence of their existence than men. Documents profiling actual relationships are scarce and differ between court and country and between the aristo-gentry and other ranks. The lower down the social scale the less material is available. The few remaining personal diaries and letters by women are held in archives, though probably more await discovery. It was a period in which few people committed personal feelings to paper, but that was changing. Cost of materials was one factor, but the culture was only slowly coming to accept that an individual's thoughts and feelings were of value. The various intersecting seventeenth-century conflicts encouraged more people to put pen to paper to express their views. The expanding print culture enabled many individuals to publish pamphlets that contributed to a war of words on religion, politics, gender issues and a multitude of other topics. Trading families needed literate heirs and from the mid-seventeenth century dissenting groups began establishing Academies that provided excellent broad education, more liberal, practical and extensive than the limited classical studies of high-end families.

It was common (among Dissenters particularly) for Christians to make a daily examination of their lives. In time this came to be written down in a spiritual journal, and subsequently more material is available. The 1600s saw an increasing number of pamphlets (many by women) offering opinions on everything from politics to horticulture to horoscopes. By the Restoration (1660) there was a slightly higher proportion of female-to-male professional writers, reflecting some easing of male repressiveness, but as a demographic percentage figures for female writing are small. Did women write but not publish? Did women just not write much? Were they unable to access reading material that triggered their own writing? Was female literacy just too low to make a showing? Much female-authored fictional work circulated in manuscript among small social networks like the court, London-based writers and literate and literary families and their friends. A number of literate all-female groups wrote, read out and published poetry or closet dramas. Prohibited from acting, women seem not to have written for the public stage until Aphra Behn, but many translated foreign plays or wrote their own for private circulation.[39] Any assessment of women in the period 1600–1620 can largely only be constructed from male perspectives, though a number of recent studies (like Schleiner's) are revealing the hidden archaeology of women's literary creation. This is confined to privileged groups. The general picture seems to be that private individuals (male and female) were increasingly writing about their lives, opinions and personal struggles. This accelerated in the Civil War and afterwards. But most of this manuscript material is locked away in scattered archives, public and private, awaiting analysis and publication.

The later Stuart period provides many spiritual autobiographies, but an interesting early example, giving insight into provincial life, comes from Lady Margaret Hoby's diary of 1599–1605. A Yorkshire heiress, educated in a Puritan school for gentlewomen, run by the Countess of Huntingdon, she married three times, making alliances with high-profile court dynasties (the Devereux, Sidneys and Hobys). Her life was spent in Hackness near Scarborough, with only few visits to London. Her diary, the earliest known written by an English woman, records her local charity work, her running of the household and estate, and her domestic activities – managing servants, paying them, mundane activities like gardening, arranging the washing and ironing, preparing medicines, and her contacts with neighbours and estate tenants. It recounts her spiritual life – organizing household prayers and her personal devotions and reading – but does not delve into her inner feelings.

At every stage of life a woman was expected to be deferential, submissive and constantly aware of her different and separate expectations. Her infant education (if she received one) would be at home and limited to letters and figures, while her brothers attended school (or were home tutored) and then, once literate and numerate, moved on to Greek, Latin, mathematics, history and geography, followed by university. In the lower ranks a schooled boy might be apprenticed or simply join his father in the family business. A girl stayed at home and learned housecraft and needlework skills. Farmers' daughters joined the women in planting, tending animals, spinning, cooking and nursing younger siblings, while brothers ploughed, reaped, herded animals, made and used tools, went to market and met the world. Once of marriageable age, whatever her rank, she might be contracted to a man of her father's choosing if it was profitable to the family, or she might remain at home unmarried as general help (i.e., an unpaid servant). If lucky she might be sent away into service. While exposing her to innumerable risks, this could open up better prospects, allowing her to climb the ladder of service from housemaid to housekeeper. A prime fantasy was that she would attract her master's eldest son and marry him. In practice parents reacted in horror at their son wishing to unite himself to a maid and gentry sons tended to see female servants as sexual provender not marriage material. Girls from the governing ranks and bourgeoisie had fewer opportunities, so simply waited to be courted. Numbers from all ranks simply never married.

The tediousness of such limited horizons is well detailed in the eighteenth and nineteenth centuries, but the bored girls of Renaissance England are relatively silent. Like their brothers, however, they had virtues to cultivate: piety, chastity, discretion, modesty, gentleness, decorum, prudence, diligence and industry. If from a comfortably-off gentry background, she was expected to join her mother in charity visits to the poor and other almsgiving. Lower down the social ladder things were better as regards active occupation, for you were expected to work and earn money to contribute to the family income. Middle- and upper-rank girls had to do much sewing, embroidery, cutting out and assembling of clothes for younger siblings or for charity children. Thousands upon thousands must have agreed to marry the first man who offered, simply to escape to another life and a home of their own to run. There were differences between how the court treated women and how they were expected to behave elsewhere. Court women were perceived (often correctly) to be promiscuous, flattering and fawning (therefore manipulative and devious hypocrites), overly interested in clothes and show, given to gossip and rumour mongering, and generally flirtatious and frivolous. Aristo-gentry young women serving a country-based aristocratic lady had more chance to form reading/discussion groups.

There were differences in how men regarded and treated women and what was expected of them according to their rank. Common girls were regarded as skivvies and sexual prey, middling ones as sexual prey and sources of fortune. A girl from a titled family could not easily be predated sexually if she had kinsmen to take revenge, but she could be courted for her money, married and left at home to nurture the offspring. Many girls in the two upper tiers did receive a good education, depending as always on parental attitudes (the father particularly) and there was a swing towards humanist ideals that saw female education as essential for the next generation of wives and mothers.

Renaissance Improvements

Richard Mulcaster, first headmaster of Merchant Taylors' School, then high master of St Paul's School, strongly favoured female education. His book, *Positions* (1581), declares that as 'our' closest 'companions', women should be 'well furnished in mind' and 'well strengthened in body'. Fathers have a 'duty' to educate their daughters. God 'require[s] an account for natural talents of both the parties, us for directing them; them for performance of our direction'. This alludes to the parable of the talents (Matthew 25:13–40; Luke 19:12–27) concerning one's God-given abilities. Mulcaster believed women's education should be selectively targeted towards strengthening virtue. He emphasized four essential skills: 'reading well, writing faire, singing sweet, playing fine', plus languages and drawing. Maths, science and divinity were less useful, but not excluded. Women, he felt, were weak by nature, but education could strengthen intellect and soul. Men should be educated 'without restraint for either matter or manner'. Countering the stereotypical view that women's education was neglected he asks

> Do we not see in our country some of that sex so excellently well trained and so rarely qualified in regard both to the tongues themselves and to the subject matter contained in them, that they may be placed along with, or even above, the most vaunted paragons of Greece or Rome?[40]

How broadly spread was female education in the upper and middling ranks is unquantifiable. While masses of boys went to grammar school then university, and scholarships, bursaries and endowments enabled poor scholars to receive an education otherwise beyond their reach, such institutional learning was generally unavailable to girls, and such home tutoring as was provided has left few examples of its existence except among high-status ladies of evident learning.

Henry VIII's daughters, Mary and Elizabeth, were very well taught. Elizabeth, with Latin, Greek, Hebrew, Italian and French, was one of the most learned rulers in Europe. Her speeches use rhetorical devices that display her classical learning, but she insisted that a prince's education should be useful to ruling the nation. The princesses were tutored by leading scholars, including Juan Vives, the Spanish humanist. Vives – conservative, wary of a classical education because some political-historical material was unsuitable and the poetry of Ovid and Catullus immoral – based their curriculum on his own *Instruction of a Christian Woman* (1524), broadened to include Erasmus's *Paraphrases* (1517–24) and More's *Utopia* (1516). He believed 'most of the vices of women [...] are the products of ignorance, whence they never read nor heard those excellent sayings and monitions of the Holy Fathers about chastity, about obedience, about silence, women's adornments and treasures.' Women had to be obedient to their duties, needed their morals shaped and their virtues developed – as did men. Only 'a little learning is required of women', while 'men must do many things in the world and must be broadly educated'.[41] Women should confine their reading to works on chastity. This betrays the orthodox anxiety about female sexuality. Men felt that independent female sexuality would lead to increased illegitimacy thus obscuring fatherhood and confusing matters of inheritance, the central concern of patriarchally controlled marriage. Erasmus (*The Institution of Marriage*, 1526), friend of Sir Thomas More and key figure in the development of Renaissance ideas, suggests education is more effective than needlework in banishing idleness, preserving virginity and enhancing matrimonial relationships.

It should not be assumed that humanist ideas greatly influenced James's court or spread very far outside. Young women attending court would already be past the education stage. Their personalities and tastes already formed, they usually had more worldly matters in mind. Away from court there was a huge variety of attitudes among the country aristocracy and gentry as regards rearing and educating daughters. Learned education (Greek and Latin) was briefly fashionable for aristocratic girls from 1520–1560.[42] Thereafter it waned. Other positive influences did emerge, though again it is impossible to chart their influence. One was Castiglione's *Il Cortegiano* (1528; *The Courtier*, trans. Thomas Hoby, 1561). This important handbook suggested a little knowledge of 'letters' (classics, modern languages, history and literature) was acceptable for women, but that the social graces (playing music, singing, dancing, drawing/painting and needlework) were more civilized and made a woman more marriageable. Hoby claimed the book was 'to Ladies and Gentlewomen, a mirrour to decke and trimme themselves with vertuous conditions, comeley behaviours and honest entertainment toward all men'.[43] Castiglione also acknowledged, in some detail, that cultured education should be more than a mere social ornament for women. He strongly endorses their virtue and their potential for positive influence in a court. This new courtly ideal promoted the self-effacing but agreeable woman – witty, cultured and chaste. Renaissance courts could be centres of high culture but were also death traps of intrigue, plotting, power struggles, assassinations, political coups, rape and seduction. Court history exemplified that double-sidedness of culture and killing: for all the poetry, madrigals and dancing, executions, torture, the rise and fall of favourites, hothouse animosities and sexual intrigues made the English court (from Henry VIII to Charles I) like the set of a bloody play. Act I Scene ii gives a brief glimpse into the laxity of Antony and Cleopatra's court.

As evidence of some shift in attitudes to women, Thomas Campion (1567–1620), explores how women's restricted social opportunities encourages a vigorous inner life, while men are easily distracted by the world's superficialities:

Women are confined to silence,
Loosing wisht occasion.
Yet our tongues then theirs, men,
Are apter to be moving,
Women are more dumbe then they,
But in their thoughts more roving.[44]

Female-authored literature was beginning to emerge. Lady Mary Wroth (c. 1586–c. 1651) from the high-status, literary Sidney family, wrote a sonnet sequence and the first known prose romance by an English woman. Both texts contribute to the ongoing gender discourse. Elizabeth Carey (1585–1639), the first woman to write a history (of Edward II), also wrote the first female-authored tragedy. *The Tragedy of Mariam* (written 1602–04, published 1613), intended as a 'closet drama' to be read in domestic surroundings, contributes to the gender debate in contrasting honest, principled Queen Mariam with devious and promiscuous Princess Salome and presenting the absolutist, violent patriarch King Herod. Another contributor to the man–woman question was Rachel Speght (c. 1597–?). A Calvinist minister's daughter, she entered the literary world with panache, stepping straight into the gender discourse controversy. Aged 19, with her name boldly attached, scorning anonymity, she published *A Mouzell for Melastomus* (*A Muzzle for Blackmouth*,

1617), an articulate, spirited, clearly and logically argued attack on the bigoted misogyny of Joseph Swetnam's *Araignment of Lewde, Idle, Froward, and Unconstant Women* (1615). Biblical and classical references reveal her religious background and education. Living at the centre of London's commercial and clerical debate, she understood the current polemical climate and had seen many examples of husband–wife co-operation among merchant families. She claims respect is due to women as children of God and sees the possibilities for companionate relationships between the sexes. Her lively style, often akin to the acerbic, insulting, combative language of male pamphlet polemics, makes her work readable, while her ideas make it convincingly sympathetic and reasonable. Marriage is a true union and married couples 'as yoake-fellowes are to sustayne part of each others cares, griefs, and calamities'. 'Marriage is a merri-age, and this worlds Paradise, where there is mutuall love […] husbands should not account their wives as vassals, but as those that are heires together of the grace of life.' As 'head' of his wife, the husband must protect her and lead her to Christ. To 'exclaime against Woman' is ingratitude to God.[45] Swetnam focuses on female vanity and lechery (traditional targets); Speght voices a new mood of companionship, shared piety and compromise between gender egotisms. Clearly there is a companionship element in the Antony and Cleopatra relationship. They would be right for each other, had they been private citizens. What they are not right for is the time and Caesar's agenda.

The entrenched history and literature of Catholic misogyny, with its horror of the physical filthiness (i.e., menstruation and childbirth) and spiritual sinfulness of women, passed into male thinking and persisted after the Reformation. In religious thought the body (a temporary house for the soul) was considered corrupt and its sinful needs and dirty functions were to be minimized so the spirit could be kept pure and nourished. Subject to fleshly temptations and the vagaries of emotion, human beings were a comic treasure. One of Castiglione's disputants says, 'In each one of us there is some seed of folly which, once it is stirred, can grow indefinitely.' Another remarks, 'Our bodily senses are so untrustworthy that they often confuse our judgement as well.'[46] Folly, the senses, unreliable judgement, in these are the sources of comedy, but also those of tragedy.

The virtue/sin, duty/desire conflict produced a body of 'sex war' literature focusing on the attraction/hostility duality between men and women – men as bullying, lascivious brutes (or gullible weaklings), women as devious, unreliable shrews, bullying in their own way (or innocent victims). Shakespeare addresses the virago–virgin polarity in *The Comedy of Errors* (Adriana and Luciana), *The Taming of the Shrew* (Katherine and Bianca) and *Much Ado About Nothing* (Beatrice and Hero). The trickiness of women is often a source of comedy, while their evil is fitting for tragedy. Contrast the polarities of the kite/tiger/wolf/monster sisters in *King Lear* with Cordelia's gentle sensitivity. *Lear* has little to say of women directly, but many negative implications resonate round the words and actions of Goneril and Regan. Both sisters are white devils – a common metaphor for hypocrites who disguised their evil. They are a study in the evil that females can perform. Cleopatra is sometimes pathetically comic in her tricks and insecurities, but their long-term effects are suitably tragic. Shakespeare often explored the failings of women, but deep evil had only been explored through Queen Tamora (*Titus Andronicus*, c. 1588–93) and Queen Margaret, a 'she-wolf' with a 'tiger's heart wrapp'd in a woman's hide' (*Henry VI*, 1590–1591). His other great study of female evil is Lady Macbeth. After *Antony and Cleopatra*, his last plays project more positive, romantically idealized images of women through Hermione, Paulina and Perdita (*The Winter's Tale*), Imogen (*Cymbeline*), Thaisa and Marina (*Pericles*) and Miranda (*The Tempest*).

Men had ambivalent, contradictory views of women. As the source of human sin they needed controlling to minimize their opportunities for tempting men. A multiplicity of pejorative terms – virago, termagant, shrew, Whore of Babylon, hussy, wagtail, punk and more – provide lexical markers of male suspicion. In opposition to the Eve/Delilah/Jezebel image, medieval Courtly Love projected an idealized woman of beauty, intelligence, elegance and chastity, while Mariolatry raised the Virgin Mary to an archetype of gentle, sympathetic womanhood and loving, nurturing motherhood, partially redeeming women. Mary became a key human intercessor in approaching Christ, and an icon of the respect men should have for women. In loving a woman you re-expressed your love and respect for your mother, showing the love you first learned from her. Martin Luther asserted that Mary was 'the highest woman' and that 'we can never honour her enough [...]. The veneration of Mary is inscribed in the very depths of the human heart.'[47] While lauding Mary's model status, Luther made very derogatory remarks about women in general.[48] Despite some easing of extreme patriarchy and improvements in the status of women, negative views persisted and progress was slow.

Medieval hagiographies (lives of saints) celebrated the virtues of women martyrs, but Protestantism had banned statues, days, prayers and oaths associated with saints. This hampered the assimilation into church dogma of any ideology applauding women, though veneration of Mary persisted in people's private faith.[49] A small amount of literature iconized particularly virtuous women and applauded romantic, rational, affectionate relationships. From the medieval period there are Chaucer's

Legend of Good Women and *The Book of the Duchesse*[50] and later Sir Thomas Elyot's *The Defence of Good Women* (1540) and Spenser's *Faerie Queene* (1590 and 1596). Notable continental contributions include Boccaccio's *De Mulieribus Claris* (*Of Famous Women*, 1374) and Castiglione's *Il Cortegiano* (Third Book), where, despite sharp misogynistic interruptions, Guiliano de Medici constructs the idealized court lady, ably acknowledges the female capacity for virtue and illustrates his case with classical and contemporary examples. There are the scattered references to courageous, faithful women in the Bible, But generally all churches were suspicious of sex and passion, encouraged men to control their own and female appetites and warned against women as the ready provokers of lust. Men were supposedly more rational, while women were more emotional and vulnerable to fleshly temptations. Polemic writing tended to highlight female failings. Literature uses the constant interplay of tension between the positive aspects (affection and love) of the appetites and the dangers of following them excessively. Love was seen as a madness, an illness caught from women. For Castiglione, 'The emotions of love provide excuse for every kind of fault.'[51] In *A Midsummer Night's Dream*, Theseus describes love's insanity:

> Lovers and madmen have such seething brains,
> Such shaping fantasies, that apprehend
> More than cool reason ever comprehends. (V. i. 4–5)

Antony is both lover and lunatic.

The Church of England's *Second Book of Homilies* (1571), which vicars used for sermons, includes 'On the State of Matrimony', defining the church's views on women and how fathers and husbands, being in authority over them and being more rational beings, should approach them:

> The woman is a weak creature not endued with like strength and constancy of mind; therefore, they be the sooner disquieted, and they be the more prone to all weak affections and dispositions of mind, more than men be; and lighter they be, and more vain in their fantasies and opinions.

They were 'the weaker vessel, of a frail heart, inconstant, and with a word soon stirred to wrath'. A commentary in Matthew's Bible (1537) says that men, being intellectually stronger and in authority, had a duty to ensure their women conformed to the demands for chastity and modest behaviour. If she was 'not obedient and helpful to him, [he may] beat the fear of God into her head, and that thereby she may be compelled to learn her duty and do it'. Corporal punishment was common in the Renaissance. Whores and criminals were publicly whipped, children caned at home and school, wives and servants beaten.[52] The Bible exhorts wives to be in subjection to their husbands, counterbalancing this by requiring that the husband should honour the wife and that they should have 'compassion one of another' (I Peter 3:8). Bishop Aylmer gave a sermon before Queen Elizabeth, outlining the best and worst aspects of women, in polarities evident in Shakespeare and most other dramatists:

> Women are of two sorts: some of them are wiser, better learned, discreeter, and more constant than a number of men; but another and worse sort of them are fond (simple), foolish, wanton, flibbergibs, tattlers, triflers, wavering, witless,, without council, feeble, careless, rash, proud, dainty (fussy), tale-bearers, eavesdroppers, rumour-raisers, evil-tongued, worse-minded, and in every way doltified with the dregs of the devil's dunghill.[53]

Legally women had few rights. Neither did most ordinary men, but they had the key ones.

There were some shifts in behaviour, but how far they penetrated society as a whole is unclear. The sixteenth century saw an increase in stern patriarchy as regards marital and parental relations. In the seventeenth century there were countermovements against both. Imperceptibly slowly, the stern, patriarchal, authoritarian father became more affectionate and considerate. Stone charts the gradual emergence of the more companionate marriage and more affective family relations: 'For a considerable period, two conflicting trends were at work at the same time, and the growing authority of the husband can only be seen in a relatively pure form during the first half of the sixteenth century.'[54]

Playwrights hint at the hope for harmonious, loving marriages at the end of comedies, but within them tend to use the dramatic possibilities of conflict between the sexes. Offering more opportunities for humour, tension and the exploration of violent emotions, it is better theatre. In George Wilkins's *The Miseries of Enforced Marriage* (1607), the character Ilford captures the orthodox misogynistic view: 'Women are the purgatory of men's purses, the paradise of their bodies, and the hell of their minds: marry none of them. Women are in churches saints, abroad angels, at home devils.'[55] Such lively possibilities are explored between Antony and Cleopatra. In John Marston's *The Dutch Courtesan* (1604), Malheureux says: 'The most odious spectacle the earth can present is an immodest, vulgar woman' (I. i. 154–5). For all her sophisticated experience Cleopatra is both vulgar occasionally and immodest often.

Marston, a member of Shakespeare's circle, worked in the same areas of problematic moral ambivalence central to *Measure for Measure*, *King Lear* and *Antony and Cleopatra*. Freevill (his name conflating evil/freedom/free will), a libertine trying to terminate his relationship with the courtesan Franceschina so he can marry Beatrice, a respectable and wealthy heiress, passes on the whore to his friend Malheureux ('the unhappy or misfortunate one'), who tries to repress his powerful sexual feelings. Freevill and Malheureux represent two significant forces in contemporary society: traditional male unfettered sexuality and the newer moral code of Puritanism attempting to control the sex impulse. Franceschina admits 'Woman corrupted is the worst of devils' (*The Dutch Courtesan*, II. ii. 201). Her remark has wider relevance than London's sex trade and some of the ladies watching *Antony and Cleopatra* would recognize their own plots and ploys in Cleopatra. Shakespeare presents the counterargument when the hitherto chaste Angelo, feeling the prickings of lust, asks, 'The tempter, or the tempted, who sins most, ha?' (*Measure for Measure*, II. ii. 164). This acknowledges partial male responsibility for lust. King Lear makes several sharps comments on lust and female lust in particular. His strictures sound as condemnatory as any Puritan preacher:

> Down from the waist they are Centaurs,
> Though women all above:
> But to the girdle do the Gods inherit,
> Beneath is all the fiends: there's hell, there's darkness,
> There is the sulphurous pit – burning, scalding,
> Stench, consumption; fie, fie fie! pah, pah! (IV. vi.)

Had Antony been more of the sort of ruler Cicero projected in *De Officiis*, he would have controlled the queen and perhaps avoided his own disasters. But he is fated to be what he is. In different ways Marston, Jonson, Shakespeare and others explored the difficulties of trying to keep to virtue's path. While others mocked the pretensions and greed of contemporary London through their theatrical satires, Shakespeare dived deep into human depravity and cruelty in a setting that is universal, removed from readily identifiable topical references, but still with targets that prompt resemblances to his time and audience.

Elizabethan-Jacobean dramatists show considerable sympathy for women in a male-dominated world, displaying their wit, virtue and sprightliness, but they are also alert to women's capacity for cunning and fierce brutality. It is disturbingly similar to men's.

Chapter 7

MAN IN HIS PLACE

First walk in thy vocation,
And do not seek thy lot to change.[1]

By God's will you were born into a particular rank (your 'lot' in life). You were expected to know your place, keep it and work at whatever calling came within the scope of your family's position. Any family might rise, through hard work and God's grace. Small status improvements were not too disturbing for one's neighbours, but great success provoked envious suspicion of overreaching ambition. Doubts about the means by which you rose might arouse accusations of bribery, magic or devilish assistance, people being all too ready to take the Bible's point of view: 'He that maketh haste to be rich shall not be innocent' (Proverbs 28:20). The industrious, careful man, slowly improving his position, was safe from negative gossip: 'Wealth gotten by vanity shall be diminished: but he that gathereth by labour shall increase' (Proverbs 13:11). The rapid increase in bourgeois wealth created an interplay between envy, condemnation of luxury, suspicion of avarice and dishonesty, and fears of an upstart, ambitiously aspirational group rivalling the traditional ruling class.

The Elizabethans-Jacobeans were suspicious of social movement. If God made the world, putting each man in his place, to alter your standing was to defy God's will. A poor man becoming poorer was thought punished for some unnamed sin, becoming richer could be a reward for hard work, but becoming very rich (and huge fortunes were being amassed) displayed greed and probable dishonesty. Some argued that God gave men abilities or talents, expected men to use them and rewarded hard work. If that meant you could climb out of your birth rank and better yourself then you could be said to be doing God's will and worshipping him by developing the talents he gave you. This was a popular view among Non-conformists for whom the work ethic was central. They believed in industry and thrift and accepted the idea of making money. But a rise in fortunes, place and public status should not be accompanied by a complacent attitude to making money at any cost. It had to be ethical and the amounts within reason. Excessive gains should be redistributed through charities and the moneymaker and his family should avoid arrogance, ostentation and snobbery – in theory.[2] A hard-working shop assistant might marry the shopkeeper's daughter or his widow, he might rise to wealth and become master of his guild or a town councillor, but he was expected to give thanks by charitable donations and to remain humble. Education could help a poor man's son to a government clerkship. Talented, active men could rise, particularly if they earned the patronage of someone of note and power. They could fall too if they became too grasping or followed a favourite who fell from favour. The court was a roller coaster of fortune where many rose by intrigues, plots, lies, favouritism and ruthless opportunism. The stakes were high and success could be expensive but profitable. Failure on the other hand was devastating. In the case of *Antony and Cleopatra*, Antony plays high and loses.

The many new men rising to prominence caused unease in conservative thinking about social mobility. Extreme reversals or improvements in rank portrayed onstage were seen as omens of impending disaster and social implosion that might engulf everyone. Subversion of any sort was disturbing and threatening to the orderliness of society. Antony is subversive in monumentally failing to live up to the demanding ideals of leadership set by Cicero, Elyot and King James. His ineptitude leads to mishandling of the tensions within the triumvirate and has universally disruptive effects. But the clash with Caesar was almost certainly inevitable however Antony behaved. He and Cleopatra help develop their own catastrophe; he rises high but his arrogance brings about a fall. As Goldsworthy points out: 'There are well-attested incidents in which both Antony and Cleopatra behaved in ways that seem irrational or at best politically unwise.'[3] It is a feature of tragedy that the doomed hero/heroine makes miscalculations that unintentionally hasten the consequences that destroy them. It suggests they are the helpless victims of an unavoidable fate.

In *Eastward Ho!*, the goldsmith's daughter, Gertrude, obsessed with becoming a knight's wife, contemplates the pleasure of having gained superiority over her father: 'He must call me daughter no more now; but "Madam", and, "please you Madam", and, "please your worship, Madam", indeed' (III. ii. 63–5). Gertrude's subversiveness is suitably punished. She marries Sir Petronel Flash for title and property, but finds he resembles his name – all show, no substance, no castle, no money. He marries her for her wealth. Each has cheated the other and their pride is humbled. In addition to pride and ambition, Gertrude shows extreme disrespect to her father, thus striking at the very root of social order and breaking a Commandment. *King Lear* shows even worse subversion of family values and many City Comedies show disturbing threats to the fundamental basis of social life – the family. It is a tenable view that Antony and Cleopatra are each punished for their offences against the gods, each being the other's punishment. Noticeably there are no family scenes. The children are mentioned as recipients of the Donations of Alexandria, but their physical absence suggests they are victims neglected by parents playing their parts in the great public-political drama.

Movement was not always upward. A third to a half of the seventeenth-century population existed at subsistence level and suffered acute unemployment. The majority of the lower sort suffered their hardship fairly stoically, but the urban underclass was always a worrying barrel of gunpowder. It took little to ignite it and regular riots occurred – in London particularly. At the other end of the scale increasing numbers of merchants, financiers, manufacturers and industrialists were making huge fortunes, becoming wealthier than some established aristo-gentry families. They copied elite cultural habits, seeking titles, estates and political power.[4] This aspiration frightened the ruling ranks. The same had happened in late-republican Rome. England's bourgeois elite was well educated, with 2.5 per cent of males aged 14–20 receiving university training. With male literacy improving (80 per cent in London), clearly life-enhancement possibilities were expanding. The middling sort was unstoppably on the move. Though the very poorest remained poor and their numbers increased due to enclosures, unemployment and inflation, those able to struggle upwards to literacy, and thereby to effective commercial activity, were also increasing. This widened the divide between those succeeding and the failing underclass with no means of reversing their downward spiral. The growth of capitalism created many different levels of sophistication and increased the need for minutely observed differentiations to distinguish between people. When a merchant's wife could afford to dress as well and in the same fashions as a lady courtier, it was human nature to seek finer status identifiers to enable those with established rank to mark themselves apart from those newly arrived.

In the 1600s voices were beginning to speak up for the lower orders. The need to do so indicates growing tensions between the ranks. At the end of his progress south James I arrived at Theobalds, Robert Cecil's magnificent palace north of London. There he was handed the 'Poor Man's Petition'. Like others it demanded the new king promise religious uniformity and the purifying of public life, particularly attacking the legal profession: 'A pox take the proud covetous Attorney and merciless lawyer! […] fye upon all close biting knaveric!'[5] Social divisions showed in other more obvious, public ways. Luxury clattered by on the streets in fine coaches. Successful men, their wives and their families displayed their newfound luxury in extravagant dress and lavishly decorated houses. Conspicuous consumption and ostentatious showing-off through carriages, horses, houses, furniture, clothes and expensive banquets were all forms of vanity. The many mocking stage representations of the purse-proud *nouveaux riches* had little effect. Sumptuary laws to control expenditure and regulate the types of clothing worn and the amounts/types of food consumed by the different ranks were ignored. Established in the Middle Ages, updated by Henry VIII and extended by Elizabeth I, they were officially claimed to restrain vain, wasteful habits and protect English trade, but were really an elite attempt to maintain the visual differences of rank. As everywhere else, there was hierarchy – in the fur trimming permitted for your level in society, the fabric you could wear, the headgear and the jewellery. To dress 'above your station' looked like pride. The laws were designed to discourage someone from one station imitating the manners and appearance of another, but were frankly a form of social control and means of identifying a person's rank, reinforcing the distinctions between the nobility and the up-and-coming entrepreneurial groups. Attempts to regulate extravagant expenditure on clothes by aspiring, fashion- and status-conscious bourgeois women were put in moral terms stressing restraint and humility. Elizabeth I's 1574 law declared the craze for fine show as

> the wasting and undoing of a great number of young gentlemen, otherwise serviceable, and others seeking by show of apparel to be esteemed as gentlemen, who, allured by the vain show of those things, do not only consume themselves, their goods, and lands which their parents left unto them, but also run into such debts and shifts as they cannot live out of danger of laws without attempting unlawful acts.

The terms 'show', 'vain', 'consume' and 'debts' suggest disapproval based on medieval ideas of moderation, evoking the Deadly Sins and stereotypes linking suitability of behaviour to rank. Rank, income and gender were the criteria that decided what you could wear. Thus dress signifiers supposedly identified social rank and preserved 'degree'. Though there were harsh punishments for sumptuary infringements they were largely ignored and the laws were repealed in 1603–04 as simply unenforceable. To some this opened the floodgates that would swamp distinction between the orders and herald social collapse. In 1583 Philip Stubbes remarked on

> such a confused mingle mangle of apparel [...] that is verie hard to know who is noble, who is worshipful, who is a gentleman, who is not; for you shall have those [...] go daylie in silkes, velvets, satens, damasks, taffeties and suchlike, notwithstanding that they be both base by byrthe, meane by estate & servile by calling. This is a great confusion & a general disorder, God be mercifull unto us.[6]

High-end fashion became more lavish and impractical as a way of saying, 'I don't need to work, so my clothes are for show only.' Snobbery drove people to seek minute markers to show their superiority. Shakespeare's drama from 1600 onwards is much concerned with how clothing disguises what people really are. In *Measure for Measure* and *King Lear* he is much concerned with the discrepancy between appearance and reality relating to clothes and office, how fine robes suggest rank and rank implies virtue, while exposing how clothes hide sin, gold covers it, and office (or authority) does not mean the man occupying it is there by merit. Clothing imagery in *Antony and Cleopatra* is much less apparent than in other Shakespeare plays of the period, but the fine shows put on by the pair as public theatre and personal projection create ironic tension with the contrast in their spiritual emptiness. Antony makes a show of buckling on his armour, yet proves an inept military strategist. He is helped to arm by Cleopatra in what is, in one sense, an affectionate and intimate moment before battle, but is, in another sense an ironic comment whereby the cause of Antony's decline as man, leader and soldier is integral to his emasculation, complicit in his arming for catastrophe. They may dress as Isis and Hercules, but are really mere flawed human beings under the finery. There would be some in the audience who were sham gentlefolk, people whose money, clothes and flattery had gained them an entrée to court circles and drawn admiring, respectful glances in the theatre. There would be some whose silks covered poxy, malodorous physical decay. Misleading appearance could apply high up the power pyramid. Brachiano in *The White Devil* suggests the Duke of Florence is all show:

> [...] all his reverend wit
> Lies in his wardrobe; he's a discreet fellow
> When he's made up in his robes of state. (II. i. 189–91)

This reminds us of King Lear's remark on 'the great image of Authority': 'A dog's obey'd in office' (IV. vi.). People perceive and treat you according to your robes and accoutrements of office, regardless of the fool or knave you might actually be: 'Robes and furr'd gowns hide all' (*Lear*, IV. vi.). Of course a fine exterior does not necessarily mean a virtuous person under the show. Appearances are deceptive in many different ways throughout the play. But fine silks paraded in public simply emphasized the fact that some were rising fabulously while most were in the mire.

Each man, as guardian of his own soul, his own virtues, was responsible for his own sins. But he had other associations to whom he owed loyalty and responsibility – his family, village, trade or craft, county, nation, church humanity and the whole of creation. Family and community were the strongest bonds, though faith might take precedence and separate him from these commitments. Each man occupied a place in the detailed stratification of society, from king to pauper. The theory of the natural order was based on harmony. Each rank, high or low, had its part to play if concord and perfect working were to be achieved.

> This is the true ordering of the state of a well-fashioned commonwealth, that every part do obey one head, or governor, one law, as all parts of the body obey the head, agree among themselves, and one not to eat up the other through greediness, but that we see order, moderation, and reason, bridle the affections.[7]

This theory of order and orderliness was conceived by those who gave the orders and wished to preserve degree. Rulers were the brains and heart, the nobles the important organs. The others – the limbs – had little else to do but obey. This often-voiced analogy is false. Society is not a body. If you cut off the head the body dies, but if you cut off the king's head or remove the aristocracy, society will continue with a new political settlement. Witness the Civil War. If the lavishly bedecked in the audience thought the play would be a celebration of high passion they were wrong. It carries in its texture warnings to the frivolous and the self-satisfied. It provokes questions about loyalty, rule, politics and misunderstanding of self. Shakespeare never wrote a lightweight play. His tragedies have comic moments, his comedies and romances have dark undertones, his love dramas are ambiguous. They all instruct in some way. In 1631 his colleague Ben Jonson wrote: 'All Repraesentations, […] eyther have bene, or ought to be the mirrors of man's life, whose ends, […] ought always to carry a mixture of profit, with them, no less then delight' (preface to *Love's Triumph*).[8] Jonson was not just referring to court masques. A classicist by education and inclination he was alluding to Horace's maxim 'He has gained every point who has mixed profit with pleasure, by delighting the reader at the same time as instructing him.'[9] How much profit and instruction would the audience take from this representation? History suggests not much.

Chapter 8

IMAGES OF DISORDER: THE RELIGIOUS CONTEXT

The sixteenth and seventeenth centuries were undeniably religious ages. Religion impacted all lives to varying degrees. The Church of England, present in everyone's life, was an arm of the established power that ruled England. The parish church, usually on the edge of the village green (with the inn and the local lord or gentleman's manor house), was visible from the fields as you worked. Its bells punctuated your day. The city parish church was likewise nearby. The priest would be visibly haggling in the market like anyone else, perhaps occupying a corner of the local tavern. He was part of the civic power structure as well as sitting in judgement over your spiritual life. He reported your civil and moral misdemeanours, convened and presided over the church court, arranged poor relief and preached. One form of socio-moral re-enforcement was the homily the priest was obliged by his superiors to read out every Sunday. *The Book of Homilies* (the first published in 1547, the second in 1571) had 33 homilies, intended to bed in the ideas of the new reformed Church of England, to educate the masses and to assist conformity. They covered doctrinal and liturgical subjects but included moral sermons: 'Against Peril of Idolatry', 'Against Gluttony and Drunkenness', 'Against Excess of Apparel', 'Of Alms [Charity] Deeds', 'Of the State of Matrimony', 'Against Idleness', 'Against Disobedience and Wilful Rebellion'.

Religion meant much to the Jacobeans, but not all those who attended church did so in a spirit of devotion. Many went simply to avoid the various punishments meted out for non-attendance, but 'there was no escaping the rhythms of the Prayer Book or the barrage of catechisms and sermons'.[1] Though it was largely a churchgoing society, there had always been those who claimed (and believed) they needed no church or priest to intercede between them and God. Increasingly Dissenters were resisting enforced church attendance, asserting they could worship in the field, the workshop or their home. One sailor expressed the view in 1581 that 'it was never merry England since we were impressed to come to church'.[2] It was a criminal offence to not attend on Sunday, though the pursuit and prosecution of non-attenders depended on the zeal of the vicar. In London, large and anonymous, it was more difficult for parish officers to keep checks on local inhabitants, especially the constantly changing lodgers in the crowded tenements. Sunday worship was theoretically a time of communal affirmation of shared beliefs and values. That excludes those parishioners with rather different thoughts in their heads while the parson exhorted them to virtue. There would always be some who were doctrinally opposed to Anglicanism but kept quiet. Though everyone was nominally Church of England, some in the congregation would be Catholics conforming to the law, others Puritans passively conforming while having more radical and aggressive beliefs about which they were mostly, but not always, quiet. Increasingly there were hostile interactions in the church that created simmering grievances in the outside community. Some vicars were too zealously reformist, some too lazily traditionalist.[3] Some Dissenters separated from the official church and formed their own unofficial congregations. These were illegal and the congregants subject to dispersal or arrest.[4] There were those who, indifferent to religion, called themselves Christian but did not allow faith to interfere with life more than they could help. Atheists tended to keep their views to themselves (or share them only with likeminded others); denial of God was punishable by arrest, interrogation, torture and imprisonment. There were always those more concerned with the pint of ale in the inn after the boredom of the sermon was over. Some chatted, snoozed, made mocking comments on the priest and his sermon, laughed aloud, flirted or transacted business.[5] Others would be more preoccupied with the members of the opposite sex seated across the aisle. Finally, there were those who had genuine faith in the Anglican Church and lived in as holy and virtuous a way as possible. It is impossible to say what proportion of the population at any one time fell into these categories. The parish church was where the community's social differences were re-enforced as much as the shared Christianity. Services were intended to celebrate solidarity and remind the congregation of the demands and sacrifices faith and virtue required. The overarching zeitgeist was religious, though like a rainbow it was of many colours. Despite the various forms of internal, external, silent and vocal opposition to imposed worship, most English men and women were regular churchgoers and those who were not, those who moved away from their village community to the anonymity of the city, would nevertheless have the vestiges of religious upbringing and the remnants of biblical teachings still in their memories.

Another aspect of this structure, that all faiths agreed on, was that the cosmos and the natural world were fantastically varied and complex yet orderly, with each part of the system working and doing its allotted job, and that all this was God's doing: 'The heavens declare the Glory of God and the firmament showeth his handiwork' (Psalm 19:1).

Unsettling Questions

Astronomers contributed to the gradual dismantling of the Ptolemaic system, but plays too could unsettle. Audiences watching the Admiral's Men perform Marlowe's *Tamburlaine the Great* (1587) at the Rose would have heard Alleyne declaim:

> Our souls, whose faculties can comprehend
> The wondrous architecture of the world
> And measure every wand'ring planet's course,
> Still climbing after knowledge infinite
> And always moving as the restless spheres,
> Wills us to wear ourselves and never rest
> Until we reach the ripest fruit of all,
> That perfect bliss and sole felicity,
> The sweet fruition of an earthly crown. (Part I. II. vii. 21–9)

This combines traditional views – man's distinguishing faculties of understanding that separate him from the animals, the glory of God's creation (the 'always moving [...] restless spheres') – with progressive, dangerously blasphemous views on man's restless search for knowledge that trespassed into the secrets of the divine. The final idea is unusual, for instead of seeing 'perfect bliss and sole felicity' as spiritual, a heavenly crown, Tamburlaine's goal is the 'earthly crown' of supreme material power – a very Renaissance ambition. This is the work of a restless, enquiring, turbulent young university man writing for an audience that would include some fairly sophisticated members. But more than three-quarters of England's population was rural – landless farmworkers and small subsistence farmers with beliefs still primitive, basic and medieval. Many large-scale landholders, farmers and nobles were similar. Centuries of Catholicism could not be erased overnight. Changes of thinking take several generations when few are literate, have no access to academic research, and in any case have closed minds. Nationwide instant communication just did not happen and the church always stood in the way of the free sharing of intellectual ideas, especially if they threatened orthodoxy. There was no organized dissemination of news; regular newspapers did not appear until the Civil War. There was also the normal monumental public resistance to change. The majority of the population was exceptionally conservative. Ignorance, fear and intellectual inertia played their parts as always. The Reformation changed the official outer world, but the private inner world of daily life and its cluster of beliefs lagged far behind. The Reformation had many fervent supporters, but was grafted onto a residue of long-ingrained beliefs and practices. Individuals, devoted to their faith, might conform to the new rites and liturgy of Anglicanism while still performing private superstitious acts.

The lines between magic and religion remained as blurred as they ever had been, but, given the growing print culture, and spreading knowledge of what the Bible said, numbers of controversial debates sprang up as to what was orthodox and what was heresy, iconoclasm, superstition, idolatry, papist mumbo-jumbo or diabolic magic. Services in English made doctrine more accessible, and as Anglicanism settled, versions of the translated Bible became more readily available and individuals could read for themselves the words that were the basis of a priest's hitherto unique quasi-mystical interaction with his congregation. This newfound capacity for personal interpretation allowed many doctrinally divergent views to spring up and worry the Anglican hierarchy. In response bishops became more repressive, demanding greater conformity from vicars and parishioners. This encouraged stronger opposition though Puritanism's rise was slow. The Puritan drive to change religious thinking was regarded with irritation and new ideas in medicine, politics and science always provoked opposition. Puritans are almost always figures of fun and derided as hypocrites in plays. The mass of people just wanted to continue living as they had always done. Regardless of this conservatism, seismic shifts were rumbling in many aspects of life. John Donne in 'An Anatomy of the World' (1611) declares:

> [...] new Philosophy calls all in doubt,
> The Element of fire is quite put out;
> The Sun is lost, and th'earth, and no man's wit
> Can well direct him where to look for it.
> And freely men confess that this world's spent,
> When in the Planets, and the Firmament
> They seek so many new; then see that this
> Is crumbled out again to his Atomies.
> 'Tis all in pieces, all coherence gone;
> All just supply, and all Relation:
> Prince, Subject, Father, Son, are things forgot.

Representing God's order, divine harmony, the Ptolemaic system gave reassuring coherence to life. To hear it questioned, to hear of old beliefs discarded by new science, was destabilizing, forcing doubts into people's heads in an age already full of changes, with a new church, a new king and new worlds being discovered, new economic practices, new towns growing (and creating new problems), and old feudal relationships breaking down. In *Antony and Cleopatra* the old Republic falls and the new imperial theme is announced. Senatorial consensus was pushed aside and one-man rule by personal whim and diktat forced into place. The story reflects the political struggles of England in reverse. The old way of absolutist monarchs was being opposed by an increasingly awkward and confrontational Parliament. The conflict between the undisciplined hedonism of Antony (bearded like Hercules) and the new, calculating ambition of Caesar ('scarce-bearded') is imagined as an earthquake event that cracks the arch of the universe. The family bond of marriage is unworkable because Antony's enchantment breaks it. Family was the commonest, closest bond for everyone. Family history, family honour and family loyalty were central to the audience's thinking and feeling. It would be painful seeing taken-for-granted relationships called into question, especially if the answers suggest family and married love are thin veneers of pretence. Antony breaks an assumed bond and besmirches his honour in marrying and then neglecting his wives – twice. But the bond with Octavia has the direst consequences.[6]

Familial and societal disassembly are active themes in the play. Antony rejects the chance for peace through family alliance represented by the union with Octavia. Cleopatra is a very different type of woman and Antony's libertinism and addiction to her draws him back. The normality of family life with Cleopatra and their children is hardly visible, but is an offence to Roman ethics and custom, and the lovers pay the price of transgression. Jacobean viewers would see their fall as punishment for fornication and adultery. The unbroken continuity of rule and order was essential. Those who knew Holinshed's *Chronicles* knew that breaks in the smooth running of royal power led to difficult times surrounding handovers to or takeovers by new dynasties. Shakespeare's history plays amply displayed the natural desire for order and peace. Political vacuums were dangerous – as was illegitimate, inefficient or corrupt rule – and usually led to bloody struggles, generating uneasiness and repression, putting into perspective the desperate anxieties surrounding a queen's pregnancy and the nervous wait for a hoped-for male heir. Cicero warned of the danger inherent in 'a situation in which more than one person cannot be pre-eminent' for 'such a power-struggle ensues that it becomes most difficult to maintain a sacred alliance'.[7] Some audience members had experienced the traumas of the Tudor continuities and discontinuities.

All remembered the recent shift into the Stuart line. Change was disturbing. From God to Earth's dust, everything had its place: man, his communities and his states were part of that orderliness. The fast-changing, apparently disintegrating world disorientated the Jacobeans, and the court was an increasing source of order-threatening discontent.

The disorderliness of courtiers was a common cause for concern, as was the unprofessional conduct of judges and justices of the peace. On 11 July 1604, Sir Philip Gawdy, MP described the Commons Speaker addressing the problem of

> Justices of Peace of wch ther wer two kyndes he founde great fault withal, the one wer such as go downe into the country, and presently fall to hawking, and other sportes, and yf any man comme about Justice, they sende him to their next neybur Justice; the others be suche as put downe one alehouse, and set vp two for it, set up one constable, and put down an other, and yf any matter be stirring whatsoeuer he must haue an ore in it.[8]

The double standard of the apparently virtuous public man whose apparent probity masked private corruption recurs in drama, in the court and in real life. Middleton's 1605 City Comedy *A Mad World, My Masters* has the mother of the courtesan Frank Gullman declare in a neat epigram:

> Who gets th'opinion for a virtuous name,
> May sin at pleasure and ne'er think of shame. (I. i. 164–5)

Part II

THE JACOBEAN PRESENT

Chapter 9

THE CONTEXT OF TRAGEDY

> Much is breeding
> Which, like the courser's hair, hath yet but life
> And not a serpent's poison. (I. ii. 199–202)

> […] the wise gods seel our eyes,
> In our own filth drop our clear judgements, make us
> Adore our errors, laugh at's while we strut
> To our own confusion. (III. xiii. 117–20)

There is perhaps something not entirely upsetting in seeing an overconfident, arrogant fool brought low. Being too grand, too successful, too full of yourself, too indifferent to moderation and the claims of humility was to court retribution. An audience may feel pity at Antony's suffering and death, but consider them deserved. Not blind to his own faults, he is addicted to his errors, aware of them but unable to amend them. We watch his clouded judgement begin to breed future poison and we witness him strut to his confusion. But he does not dance alone to his destruction. This is a duet of death. We witness the fall of two larger-than-life characters and inevitably we may try to apportion blame. Is it a case of a fool fooled by a strumpet who survives him but ends her own life rather than be held captive, deposed from her throne and made a public show? Or is it a tragedy of true lovers destroyed by their own inability to rule wisely, who prioritize pleasure over duty and cannot combat a ruthless, clinical power seeker with an unstoppable military machine behind him?

A feature of Aristotle's definition of tragedy is that it should fill the audience with pity and fear. Pity is evoked for those who, while not totally evil, are flawed enough to bring down suffering upon their heads. Fear originates in the awareness that if such things can happen to men and women of special ability and charisma, with power and money behind them, how much more easily can disaster befall us ordinary men and women. In *Antony and Cleopatra* some of the grand names of history parade before us. How petty, spoiled, devious, corrupt and sinful they appear – in other words, how disturbingly human. We see a drunken lecher, a dissolute libertine, hypnotized by an untrustworthy, selfish, promiscuous trull – not an evil man, only weak and foolish. By their own choice or by the weakness of their wills both are caught in a series of binary opposites: Rome/Egypt, duty/appetite, business/pleasure, masculinity/femininity, stoicism/hedonism, love/war, youth/age, naiveté/deviousness. Other contrasts are set up too: e.g., Octavia and Cleopatra, Antony and Octavius. No polar factor in these opposites is entirely good and the other evil, for both have their negatives and positives. Each end of a spectrum is an extreme position and the Roman and Jacobean worlds both believed that reason and harmony were achieved by a sensible balance, what the Greeks called *sophrosyne*. Antony lacks what Montaigne called 'pliableness'. He is too extreme, gives himself entirely to his pleasures and neglects his duties. This was true of the historical Antony too. The Epicurean concept of flexibility, adjusting to the different needs of life at different times, was seen as the key to surviving and living life well (in the sense of morally, rightly, not indulgently). Antony and Cleopatra are both a unity and a disparity. Though the play links them together (and they are, in respect of their weaknesses and some shreds of love, inextricably joined), the play also presents them as two separate figures. Though they are coupled by some sort of passion they are different types; though they have many similar personality traits they have differing ones too. Antony has some sense of his failure to carry out his duty to Rome and live up to his own image of himself. Cleopatra seems almost entirely self-centred, concerned to have her own way and be the centre of everyone's focus. She never seems to doubt that she is right to act as she does. The historical Cleopatra was very involved in conserving her state. Though dearly loved by her people, she was not especially attached to them. The theatrical figure shows no sense of political duty and clings to power for her own sake and not for her subjects. She shows minimal understanding of Antony's wider role in the world. Though they have a family, live together and are traditionally thought of as the world's most iconic lovers, they spend much of the play arguing, recriminating and being apart. Plutarch and Shakespeare present her as a fascinating woman, but also as a voluptuary and siren. She is overemotional and neurotically sensual (particularly in Shakespeare). She is an amalgam of those female characteristics that have, through the ages, both attracted and repulsed men. Historically Antony deserted Cleopatra during his marriage to Octavia (which produced two daughters), before drifting back into the relationship. These and other features of the marriage are stripped out by Shakespeare. They would dilute the focus on the fatal intertwining with Cleopatra. Antony expresses much dissatisfaction with Cleopatra, is sharply critical, but cannot keep away. As Enobarbus acutely remarks, foreseeing the inevitable: 'He will to his Egyptian dish again' (II. vi. 128). His desertion of Octavia is the tipping point for her brother's anger against Antony; it blows 'the fire up in Caesar', it is 'the immediate author of their variance' (II. vi. 129, 131) and precipitates the military action that destroys the lovers. Both are too obsessed with satisfying their own physical pleasures. They are addicted to pleasure, they know they should realign this to a more balanced state, but are drawn back into their obsession by each other. In Jacobean thinking, this addiction to satisfying their appetites is both sinful and a prelude to inevitable doom. Both are weak characters and keep each other weak. Are such personages a fit subject for tragedy? They are, because they are instructive of how unrestrained appetite in people of power destroys not only them, but those who rely on them. This gives them a political dimension.

Another framework in which both are situated is the network of vices and virtues that was fundamental to Jacobean judgement of all personal, social and political conduct. Both Antony and Cleopatra would have been seen as manifest sinners and the play combines their fall as flawed individuals with a broader picture that expresses a deeply cynical sense of the general decay of society. The Christian ethos shared many of the ethical values of the ancient world and the starting point for the tragedy is that, like other tragic figures, they have committed some sort of offence. Cicero and Plutarch regarded them as offending not only Roman virtues but the gods. For all their parading as Isis and Dionysus, their arrogant pursuit of their own wills cries out for punishment. Shakespeare's audience would agree.

Tragedy as a genre is as old as human sorrow. The medieval concept was of a great man's fall due to the instability of all human affairs. This focused on the caprices of Fortune as the cause of personal disaster and the vicissitudes of life. The Florentine Giovanni Boccaccio collected 56 stories of such falls in *De Casibus Virorum Illustrium* (*On the Fates of Illustrious Men*, 1355–74), which provided a model for subsequent authors. Book VI recounts the destiny of Antony and Cleopatra, with a single entry for Cleopatra and another on Mark Antony, the Triumvirate and Cleopatra.[1] The companion piece, *De Mulieribus Claris* (*On Famous Women*, 1374), reinforces the negative assessment of the queen.[2] Renaissance tragedy, similarly concerned with 'the Fall of Princes' and acknowledging the erratic, unjust turning of Fortune's wheel, additionally explores the central character's *hamartia* (the fatal individual psychological flaw or weakness) and the degree to which humans create their own disasters. Elyot's *The Boke*

Named the Governour (1531) provided a programme of idealized conduct for any man that governs people. The verse stories in *The Mirrour for Magistrates* (1559) illustrate, from history and legend, the different disasters that have befallen prominent figures. Both works are mirrors for rulers of whatever status (from father to king) to see how they may resemble famous figures from the past. Both indicate interest in the means by which power may be lost. Shakespeare's tragedies all focus similarly on the personal psychology that puts a powerful figure in a vulnerable position. There are other external factors like other men's power plays or the plotting of malevolent antagonists that can accelerate or exacerbate the fall of an otherwise good and strong ruler, but essentially it is the central figure's own weakness(es) that precipitate his fall. People in the 1600s were particularly interested in stories portraying the decline of men of power and place. They saw it regularly in their own socio-political milieu and looked to famous people of the past as instructive *exempla*. The vacillating fortunes of the Earls of Leicester and Essex were recent memories and the recurrent rises and falls of Sir Walter Raleigh were an ongoing saga. The decline of such figures still had huge impact on the mass of people and their failings are thus of importance as warnings and instruction. In *Antony and Cleopatra* two figureheads fall, and their fates being intertwined raises the question whether this doubles the impact for the audience or dilutes it.

The theoretical basis for tragedy came from classical sources, the chief being Aristotle's *Poetics*. This collection of lectures defines and analyses the key features of Greek tragedy. It was known in the Renaissance through a Latin translation from Arabic and was increasingly becoming part of European thinking about tragedy. A tragedy is a representation (*mimesis*) in action and words of the fall of a great man (the *protagonist*) from prosperity to misery, not necessarily ending with his death. It presents a story (*mythos*), complete in itself, with a beginning, middle and end, employing dignified language suitable to its serious theme and including a degree of spectacle. The tragic process is defined as follows: a man of power, at the height of his prosperity, of otherwise good qualities, thinking his world is safe and he is happy, makes a mistake of judgement and action (knowingly or unknowingly). His miscalculation comes about because of a weakness or flaw (*hamartia*) in his personality and is caused by an excessive pride (*hubris*) in his ability to judge and act without due attention to morality and the gods (or God). His pride in himself will falter, due to his flaw: a tendency to jealousy, ambition, irascibility, impulsiveness, lust – any emotion experienced to an irrational extreme. In any event it will transgress the moral boundaries of his time and offend the gods. Unaware of the mistake initially, the character continues his life. Gradually a problem emerges as a result of his mistake. It may be military, political or personal. Matters deteriorate, his fortunes begin to reverse (*peripeteia*), complications become inextricable, the hero becomes aware of the mistake and recognizes his fault (*anagnorisis*) before disaster (*catastrophe*) strikes (perhaps his own death at the hands of the opponents [*antagonists*] he has aroused, but death is not a necessary outcome). The progress towards the outcome (*dénouement*) involves escalating suffering (physical, emotional, mental or any combination) and creates in the audience a sense of sorrow for the protagonist and fear that if such things can happen to men of special abilities, with power, privilege and wealth, they can wreck our lives too. This pity and fear creates such strong feelings in the audience that they are purged of emotion, washed out and exhausted, but also filled with a sense of how little their own problems are by comparison. This process is called *catharsis*. One other feature of tragedy is the sense the protagonist (and the audience) has of being hopelessly entangled, trapped in a process he cannot stop. He is fated to disaster whatever he does.

Antony's fall and the question whether it fits Aristotelian or medieval-Renaissance concepts of tragedy will depend to some extent upon how we feel about him as a person and whether we feel he deserves what happens. It is possible to separate his tragic status from our personal assessment of him and say that he does fit the tragic criteria, but that we are not moved by his suffering and death. His suicide is a botched farce, his removal to the monument undignified, even absurdly laughable. We may see the pathos of his suffering but not feel sorry for him other than the general sadness we feel at any human being dying in pain. Being an eponymous play might suggest we are being encouraged to identify with and therefore feel pity for the two named characters. Yet this is not true of *Titus Andronicus*, *Richard III*, or *Macbeth*, though each character does elicit admiration for their courage and tenacity in the face of death. There is the inevitable question whether the punishment for his sins is disproportionate or just. A Jacobean audience might well feel he is suitably punished for his gluttony, pride, lust, adultery and fornication. But alongside the fall of a great man (or a man with great power) are the interconnected subsidiary traumas experienced by others around him – sometimes innocent victims, collateral damage in a state's collapse. There are the soldiers and sailors killed in the battles, Iras and Charmian choosing to die with their mistress, and Enobarbus and Eros, the unintended, undeserving victims of Antony's chaotic career. A moralistic Jacobean might say Enobarbus too deserves death for his disloyalty. He certainly feels he is 'alone the villain of the world' (IV. vi. 31) and his 'revolt is infamous' (IV. ix. 22). Loyalty in a warrior culture was highly prized. In a political court culture it was equally regarded, though rare. Betrayal of state, lord, family and guest was regarded as especially sinful; Dante put these traitors into Nether Hell.

Antony is a prime traitor, betraying Fulvia, his duty, his self-image, his co-partners in the triumvirate, Octavia, his men and Cleopatra.

The progress of the drama follows the sequence indicated in Freytag's Pyramid. The rising action introduces the initial problems: Antony's obsession with Cleopatra leading to neglecting his duties as Roman leader of his third of the empire, his wife leading an army against Caesar, his co-partners needing him in Rome and Cleopatra unhappy about letting him go. Determination is needed, but Antony lacks the courage to stand up to Cleopatra. Once it is set going, the action builds through a series of minor climaxes and disasters, before the climax of the final battle and a series of deaths. The early stages concern a general neglect of duty. This is exacerbated by the perceived insult in not listening to Octavius' messenger. The crucial disaster is the agreement to marry Octavia. His casting her away and return to Egypt provide the motive for Caesar to do what he has long desired to do: deal with Antony once and for all and become sole autocrat of the empire. The emotional graph is a steep and steadily climbing anguish, the scenes becoming incrementally more disturbing as Antony helplessly approaches destruction. It is a staged fall: the marriage and separation, the return to Cleopatra, Actium, the land battle in Egypt, the final sea battle, the botched suicide, discovering Cleopatra alive, and finally death. The downward course is made worse by Antony's courage and persistent optimism.

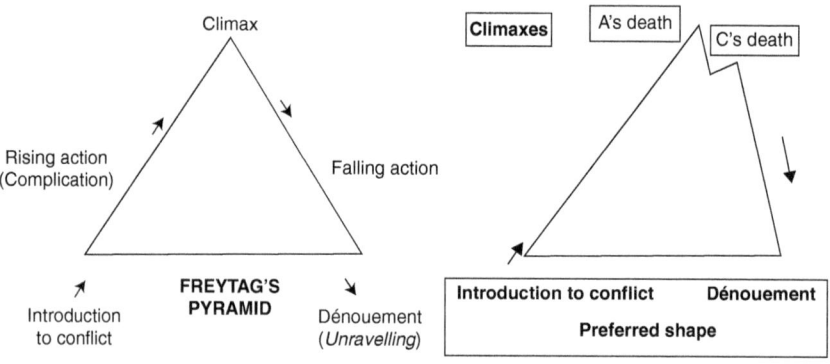

After each mishap he is cast down, rouses his spirit, only to be pushed down further. The shape of the action is less an isosceles triangle than an irregular one with a steep, double-peaked fall from climax to *dénouement*. Shakespearean tragic climaxes usually come in the final scene. In *Romeo and Juliet*, a mere fifty lines intervene between Romeo drinking poison and the heroine killing herself, with ten lines between her finding Romeo dead and then stabbing herself. In *Antony and Cleopatra*, the hero fatally wounds himself in Act IV Scene xiv (line 103), while Cleopatra dies in Act V Scene ii (line 311).

Antony dies 104 lines after his stabbing and Cleopatra another 415 after that. In between his death and hers she negotiates with Caesar, hardly a passionate response to the death of the man she is supposed to love. This not only dilutes the tension, but suggests that if she had been satisfied that Caesar would not show her off to the greasy Roman populace ('the shouting plebeians' [IV. xii. 34]) in his triumph, she would not have killed herself. Mardian, the eunuch, delivering the false message of Cleopatra's death, declares to an angry Antony, 'My mistress loved thee and her fortunes mingled/With thine entirely' (IV. xiv. 24–5). There is an intriguing ambiguity here. 'Fortunes' means both material wealth and the course of one's life – good and bad luck, success and failure. Certainly it suited the queen to mix her money with Antony's. He had access to taxes and other imposts from the whole Middle East. Shared finances meant double the pleasure. They also shared their fortunes, the ups and downs, the good times and the bad. But ultimately she was seeking a way of surviving. The stark fact is that 50 lines after Mardian's announcement of the queen's death Antony asks Eros to kill him. When Eros kills himself it only takes 8 lines before Antony does his own deed. He still affects the play. His prolonged dying has a noticeable effect on Cleopatra, if her words are sincere:

> O sun,
> Burn the great sphere thou mov'st in! Darkling stand
> The varying shore o'th' world! O Antony,
> Antony, Antony! (IV. xv. 10–13)

Or is she play-acting again, milking a sad situation in order to dramatize herself? Her passionate desperation seems evident as the body is hoisted into the monument:

> Quicken with kissing. Had my lips that power,
> Thus would I wear them out. (IV. xv. 40–41)

Shakespeare judiciously omits a detail from Daniel that has Antony's blood splattering those below as he is lifted up. This might provoke inappropriate laughter. Antony's plaintive 'I am dying, Egypt, dying' is repeated twice. This (and her fainting) helps realize what Plutarch describes:

> Those who were present say that there was never a more pitiable sight than the spectacle of Antony, covered with blood, struggling in his death agonies and stretching out his hands towards Cleopatra as he swung helplessly in the air.[3]

Antony calling for a cup of wine is also in Plutarch, but what Shakespeare omits is how Plutarch's Cleopatra beat and lacerated her breasts, smeared her face with Antony's blood and called him 'her lord and husband and emperor'.[4] This Eastern-style reaction to death is stage business that might have been added to piece out the limited stage directions. Cleopatra had Antony's body cremated and put in an urn that was then placed in his tomb. Several days later, when her negotiations for survival failed, she visited the tomb and 'crowned the urn with a garland and kissed it'. She addressed Antony's ashes:

> My beloved Antony [...] although in our lives nothing could part us, it seems that death will force us to change places. You, the Roman, have found a grave in Egypt, and I, unhappy woman, will receive just enough of your country to give me room to lie in Italy. [...] Do not abandon your wife while she lives [...]. Hide me and let me be buried here with you, for I know now that the thousand griefs I have suffered are as nothing beside the few days that I have lived without you.[5]

This speaks of a love not always believable or visible in Shakespeare. She was accompanied by her female attendants, Charmian and Iras. As they die with her presumably others were there to report these incidents, but it is difficult to believe someone overheard and remembered all that Plutarch reports Cleopatra saying.

There is also the problem raised by the dispatching of Antony nearly five hundred lines before the end of the play. Is audience sympathy dissipated through the two remaining scenes? Shakespeare was content to change history if it suited his purposes. In *King Lear* he kills off the king and Cordelia when the sources all have them win their battle for restoration and live on for some years. But Shakespeare having them die in the final act has tremendous impact.[6] Antony's body is carried off at the end of Act 4 and focus shifts to how Cleopatra reacts. This is significant in several ways. There is no passionate and moving suicide by the queen in spontaneous reaction to the death of her lover. That is delayed and is in reaction to distaste at being made a circus curiosity in Caesar's triumph. There is a discussion whether the new dispensation can accommodate Cleopatra. The gap between their deaths can be seen as a physical marker of the emotional gap between them, marking his infatuation with her (and immediate suicide on hearing she was dead) and her infatuation with herself (only turning to suicide once negotiations with Caesar seem hopeless). However, it is only after the death of Antony that we get a sense that perhaps Cleopatra did love him – in her way – and only expressed it when it was too late. Theatrical to the last, in her final staged spectacle, she dresses in her royal finery and is laid out crowned on a golden couch. Caesar was struck by the 'nobility of her spirit' and follows her wishes for burial with Antony. She was 39, had reigned for twenty-two years and been with Antony for something over ten. Her death has a dignity she does not often show in the play. It has spectacle too, features included in Aristotle's prescription for tragedy. It is typical of Shakespeare that the lofty poetry of their deaths is partially interspersed, but not dispersed, by the down-to-earth comments and *double entendres* of the clown who brings the asps. It is a reminder, like the apothecary in *Romeo and Juliet*, the gravedigger in *Hamlet* and the porter in *Macbeth*, that whatever high-flying pretensions the so-called great and good adopt, they are but flesh and blood and they live cheek by jowl with the inescapable gritty realities of life and death; laughter co-exists with tears.

Cleopatra's tragic trajectory can similarly be traced. Her decline begins with her at the height of her power and happiness and follows a series of reverses, some induced by her own actions, some imposed upon her by outside forces she is unable to manipulate. Her kingdom is safely under the guardianship of the Roman state and she has the Roman leader under her control. But practical realities intervene; duty and necessity call her lover to Rome. This precipitates all sorts of undignified outbursts on her part. Reminiscent though they be of Queen Elizabeth, they are also resonant with conduct unbecoming a monarch that a Jacobean audience would readily identify. Some may even have seen echoes of King James's behaviour in her antics. Cleopatra (and to a slightly lesser degree Antony) has failed to understand that a ruler cannot live for themselves; they are expected to live for their people and their state.

Chaucer's prologue to *The Monkes Tale* in *The Canterbury Tales* gives a standard medieval definition of the subject matter of tragedy:

Tragedie is to seyn a certeyn storie,
[...].
Of him that stood in great prosperitiee
And is y-fallen out of heigh degree
Into miserie, and endeth wretchedly.

The Monk lists a sequence of famous men who fell: Lucifer, Adam, Samson, Hercules, Nebuchadnezzar, Belshazzar, Zenobia, Nero, Holofernes, Antiochus, Alexander, Julius Caesar, Croesus, etc. This standard recital of mythical, classical and biblical figures is augmented by more recent instances of misfortune: King Pedro of Spain, King Peter of Cyprus and Count Ugolino of Pisa (who figures in Dante's *Inferno*). Unlike Boccaccio, Chaucer does not include Antony. The Monk is stopped short by the Knight, uneasy at hearing this 'hevinesse', preferring tales of poor men who 'clymbeth up, and wexeth fortunat'. This gives a sense of the depressing effect of tragedy, purging audiences of all taste for gloom and making them all the more ready to be thankful for good fortune. The fall of a prince was seen as the most apocalyptic event, since the collapse of central one-person rule (liberal or despotic) affected the whole polity. Given too the quasi-divine status accorded kings and the awed reverence shown to them, for them to fall was shocking. If God's elect could be toppled – by treason, murder or self-inflicted failing – what hope was there for the security of lesser men? A prince's fall was a warning, a reminder of the precariousness of human life. Such a subject demonstrated those personal or political faults to avoid, applied by extension to anyone with power to lose – noble, MP, judge, magistrate, general, ship's captain, head of commercial enterprise, lord of the manor or father of a family. Recent history alone provided copious examples of the intrigues, betrayals, bloodthirsty ambitions, attempted coups and outrageous bids for power that led to the toppling of rulers and traitors alike. The Wars of the Roses and recent English history apart, the sensational violence of political struggles in the Italian city-states and elsewhere proved an exotic, endlessly fascinating source of settings and stories to explore. Catholic Europe was connected in English minds with devious plots and ingeniously cruel methods of killing. Thomas Kyd's *The Spanish Tragedy* (1581), *the* play that captured the popular imagination, regularly recalled for performance (unusual in those days), set the mould for violent tragedy and the fashion for dramas that centred on revenge. The element of revenge in *Antony and Cleopatra* is minimal in plot terms. Revenge for the insult to his sister is what motivates Caesar to finally move against Antony. It is a trivial and paltry excuse. There is, more importantly, the extra-narrative revenge of the gods for a life lived badly. Elizabethan-Jacobean tragedy's great contribution is in the subtle psychological dynamics of heroes and villains. In *Antony and Cleopatra*, while clearly the protagonists are not to be applauded morally, the complexity of their personalities and the possibility that they do not deserve to die for their sins adds an intriguing dimension to the plot. We may deprecate Antony's libertine life but feel being deposed and forced into exile are more suited to his crimes. Though sympathy may build for him, as inept actions and hollow optimism hasten his decline, we may also feel that exile and anonymity would be intolerable for such a big character.

The model for early Elizabethan tragedy was the work of Seneca. Francis Meres links the Roman writer with the rising star of English theatre: 'As Plautus and Seneca are accounted the best for Comedy and Tragedy among the Latins, so Shakespeare among the English is the most excellent in both kinds for the stage.'[7] The stories that were the bases for the great Greek tragedies (Aeschylus's *Oresteia* and Sophocles's *Oedipus* trilogy) were often known through other sources than the originals – Chaucer's poetry and Ovid's *Metamorphoses* for example – but in the early 1500s, the Greek texts of Sophocles and Euripides were becoming available. By the 1550s Seneca too was gaining ground as a model for classroom translation and study. His prose works initially attracted interest for their liberal *sententiae* contemplating matters relevant to men in public office. His meditations on personal loss and exile appealed too. *De Ira* (*On Anger*) has relevance to *Antony and Cleopatra* in its powerful plea for the control of the lower, baser emotions. This ethical line and the stoic approach coincided with the religious views of the time and the tradition of Christian quietist endurance of suffering. Gradually, Seneca's tragedies too gained attention. Tragedies, in Latin, written in European universities, owed much to the influence of Seneca's flamboyant rhetoric. Rhetoric was still a major part of the undergraduate degree course. Public speaking competitions and dramatic performance were seen as suitable training, for many students would become public leaders or priests. The earliest evidence of Seneca performed in English was *Troades* at Trinity College, Cambridge (1551), followed by *Oedipus* and others. But another impetus came from the developing public theatres, where dramatists (many from Oxbridge) exploited his sensational and bloody storylines. The later dominance of Revenge Tragedy is traceable to Seneca's influence, its persistence evidenced by recurrent quotation and parody of his work far into the period. He provided three examples of the ghost device, whereby a returning spectre informs the hero/revenger of the cause of his or some other person's death. This incites the action. The ghost of Hamlet's father is well known, but many other plays rely on this Senecan device. No ghosts occur in *Antony and Cleopatra*, but the music of hautboys played under the stage in Act IV Scene iii is said, by a superstitious soldier, to be the god Hercules leaving Antony. Revenant spectres represent nemesis from the past; the past is still vibrantly active in the politics of the present and shadow figures (Julius Caesar, the assassins of Caesar, Fulvia, Antony and Cleopatra's own pasts) still influence the narrative. Other Senecan features appealing to English playwrights were the passages of lyrical description and the flourishes of oratorical language used for dramatic moments. This explains the presence in so many early Elizabethan tragedies of long, action-stopping speeches. Audiences used to long sermons were attuned to listening to and untangling the meaning of sometimes turgid descriptions. By the time of the Great Tragedies, however, Shakespeare's experience had taught him how to break up long speeches with dramatic interjections. The lively fluidity of the language in *Antony and Cleopatra*, with few lengthy speeches, is an indicator of how mature a craftsman Shakespeare had become.

The Tenne Tragedies, edited by Thomas Newton (1581), collected the translations of Seneca's dramas.[8] In this edition, writers discovered plots focused on revenge carried out in highly bloodthirsty ways. Seneca's implicit critique of high-handed autocratic rule by absolutist monarchs/emperors was much to the taste of English dramatists, as was his condemnation of courts corrupted by favourites and parasites, scheming ladder climbers and hangers-on. This, and the examples from contemporary and recent political history available in Holinshed, created a taste for violent stories involving redress of personal wrong. Court settings offered satirical opportunities aimed at the sycophantic toadyism found in myth and history that inevitably evoked identification with contemporary life. In the claustrophobic domestic setting of *Othello* and the closed, court/family setting of *Hamlet*, Revenge Tragedy is given its cleverest and most psychologically complex treatments, but since Christianity demanded retribution for all wrongdoing, a way of reinforcing God's omniscience and omnipotence, literature was required to demonstrate that sin would be punished, and so in *Macbeth* and *King Lear* we see the bad punished in a public space – the field of battle. *Antony and Cleopatra* is curiously lacking in bloodshed. It is implied in the background with the battles, but only with Eros and Antony is blood spilled onstage. Given the hothouse pleasure of the Alexandrian court, it is fitting that Antony and his partner, having lived so much for themselves within this closed location, should die private deaths. Believing that God knew of all sins committed, people expected villains to be punished sooner or later. A Latin saying '*Cave, cave, deus videt*' ('Beware, beware, God is watching') and innumerable biblical texts reminded ordinary Christians they lived in a culture where sin was expected to be discovered and followed by retribution. People tended to want to take revenge themselves, in the ancient tradition of the revenge vendetta – the *lex talionis* (law/right of retaliation). Vengeful people very reluctantly hand over this traditional 'duty' to the courts. Christianity tried to control the 'eye for an eye', 'take the law in your own hands' instinct. Theology stressed vengeance as the prerogative of God: 'Vengeance is mine; I will repay, saith the Lord' (Romans 12:19). But the desire to retaliate personally against those dishonouring or murdering a member of the family persisted, especially among the aristo-gentry, with their warrior-culture background and their oversensitive 'code' of 'honour'. Conveniently, Caesar is handed this excuse by Antony's treatment of his sister. Nodding deferentially in the direction of law, order and Christian values, the Revenge Tragedies, from *Horestes* (1567) to the derivative bloodbaths of Caroline drama, took advantage of the public's love of gory payback stories acted out onstage. Revenge Tragedies involve disguise, intrigue and plotting, as the murderer and the avenger scheme to outwit each other. Real or pretended insanity is common and numerous secondary deaths obligatory. Antony, though not clinically insane, acts irrationally at times, stupidly courting difficulties by persisting in his relationship with Cleopatra, and displaying a number of outbursts of quite extreme anger. After the second naval fiasco and a second betrayal by the Egyptian navy, Cleopatra describes Antony as 'more mad/Than Telamon for his shield' (IV. xiii. 1–2). Telamon was the patronymic of Ajax (a Greek leader in the Trojan war) and this comment makes another connection between him and the brute fool of *The Iliad*, more recently mocked as the more-brawn-than-brain soldier Ajax in Shakespeare's *Troilus and Cressida* (1601–02).

For Aristotle tragedy concentrates its effects by having one plot, one setting and a timescale of 24 hours (the unities). The language should be dignified, in keeping with the lofty subject, and the cause of the 'fall' should similarly be serious, not trivial. Because Greek drama in general (and tragedy in particular) was a public religious celebration, there is an ethical underpinning that honours and supports the gods. Non-normative behaviour is punished as a reaffirmation of community-held values. Noticeably, Shakespeare deviates from these rules. The plot of *Antony and Cleopatra* is largely focused on the fall of the lovers, but has input from the rise of Caesar. The timescale of the action is far beyond a day and the settings are exceptionally varied even for Shakespeare. He is, of course, constricted somewhat by the facts of history. The lexis has multiple registers, moving from the high rhetoric of formal ceremony delivered in blank verse (which is the bulk of text), to bawdy chit-chat in the Alexandrian court, drunken banter aboard Pompey's galley, soldiers' talk and the rustic who brings the asps. It is, however, much less mixed than other tragedies. Within the dominant blank verse, there is considerable variety of pace and lineation. There are many broken lines and run-on lines, indicating extreme emotion and giving varied pace. Much of this comes from Antony in his different incidents of fury at Cleopatra. There are prose exchanges, a song and an example of peasant dialect. Mixing diverse language forms – structurally and lexically – reflects a little of the social mix but it is very largely the leaders of society who speak and declaim in formal verse. This skilled use of language reflecting the actions and moods of the plot is an identifiable feature of the mature craftsmanship Shakespeare displays at this phase in his career. It contrasts graphically with the more straight-laced, dull, unvarying formality of many plays from the early Tudor period. The circumspect and magnanimous closing words to this 'pair so famous' (V. ii. 359) are given to Caesar. His army will 'in solemn show attend this funeral'. This indicates a return to Roman propriety and his final order to Dolabella (Antony's enemy) is that he 'see/High order in this great solemnity'.

The disorderly and transgressive conduct of the 'famous pair' put the Roman world in peril. That hierarchical order is now restored.

The theme of retribution is another feature are commonly found in tragedy. Nemesis, the ancient Greek goddess of retribution, represents the belief that whatever wrong you do will be done back to you, through the gods or a human agent of punishment. Nemesis (from the Greek for paying what is due) was a remorseless goddess pursuing perpetrators, for years if necessary, until vengeance was taken. The wrong done initially might be against the hero or another person (as in Clytemnestra's murder of her husband, Agamemnon, in *The Oresteia*). The gods then sent someone to avenge the wrong (like Orestes, son of Clytemnestra, and Agamemnon, deciding his duty to his father was greater than to his mother). The initial wrong might also be committed by the protagonist somehow dishonouring the gods, as is the case of Antony and Cleopatra in their self-obsessed pursuit of pleasure. This pride, arrogance and overweening confidence (*hubris*) was the pride that goes before a fall. Overconfidence in yourself (like Antony's declaration that 'the nobleness of life/Is to do thus' and that they 'stand up peerless' [I. i. 37, 41]) is a weakness, a flaw. Other personality defects could be flaws. A particular weakness might not inhibit performance as a leader at all until circumstances activate the flaw. It could be a flaw you are completely unaware of until it begins to destroy your peace of mind, your world or your life. The tragic flaws that destroy the heroes of Shakespeare's Great Tragedies are variously defined. Antony's weakening flaws might be defined as passion (anger), wantonness, gluttony, lust, and a lack of balance between reason and appetite. Cleopatra's are the same, though we may add a hubristic sense of her mastery of Antony, and her desire for that mastery. Both would be seen as sins. The Romans saw retribution as linked to *invidia* (envy). A ruler brazenly believing every decision he makes is divinely inspired would arouse the gods' envy, incurring punishment for thinking he was untouchable, invincible and irreproachably right. *Invidia* can be seen as a sense of injustice that needs righting. A king who is too autocratic needs to be humiliated. A ruler who thinks he is above restraint, above right conduct and has a right to indulge in all the fruits of the Earth is setting himself up for humiliation. Punishment and humbling underlie much of what happens in the play. Antony's suicide is a painfully prolonged physical humiliation rather than swift, heroic or moving.

Dénouements (conclusions; literally 'unknotting') are catastrophic in tragedies. The double catastrophe in *Antony and Cleopatra* is less stunning than the deaths of Romeo and Juliet, but the reunion effected has power and gives Cleopatra the opportunity to express her depth of emotion with regard to the loss of Antony. Death, not always the inevitable end of a tragedy, is a common and useful device. It is not tragic if the hero is destroyed by a sudden disaster from outside or if, like a puppet, he is manipulated by outside forces. The destruction is only tragic when set in motion by a self-initiated action stemming from the protagonist's inner weakness, setting the tragic machine on its path. Once reconciliation is impossible between Caesar and Antony tragedy becomes impossible to halt, given Antony's impulsive nature

With domineering hand she moves the turning wheel,
Like currents in a treacherous bay swept to and fro:
Her ruthless will has just deposed once fearful kings
While trustless still, from low she lifts a conquered head;
No cries of misery she hears, no tears she heeds,
But steely hearted laughs at groans her deeds have wrung.
Such is the game she plays, and so she tests her strength;
Of mighty power she makes parade when one short hour
Sees happiness from utter desolation grow.
(Boethius, *The Consolation of Philosophy*, II. I.)

and his passion for Cleopatra. He is unlikely to conduct a campaign with clear judgement. The exposure of a leader's vulnerability reminds us of the insecurity and precariousness of all life. For the audience – helpless to help, witnessing another being's life falling apart – the experience is harrowing. To watch a man make such foolish decisions about battle tactics, to watch him provoke his own tragedy, is almost unbearable. Having set up his own downfall the hero is increasingly subject to situations he cannot control and which overwhelm him. The machine is unstoppable. Through suffering, the hero, punished and purified, may emerge sadder and wiser. But it is doubtful Antony has learned anything of himself from his defeats. He is more focused on his love. That is, perhaps, his final tragedy.

Part of the helplessness that spectators of tragedy experience is the sense of the protagonist(s) being in the hands of Fate. They are destined to this fall and each action they take moves them closer to catastrophe, however they try to avoid it. The hero's helplessness is likened to being on a wheel that spins them up to greatness but can equally, unexpectedly and undeservedly, spin them down to misfortune. The Wheel of Fortune (*Rota Fortunae*) was a popular image reflecting the unreliable and capricious nature of success. It was how the classical world explained the workings of Fate, providing aptly the image of great men falling from power to misery and/or death that was central to the idea of tragedy. Fortuna, goddess of Fate (a woman, i.e., a symbol of arbitrary changeability), was often imagined as blindfolded to express the arbitrariness and impartiality of good or bad luck. In the Middle Ages, though the wheel image was often invoked, it was increasingly connected not with an unpredictable goddess but with the will of God. God – omnipotent, omniscient – planned everything. A fortunate rise or an unforeseen disaster were not the work of untrustworthy Fate but of Providence. John Knox rejected the idea of Fortune as heathen. The Elizabethan Bishop Thomas Cooper summed up the Anglican view: 'That which we call Fortune is nothing but the hand of God, working by causes and for causes that we know not'; nature was 'nothing but the finger of God working in his creatures'.[9] He saw plagues not as a natural, preventable medical problem: 'Whensoever misery or plague happeneth to man, it cometh not by chance or fortune, but by the assured providence of God.'[10]

Caesar's role in destroying Antony is suggestive of a new development in thinking associating punishment with human agents acting on their own behalf, but the soothsayer's warning to avoid any competition with Caesar is based on a concept of Fate:

> If thou dost play with him at any game,
> Thou art sure to lose; and of that natural luck
> He beats the 'gainst the odds. (II. iii. 24–6)

The gods have ordained that Antony's spirit will always be subordinated to Caesar's. Tragedies in general remind men how fragile their hold on life and happiness is and how devastation is a judgement on their conduct. The moment when the hero finally realizes the mistake(s) he has made, how events are leading towards collapse, can be heart-rending. Antony numerous times expresses awareness of the malign influence Cleopatra has on him and how the Roman world judges him. He uses a lexis connected with enchantment and betrayal. Betrayal has a political association, but its moral dimension involves her leading him into profligacy as a diabolic betrayal of his soul to damnation. The ending itself is meant to bring about feelings of pity and fear that effect a purging or *catharsis*. The idea is that in witnessing such horrific events happening to people who, while making foolish judgements, are not essentially bad, the play appeals to our sympathy and so works upon our emotions that we are completely purged of emotion and feel helplessly battered into dumbness.

Relevant to a play involving another civil war is Richmond's plea for healing and reconciliation at the end of *Richard III* (1592–93):

> England hath long been mad, and scarred herself;
> [...].
> Abate the edge of traitors, gracious Lord,
> That would reduce these bloody days again,
> And make poor England, weep in streams of blood!
> Let them not live to taste this land's increase
> That would with treason wound this fair land's peace!
> Now civil wounds are stopped, Peace lives again:
> That she may long live here, God say Amen!

The double death moves Caesar to deliver a brief eulogy at the end of Act V. It was a Roman custom to give a speech of praise over a dead body before burial., but this is curt in the extreme, especially if compared with the famous 'Friends, Romans, countrymen' speech Antony gave over the body of Julius Caesar. This is businesslike, commenting on Cleopatra having studied 'easy ways to die', and ordering the bodies to be removed. He does offer some praise:

> She shall be buried by her Antony.
> No grave upon the earth shall clip in
> A pair so famous. (V. ii. 357–9)

But he cannot forbear from drawing a moral from the events and their outcome; he mean-spiritedly declares that they brought the catastrophe upon themselves and that the pity he feels for them is counterbalanced by the glory he has won in bringing them down:

> High events as these
> Strike those that make them, and their story is
> No less in pity than his glory which
> Brought them to be lamented. (V. ii. 59–62)

It is an apt assessment, but a magnanimous spirit would not have glorified himself at such a moment.

Antony and Cleopatra were always a tragedy waiting to happen. In the words of Anouilh's Chorus in his tragedy *Antigone*:

> The spring is wound up tight. It will uncoil of itself. [...] The least turn of the wrist will do the job. Anything will set it going [...] and the tragedy is on.
>
> The rest is automatic. [...] The machine is in working order; it has been oiled ever since time began, and it runs without friction. Death, treason and sorrow are on the march; and they move in the wake of storm, of tears, of stillness.[11]

The sins of the protagonists, speedily portrayed in the opening act, have set up a dangerous situation – morally and politically. The careless pair, on the edge of catastrophe, continue in their revelling. The tragic machine waits throbbing; its horrific, destructive path will unfold swiftly and inexorably.

Chapter 10

'O'ERFLOWING THE MEASURE': RESTRAINT AND EXCESS

The Character of Antony

Next to Romeo and Juliet the story of Antony and Cleopatra is probably the second most famous love story in the world. It is questionable whether a Jacobean audience would have seen it quite as simply as being the sad tale of a great passion destroyed by Caesar's ruthless ambition. While the human and personal disasters that befall the two are moving, dramatic, perhaps even tragic, there is an unavoidable aspect that would not have been disregarded by seventeenth-century audiences: the political dimension is inextricably entangled with the personal, and the personal has wrongfully been allowed to distract from the public duties of both title characters. Both leading characters are no longer private individuals; their roles as leaders should supersede their private lives. But they make the mistake of blurring the line between personal and public, letting their lives as a couple spill over into their lives as leaders. Their roles involve privilege, power and access to wealth, and in return for these advantages both had a duty to prioritize the security of thousands of dependent subjects. Shocked by news of the hitherto loyal Enobarbus's defection, Antony asserts his awareness of the collateral damage his decline is creating: 'Oh, my fortunes have/Corrupted honest men' (IV. v. 16–17). Yet he shows a small glimpse of the greatness of which he was capable in an act of nobility – sending Enobarbus's treasure after him. At the same time, his once-loyal follower is shamed by the desertion he felt he had to make and the generosity of Antony, that 'mine of bounty' (IV. vi. 3). Open-handed munificence in rewarding service is the sign of a fine leader, a noble spirit. That benevolence, even to someone who has betrayed him, shows greatness of heart. At the same time it displays what Antony's poor conduct has done. His personal life has been excessive and profligate. His public life too has been excessive: assuming identification with Dionysus and Hercules, giving away Roman land, behaving generally in a hubristic manner. His arrogance has transgressed the requirements of moderate humility. Balance, moderation, self-control and modesty of manner and lifestyle were high priority values in Roman/pagan and Jacobean/Christian times. Despite the warnings of others Antony goes ahead and makes his own decisions, increasingly courting opposition from Lepidus and Caesar, general disapproval by the Romans, and certainly condemnation by the theatre audience of Shakespeare's time. He flirts with disaster by proudly persisting in his adultery with Cleopatra, his decadent lifestyle, and his indifference to the business of running the Eastern empire sensibly and in line with Rome's interests. Having survived many dangers in his life he seems to feel now that he is untouchable, irreproachable and invulnerable. These ingredients – this *hubris* – invites potential tragedy. In pagan terms he offends the gods; in Christian terms (by which the Jacobeans would judge him) he shows no humility, no respect for the duty with which God has honoured him. Either way he faces the risk of being brought down.

The idea of measure, of acting within the prescribed bounds of balance, common sense and virtue, was highly important to the Jacobeans. It related to all aspects of life – secular and spiritual, domestic and communal. Eating and drinking beyond measure was gluttony, spending extravagantly was ostentatious pride in array (clothing and other visible signs of status), extreme cruelty was barbaric excess, loving beyond normal attraction was madness. All were sins, all folly, and all ran the risk of disaster. Both protagonists neglect their public duty in favour of their personal involvement, imperilling the stability of the Roman world and throwing into doubt whether they should be judged as famous lovers or as infamous and irresponsible fools. Their lives are a continuous drama, mostly generated by themselves. Every action is a piece of theatre, their very language is hyperbole. Normal conduct and moderate language seem impossible. In the end they become stereotypes of themselves, puppets manipulated by their own manipulations, prisoners of their own self-fashioned images. Lucy Hughes-Hallett, in discussing seventeenth-century views of Cleopatra, makes the point that 'to the Protestant and most particularly to the bourgeois English mind' the famous queen was 'in a state of lamentable sin'.[1] To the Jacobeans, according to Hughes-Hallett, she is contriving, devious and play acting. To be a heroine she had to be not only charismatic and great but also virtuous. Both she and Antony are examples of the dangers of uncontrolled appetite. The queen was adept at self-image invention, perpetually changing shape to adjust to circumstances and for her own advantage. She was 'a skilled self-publicist who stage-managed the crucial events of her own career with a consummate sense of the persuasive power of spectacle and symbolic action. Even her death was a show.'[2] She 'rewrote her life as she went along'.³ Antony too has created a macho image of himself as an amalgam of Mars, Hercules and Dionysus. So immersed are they in these parts, they have lost touch with reality; they believe the fiction they have created for themselves. The audience too is unsure whether what they say is ever true or part of their image. What would have been clear to the Jacobeans is that neither behaves as a ruler should – with dignity, circumspection and moderation.

The opening words set out the ethical values of Rome and of Jacobean times. As a general, Antony has power, position and responsibility for his soldiers. But his behaviour is described as 'dotage' that 'o'erflows the measure'. 'Dotage' refers to the weakness of age diminishing mental judgement. The verb 'to dote' means to be inordinately fond of someone or something. Both meanings indicate disability, ineffectiveness due to the mind being obsessively focused elsewhere. Philo is saying that his senior officer is behaving like a foolish old man in his excessive feelings for Cleopatra. 'O'erflows the measure' connotes excess, some form of behaviour that does not conform to what is thought to be balanced, measured and virtuous. Many times Antony behaves in ways that are not measured, not carefully thought about and not very well judged. He is a man who acts spontaneously according to whim, will and appetite. To the Jacobeans the appetites were dangerous. They could lead one into folly – or worse, into sin. Donne calls them 'beasts' and 'brutish affections', that cause us to 'lose this dominion over our selves'.⁴ Antony's petty follies accumulate to dangerous levels. He is a man given to readily satisfying his appetites, is aware of this, knows he should be more circumspect, knows he should break away from the snare of Cleopatra – but cannot. As a flawed colossus he is thus marked for disaster.

The language of the play reflects this contrast and conflict of restraint and excess. The Nile's annual flood contrasts with the measured tidal fluctuation of the Tiber. The Nile is erratic, like Cleopatra; sometimes it will not flood, therefore not bringing the rich silt to fertilize the land and leaving the fields desiccated, leading to famine; sometimes it floods so extremely as to inundate and devastate the fields and drown the people working and living on the land. The life-giving/death-bringing Nile has another aspect: it is the source of other dangers – crocodiles, disease-bearing flies and the snakes that breed there. It is significant that Cleopatra is called 'the serpent of old Nile' for she is both life-enhancing and death-dealing. Much of the phraseology, metaphor and lexis is on a grand scale, relating to the world, the universe, oceans, kingdoms, colossi, armies and fleets. The central characters are actors on the world stage. Their actions and decisions have enormous consequences.

The quiet demeanour of Octavia and her brother reflects not only how the Renaissance thought of Roman culture (as understated, preferring calm reason, duty and virtue), but what the Jacobeans as Christians valorized too. There is some ambiguity here. Rome was a bizarre mix of the civilized and the barbaric, though the schooling of most of the educated part of the audience would have focused on those classical writers whose philosophical and ethical views most fitted sixteenth- and seventeenth-century religious prejudices. Yet the histories of Tacitus, Livy and Caesar were replete with violent incidents, wars, beheadings, poisonings, rivalries and plots. The plays of Seneca were similarly focused on bloody revenge. Renaissance courts, including that of James I, were a similar blend of high culture and low morals, courtesy and conniving. As Nashe put it, where there was 'much curtesie' there was also 'much subtiltie'.[5] 'Subtiltie' means double-dealing and cloaked insincerity – deviousness masked by good manners.

The language of the lovers is excessive, emotional hyperbole. They are always in a state of high drama – either overly expressive of their affection, quarrelling or playing teasing games. Their lives are lived at high pressure emotionally. They are always revelling, overeating and overdrinking, everything is either a laugh or a tragedy. Kott defines the play as

> the story of love as experienced by mature adults. Even their embrace is bitter: they know it as a challenge and that they will have to pay for it. A seed of hate is inherent from the start [...]. Neither Antony nor Cleopatra want to give up their freedom; they accept love as if under duress, and want to gain the upper hand over their partner.[6]

This hysterical swing from levity to personal overemotionalism in public (or at least in front of the court) recalls William of Malmesbury's comment about the antipathy of majesty and love and is not dissimilar to the theatrics of James's court, with its love of pleasure and leisure, masques, plays, dances, banquets and the intricate intimacies and public dramas of the constantly changing love/lust liaisons of several hundred people (many of them young) drawn together in one place and with little to do. In the first of many overinflated, rhetorical declamations Antony unwittingly damns himself:

> Let Rome in Tiber melt, and the wide arch
> Of the rang'd empire fall! Here is my space,
> Kingdoms are clay: our dungy earth alike
> Feeds beast as man; the nobleness of life
> Is to do thus: [...] [*Embracing*] (I. i. 33–7)

Cleopatra voices a similarly inappropriate sentiment when she learns of Antony's marriage to Octavia:

> Melt Egypt into Nile, and kindly creatures
> Turn all to serpents! (II. v. 78–9)

Is this disappointed love or an angry, hurt ego? Either way, it shows a less than loving attitude to her subjects and an elevation of her desires above their well-being. She is largely unaware of her misconduct yet (after striking the messenger) acknowledges that 'these hands do lack nobility that they strike/A meaner than myself' (II. v. 82–3). She promises excessive reward for good news and delivers violent attack for bad. She wishes the messenger had lied even if it meant 'half my Egypt were submerged and made/A cistern for scaled snakes!' (II. v. 94–5). No proper monarch should wish harm on their subjects even in jest or as a piece of insincere rhetoric. Antony's similarly overblown declaration that Rome can simply dissolve into the Tiber is an unacceptable expression for a ruler. It may simply be disingenuous posturing to please Cleopatra, but it soon appears to be how he treats his allegiance to his *patria*, his fatherland, too. Such views might be more acceptable in our individualistic age, but were anathema to Shakespeare's, when civic duty came before all personal ties. It was an age, however, when self-interest was on the rise. Antony seems more aware of degrading of his own self-image than Cleopatra is, yet both go ahead and persist with their relationship. They are locked in a tragedy of folly, a *folie à deux* where among their shared delusions is thinking that letting the personal intrude into the public is somehow acceptable. Both are so imperfect they have to be annihilated. Simple removal from power would not work with such egos. No state can afford to be ruled by such pantomime actors. As a man with a public role of immense importance, Antony's easy dismissal of his duty marks him as a protagonist ready to fall. Serious-minded, pious spectators would not condone such destructive views, even in private life. It is excessive and excess is always sinful. They would see Antony as caught between reason and appetite, Cleopatra as mired in appetite entirely. This is a story of fatal obsession: he with her, she with herself.

The more educated in the audience might remember from school or university a comment by Cicero in the opening pages of Book I of *De Officiis*: 'He that accounts pleasure the highest good cannot be self-controlled.'[7] This contrasts starkly with a kiss being regarded as 'the nobleness of life'. The struggle between common sense and emotion threatening to get out of proportion is almost a given theme in every Elizabethan-Jacobean play. It represents the great ethical struggle of life. It was central to Christian thinking that the passions (appetites or affections) were dangerous and sinful and needed to be kept in control by exercising restraint, abstinence, prayer and, above all, by exercising the reasoning faculties that made man superior to all other creation. It was a continual battle, every moment of every day. Many of the terms theologians and moralistic writers used were those employed by classical authors, and the way Antony offends right conduct in the eyes of a Jacobean audience would have accorded with Roman assessments of him. He is betraying his state ('Let Rome in Tiber melt') and betraying his rational male self in embracing the female principle that diminishes his expected dominance. It is a subversion of gender roles, a transgression of hierarchy, and a moral dereliction of the requirement of moderation in male–female relationships. As such it would have horrified many in the audience and been a proleptic marker of disaster. Whenever excess was displayed and hierarchy subverted, catastrophe was the most likely outcome. In declaring that 'nobleness' resides in two lovers embracing, he is offending what many in the audience believed about the Adamic flaw of uxoriousness (excessive fondness for one's wife) and subverts the belief that male dignity was expressed in reserved, emotional control. Antony displays himself this early in the drama as a libertine with anarchic values overprioritizing sexual gratification and personal relationships. He is a man out of control both as a political figure and in his personal life. In the middle of the play he exhibits the same weakness, aware one moment of his feminized situation ('My sword, made weak by my affection' [III. xi. 67]), but then four lines later kissing Cleopatra and saying, 'Even this repays me' (III. xi. 71). This is the depth of his shame and emasculation – a kiss is just recompense for losing a battle. His weakening is reflected in Cleopatra's joke/boast that she has dressed the drunken Antony in her clothes and worn his sword. According to Roman and Jacobean thinking a king or queen is duty-bound to put their public role before their private desires. Queen Elizabeth had done exactly that in 'marrying' her realm. King James was much less 'wedded' to his people, despite his early proclamations and promises. Part of the view that society was in decline saw men as becoming more effeminate. This was particularly seen as happening at court and in the upper ranks. Antony's enslavement to Cleopatra would be judged in just such a light.

Moderation, restraint and decorum are all terms Cicero regularly uses in his guide book to proper behaviour for men in leadership roles. The same key concepts emerge in the conduct literature produced in the Elizabethan-Jacobean period. They carry religious connotations suggesting there was order and balance in all things, that order was God's doing, and that losing balance, upsetting order and incurred danger and was sinful. These moral dangers are implied in Philo's opening words as he establishes the key transgression – loss of rational balance: there is 'dotage', loss of due 'measure', a soldier has neglected 'office and devotion' to become a 'bellows' to fire up and the 'fan' to slake or cool 'a gipsy's lust'. His heart has rejected all restraint ('reneges all temper'). It is significant that Antony uses the same word in an expression of self-awareness:

> These strong Egyptian fetters I must break,
> Or lose myself in dotage. (I. ii. 122–3)

The nature of the excess that has overflowed the healthy, natural measure of normality is quickly contextualized as sexual addiction when Philo talks of his leader as 'like plated Mars' bending and turning his 'good eyes' on 'a tawny front' – a once reputed, effective warrior now subjugated by a strumpet. This is not the standard temporary attraction of a soldier to a woman for a passing sexual liaison, but a deep-seated involvement in which the man has become besotted and cannot break free. It is the common male weakness, lust, fixated on one object. The problem here is that the object is not a public prostitute or anonymous private mistress, either of whom could, as so often, be paid off and left behind, but a very public, high-profile figure. In his infatuation, Antony has compromised Rome's interests. This brings into play all sorts of problems that would be serious enough in a private citizen.

The allusion to Mars besotted with a female hints at the famous mythological story of the god of war weakened and emasculated by Venus. Shakespeare would have known this story from his favourite text, Ovid's *Metamorphoses* (Book IV). It involves the adulterous fornication of the married goddess of love with Mars. The 'shameful behaviour' is publicly punished when the pair are trapped in bed and the gods come to mock them.[8] Adultery, a serious offence in Jacobean times, was commonly punished in public and was the focus of a moral crusade by the church to reduce its frequency. (The majority of cases brought before the church courts involved sexual misconduct.) The allegorical image of Love subduing War is potent – who would not wish to see war averted by love? But it also has connotations of the male subdued and weakened by too strong an attachment to a female. In reality Antony, representing the occupying power, has become subordinate to the queen who should be his subject. Her rule of him, blatant as it is, offends Roman political requirements and Jacobean ideas of the true order of things, which make the man the principal both hierarchically and in gender terms.

In the classical myth Venus (goddess of the erotic aspects of love) is married. Here it is the male who is married, but the sin is the same. Ovid calls it 'shameful behaviour', while Philo (whose name derives from the Greek for love and who is a loving, loyal follower of his 'captain') sees it as contrary to his master's courageous, warlike nature to 'become the bellows and the fan/To cool a gypsy's lust' (I. i. 9–10). Lust, seen as potentially dangerous by the Romans, was a Deadly Sin to the Jacobeans. The bellows and fan are markers of a scullery maid whose first morning task was to set the fire blazing from the embers kept covered overnight. This indicates a demeaning of Antony's high status to one of the lowliest household menials. In doing this Antony 'reneges all temper'. To be in temper meant to be in a balanced, healthy state. To abandon all balance (renege all temper) was dangerous. It is what Othello and Lear do and it draws down their tragic fates. This is another image of rational restraint overturned and there are many in the play. The epithet 'gypsy' refers to the Renaissance belief that gypsies originally came from Egypt, thus associating them with the deceitful 'other', the demonized East, and linking Cleopatra to the perception of gypsies as untrustworthy thieves. It resonates with their connection to fortune telling and the occult and therefore with diabolic corruption.[9]

Most Romans would have regarded Antony as a man diverted from his duties. Most Jacobeans would have seen him in this light too, though perhaps blaming Cleopatra more as a stereotypical conniving woman entangling a naive man with her wiles. Many would blame Antony for being so weak. Politically the stronger person in the relationship, he portrays the stereotypical man who is weakly allured by sex into a submissive addiction. Philo's anger rises in (ex)plosive fury as he spits out:

> Take but good note, and you shall see in him
> The triple pillar of the world transformed
> Into a strumpet's fool. (I. i. 12–13)

Phrases like 'tawny front', 'gipsy's lust' and 'a strumpet's fool' suggest a hardened soldier's cynical view of a brave leader lured into effeminate affection for a woman no better than the usual low female camp followers. Antony too has some sense of his weaknesses and tells the messenger from Rome to 'taunt my faults' (I. ii. 113). But Antony lacks the Fool who tries to jerk King Lear out of his folly by his cruel satirical quips. While aware that 'we bring forth weeds/When our quick minds lie still' (I. ii. 115–16), he only intermittently sees his own folly (usually when alone) and has no one round him to jolt him out of his sexual hypnosis into correct action. As he spirals into disaster Antony admits 'I have fled myself' (III. xi. 7). This recognition of his faults (*anagnorisis*) smacks of self-pity and is difficult for an audience to sympathize with. Enobarbus, a clearer-sighted judge, observes coolly from outside (though he is loyal to Antony), attempts to put leaving Alexandria into perspective and offers a rational view of the influence of women: 'It were pity to cast them away for nothing, though between them and a great cause they should be esteemed nothing' (I. ii. 145–7). Clearly the need to attend to the threat of pirates ravaging the Italian coastal towns and to smooth over the tensions caused by Fulvia's wars has greater priority than pleasing Cleopatra by staying in Egypt. As a ruler Antony must attend to political business. His exit from Egypt is, however, hard won against the persistent demands and taunts from Cleopatra.

There is something pitiful in Antony's knowing how foolish he is being, but being unable to break the fetters. Maecenas, admittedly Caesar's man and therefore biased, describes the situation to Octavia without embellishment:

[…] th'adulterous Antony, most large
In his abominations, turns you off
And gives his potent regiment to a trull (III. vii. 95–6)

Others too see how Antony has lost his sense of self (or what they consider to be his true self). Canidius says, 'Had our general/Been what he knew – himself – it had gone well' (III. x. 26–7). Even Iras (waiting gentlewoman to Cleopatra) sees Antony as 'unqualitied with very shame' (III. xi. 44).

While Philo's remarks clearly prejudice the audience prior to assessing the two characters for itself, the couple's behaviour seems initially to endorse his judgement, as witness Antony's readiness to abandon Rome, to see it melt away, while he submerges himself in the pleasures of love. It was seen as a perpetual problem that women wanted men to attend less to their work and spend more time with them. If Cleopatra truly loved him and was rational she would encourage Antony to do what he must to maintain both his power and his peaceful relationship with Caesar. Both are vital to her security. As it is, she persistently mocks, teases and criticizes his explanations about Fulvia and his return to Rome. Is this emotional insecurity or simply the irritating attempts of a spoiled child to get her own way and disrupt what needs to be done because it thwarts her desires? In any event, Antony is caught in the middle trying to defuse Cleopatra's taunts and tantrums, trying to convince her of his love for her, and trying to get away to Rome to defuse another volatile situation. Throughout the play she can be seen as a disastrous distraction, but this is because Antony has little knowledge of himself and so little self-control. As an educated man who spent time in Athens in his youth, he could not have been unaware of two key tenets of the Apollonian religion. Inscribed on the vestibule entablature of Apollo's temple at Delphi are two dicta: 'Know thyself' and 'Nothing in excess'. Sadly his life never showed regard for these two ideas. Antony knows that he should in wisdom leave Cleopatra:

> I must from this enchanting queen break off.
> Ten thousand harms, more than the ills I know,
> My idleness doth hatch. (I. ii. 135–7)

He is bewitched and like King Lear is bound upon a wheel of fire. This is his destiny. An early seventeenth-century proverb declares, 'Whom the gods would destroy they first make mad.'[10] This may be related to an anonymous scholiast's annotation to Sophocles's *Antigone*: 'Whenever God prepares evil for a man, He first damages his mind.' It is clear that much of the time Antony does not think rationally. If he did so he would act more circumspectly, attract less attention to his behaviour in Alexandria and be more wary of outright conflict with Caesar. Antony, all his life, 'overflowed the measure' and it is an aspect of tragedy that opportunities for rational decision are ignored, as if the hero has a death wish and simply careers on making wrong choices, drawing down closer and closer the unavoidable catastrophe.

Confused identity and a lost sense of self occur in different ways in many of Shakespeare's plays. King Lear asks, 'Who is it that can tell me who I am?' and his voice of conscience and reason, the Fool, answers him: 'Lear's shadow'. Early in this play, in contemptuous response to Antony's assertion of the nobleness of life being when they embrace and 'stand up peerless', Cleopatra answers:

> Excellent falsehood!
> Why did he marry Fulvia and not love her?
> I'll seem the fool I am not. Antony
> Will be himself. (I. i. 41–4)

This resonates with the sense of his and her identities being continually blurred and shifting. Apart from being a typical response from her, never satisfied always wanting more, this carries an interesting possible meaning. 'Antony will be himself' is not what she means, only what she pretends to mean. She claims that she will pretend to believe Antony's declaration of love ('Here is my space!') and seem to be a fool in believing it, though she is not a fool. 'Antony will be himself' appears to mean he will be what he usually is, a man getting on and doing just what he wants, marrying Fulvia, cheating on her, telling Cleopatra he loves her, but really loving his wife. It is possible too that what she actually means is that she will appear to be a fool and believe him, but actually not believe him, while he will be the fool he is.

The ambiguity suggests the appearance/reality duality that is recurrent in the play and is a common motif in Shakespeare. Antony is a fool. His followers see him as diminished, changed and degraded. He too is aware of having lost his way. He tells Caesar he postponed seeing a messenger from Rome because he 'did want/Of what I was i' th' morning' (II. ii. 81–2), meaning he was drunk and not himself, but the phrase carries the suggestion of having lost his sense of his true self. He claims his 'honour is sacred' (II. ii. 91) – though he often behaves dishonourably – and neglected his duty to lend arms and aid to Caesar because 'poisoned hours had bound me up/From my own knowledge' (II. ii. 96–7). This hints that he is beginning to see Cleopatra has poisoned his life. After Actium, Scarus talks of Antony as 'the noble ruin of her magic' (III. x. 19) and his comrade Canidius asserts that Antony does not know himself, echoing the idea of Antony having lost identity. A curious irony resides in Caesar's twisted idea of putting the defectors from Antony's army in the vanguard (the front troops) of his battle formation, so that 'Antony may seem to spend his fury/Upon himself' (IV. vi. 10–11), yet Antony wins. It is as if seeing his own troops against him rouses him to fury, remembering how loyal they once were to him and what he once was. Image after image suggests that Antony is no longer what he was.

If Cleopatra is a witch then she has possessed him and he is not himself. His chasing after the fleeing queen is a disastrous move, but, as Enobarbus said, at Cydnus Cleopatra 'pursed up his heart' (II. ii. 97). It was a common belief that if a witch possessed part of you (hair or fingernails usually) she could control you. The historical Antony had wanted to send her away from battle, but Canidius (one of his most trusted and experienced officers) advised it would enhance the morale of the Egyptian naval and land forces to keep her with them. This transgresses military practice and superstition about the presence of women in battle. Antony's retreat, chasing after his mistress, also runs counter to all the patriotism, loyalty and fortitude instilled in the patrician Roman male. It implies cowardice, feminization, even effeminacy, and indicates the degree to which Antony has been Egyptianized. The ignobleness of life is to do thus. His later desperate courage, like Macbeth's, will not cancel the shame of his previous actions, but it has a heroic magnificence that may make the audience admire him. He is brave in the face of disaster. There is *hubris* in his vaunting claim that he will fight the enemy in the fire or the air, but his courage in the face of difficult odds gives a glimpse of why so many soldiers were loyal to him. Just before the Egyptian fleet surrenders, Scarus reports how 'his fretted fortunes' make him 'valiant and dejected', hopeful yet fearful (IV. xii. 8, 7). It is a merciful release when he dies. He had earlier felt he had lost everything and Fate turned against him ('my good stars [...] my former guides/Have empty left their orbs' (III. xiii. 150–51). Cleopatra responds with what is perhaps the first sign of genuine tenderness (III. xiii. 163–72), but it is expressed in such extreme language its sincerity may again be doubted. He recovers some confidence and proposes 'one more gaudy night' (III. xiii. 183–90). They are brave words, the defiant bluster of a failing man, but it is not wise preparation for the next day's battle. Enobarbus sees how fine words mask a precarious state: 'When valour preys on reason,/It eats the sword it fights with' (III. xiii. 204–5).

The changed identity of Antony, his loss of self, his Egyptianization, is famously focused in the story of Cleopatra dressing him in her robes. Antony too, after the fiasco of the sea battle, looks at what he was and what he is:

> O, whither has thou led me, Egypt? See
> How I convey my shame out of thine eyes
> By looking back what I have left behind
> 'Stroyed in dishonour. (III. xi. 51–4)

He is not just referring to deserting his fleet to sail after her fleeing ship, but is expressing a sense of lost honour. Bevington states, 'Despite their pretensions to mythic grandeur, Antony and Cleopatra are mere stage figures.'[11] Their multi-flawed humanity creates an ongoing dramatic tension between what they say of themselves, how they see themselves, the images they project of themselves and what they actually do. Antony was always a tainted character, morally weak, given inordinately to sensual pleasures, always in debt, chasing women (usually married ones) and inefficient as an administrator. But he had shown great qualities too. He saved the Republic after Julius Caesar's murder and rescued Egypt from the garrisons Pompey left there. This Egyptian campaign reinforced Antony's reputation for courage and dash. It also endeared him to the occupied population when he saved and freed native prisoners held by Pompey's forces and facing death penalties.

Such was his prestige after defeating Julius Caesar's opponents at Philippi (where Brutus committed suicide) that he could choose which region of the Roman world to rule as triumvir. He chose the East because of its huge and varied wealth; as always he needed money and most immediately needed to pay his soldiers. The Antony of the play is, however, a wreck of a man, tied by the heart strings to an impulsive, selfish neurotic. What makes it worse is that he knows it and can only watch himself falling into catastrophe. The audience may well feel he gets what he deserves, but they may also pity him. It is upsetting to see any human being destroyed. It is worse when that person was once of great spirit. This was a consideration for Dryden when writing his version of their fall:

> That which is wanting to work up the pity to greater height, was not afforded me by the story: for the crimes of Love which they both committed, were not occasioned by any necessity, or fatal ignorance, but were wholly voluntary; since our passions are, or ought to be, within our power.

He was aware that the time/place unities would be impossible to adhere to, simply due to historical facts and because 'all reasonable Men have long since concluded, That the Heroe of the Poem, ought not to be a Character of perfect Virtue, for, then, he could not, without injustice, be made unhappy; nor yet altogether wicked, because he could not then be pitied'.[12]

Counterbalancing Antony's sense of identity loss are those moments when clarity seems to strike him as to just what Cleopatra is: 'half blasted', a 'boggler' a 'morsel', 'one that looks on feeders'. One of the most telling moments of clear-sightedness is when he announces how

> The wise gods seel our eyes,
> In our filth drop our clear judgements, make us
> Adore our errors, laugh at's while we strut
> To our confusion. (III. xiii. 117–20)

He has summarized precisely his own situation.

The question remains: how much pity do we feel for either central character, given that their downfall is largely self-inflicted? There may be more sympathy for Antony, the victim of a cruel trick that misfires (the false news of Cleopatra's suicide). The inflated rhetoric of their death scenes does nothing to rescue their vaunted greatness. It is just more fine poetry to varnish over the folly, degradation, impulsive decisions, pride, gluttony, lust, sloth and persistent self-delusion and self-aggrandisement. This automatically raises the question of how much sympathy the audience can have for two such self-destructive sinners. The tragic hero is to a degree responsible for the mistakes that help to destroy him, but other forces and other characters act upon him too as Fate conspires to bring punishment. Though Caesar is the means by which Nemesis executes retribution, making them the targets obstructing his ambitious rise, Antony and Cleopatra's faults are so much of their own making that pity may well be in short supply.

Hercules or Ajax?

> [...] a drink-sodden, sex-ridden wreck. (Cicero, *Second Philippic against Antony*)[13]
> None of these rogues and cowards
> But Ajax is their fool. (*King Lear*, II. ii. 125–6)

Is Antony a hero or a fool? Or both? Ajax, the Greek warrior in Homer's *Iliad*, was a byword for bullish brawn and stupidity. Shakespeare had already presented him as such, the stock braggart soldier, the *miles gloriosus*, all muscle and no brain, in *Troilus and Cressida* (1601–02). He is referenced several times in *Antony and Cleopatra*. Hercules, the legendary strongman of Greek myth was also on occasions a drunken fool. As a penalty for an accidental murder the hero is made to serve the Lydian queen Omphale. Various sources tell how he was made to wear women's clothing while the queen wore his iconic lion-skin cloak and wielded his club. This gender reversal, humiliating and foolish in itself, denotes a strong man brought low by subservience to a woman and how men's stereotypical weakness for women destroys their dignity and status. The swapping of clothing and the emasculation of giving up his weapon are repeated in Cleopatra's comments to Charmian as she remembers playing a trick on Antony:

> I laughed him out of patience, and that night
> I laughed him into patience, and next morn,
> Ere the ninth hour, I drunk him to his bed,
> Then put my tires and mantles on him, whilst
> I wore his sword Philippan. (II. v. 19–23)

On the surface this is just a picture of two lovers laughing, playing drunken tricks, but it betokens something more significant to a Jacobean. The gender reversal signifies danger, the danger of a woman, a subject of the Roman polity (albeit a queen), subverting the established political order and subverting what was regarded as the natural order of the universe that men ruled and women were subservient. It suggests too that Antony is a drunkard, or at least often and easily made drunk and very much ruled by Cleopatra. Her wearing the sword he used at Philippi is not just gender reversal but symbolizes penis theft. She has become the man and assumed his phallic power. North's translation says, 'Cleopatra oftentimes unarmed Antonius, and intised him to her, making him lose matters of great importance.'[14] This Antony, a clown and a fool, completely under a woman's thumb, is no hero, and his story is an *exemplum* demonstrating the typical medieval/Renaissance view of women.

Plutarch reports Antony receiving and reading love letters while administering justice and once leaving the tribunal (judge's seat) to run after Cleopatra's litter as it passed.[15]

Antony prided himself, as many Jacobean gentlemen did, on his ancestry. It was, as many seventeenth-century family histories were, partly a fabrication. He claimed that the Antonii were descended from Hercules. What North translates as 'the likenes of his bodye' encouraged Antony to cultivate the Herculean fiction, wearing a thick beard, sometimes even wearing a lion skin.[16] Physically he was well built, broad shouldered and with a muscular neck. Like the Greek hero his courage was never in doubt but his intelligence and subtlety were – constantly. His private life before he met Cleopatra was littered with affairs (often messy), debts, drunken sprees (including vomiting in the senate after a night of revels) and varied fortunes in his public roles. A larger-than-life character certainly, but weak. A man with talent, the ability to generate loyalty, but without the intelligence and genius of Julius Caesar. It is the view of one historian that while the Egyptian queen was 'a charismatic personality [...], a born leader and vaultingly ambitious monarch', she 'deserved better than suicide with that *louche* lump of a self-indulgent Roman, with his bull neck, Herculean vulgarities, and fits of mindless introspection'.[17] The Herculean image (with connotations of physical strength but mental weakness) is alluded to several times in the play. After the queen's fleet surrendered to Caesar, the angry Antony talks of the shirt of Nessus being upon him. This references the death of Hercules maddened by a poisoned shirt. The story is in Ovid's *Metamorphoses* and tells of a centaur, Nessus, who attempts to rape Hercules's wife, Deianira. The hero kills him with a poisoned arrow and the dying creature gives Deianira his shirt (secretly impregnated with poison) as a charm to win back her husband's love. She later gives the garment to the errant Hercules and it burns his flesh with such fierceness he thinks he will die, though Zeus saves him and takes him off to Olympus. The night before the last battle the music heard by Antony's soldiers signifies the departure of 'the god Hercules whom Antony loved' (IV. iii. 21). Shakespeare changes Plutarch here, for the historian says the guardian god is Bacchus deserting the fated Roman, though either would be appropriate. Antony, a devotee of the wine god, had dressed as Dionysus (the Greek version of Bacchus) when in Athens.

In his own time Antony was regarded as a leader of variable ability – not a brilliant strategist, but occasionally a brave and effective tactician largely due to his personal courage. He lived in a time of violence; the Republic was in decline, with constant power struggles, coups and assassinations. The play represents the death spasm before Octavius (soon to rename himself Augustus) became the first emperor. Antony made bad friends – personally decadent and corrupt in their civic posts – and emulated them, running up huge debts and not performing his public roles very effectively. He epitomizes the seventeenth-century man-about-court. In Julius Caesar's absence Antony (as Master of the Horse) was virtually the ruler of Rome. He abused this power, permitting officials to bribe and blackmail, while he showed off his wealth, parading with his mistress heading his huge train. His wealth was largely a sham, a show of goods, clothes and banquets purchased on credit. He was unstable, a prey to his appetites, and politically inept. Boccaccio called him 'an extremely sensual man', a 'weakling', a 'gluttonous fellow', and 'a man of the vilest character'.[18] The stoic virtues of duty and self-discipline were unknown to him. He became dependent upon Cleopatra both politically and personally; Plutarch asserts that he was physically and emotionally addicted to her to a point where he could not live without her. She needed his military and political power, but whether she truly loved him is difficult to determine. If she did love him it was also true that she needed his military presence. Part of his tragedy is to have gained power at a time when a ruthless power seeker was looking to rise. Caesar is perhaps less than sincere not to grant it amiss to 'tumble on the bed of Ptolemy,/To give a kingdom for a mirth' (I. iv. 17–18), drink with slaves and roll around the streets drunk at midday, filling 'his vacancy with his voluptuousness' (I. iv. 26). But Antony is like a boy who knows he should not disregard virtue simply for 'present pleasure', especially when 'we do bear/So great weight in his lightness' (I. iv. 24–6). Caesar feels, as others do, that Antony has rebelled against judgement (I. iv. 33). His libertinism is indecorous, inappropriate in a man of such power. Caesar calls upon him to 'leave thy lascivious wassails!' (I. iv. 57) and 'let his shames quickly/Drive him to Rome' (I. iv. 73–4). Does he mean it? It would suit him if Antony stayed in Egypt. It would strengthen his case for removing him. As with Cleopatra, it is difficult to tell whether his statements are genuine.

Dryden called his realigned version of their story *All For Love, or, the World Well Lost*. Many Jacobeans would have considered Antony's story that of 'A Fool for Love and the World Ill Lost'.

Chapter 11

INFINITE VARIETY: ISIS OR STRUMPET?

The Character of Cleopatra

> Everyone sees what you appear to be, few experience what you really are.[1]
>
> How are we to arrive at the solution of this glorious riddle, whose dazzling complexity continually mocks and eludes us? What is most astonishing in the character of Cleopatra is its antithetical construction – its *consistent inconsistency*.[2]

What would the Jacobean audience have made of Cleopatra? Antony's complexity is simple in comparison. Churchill once described Russia as 'a riddle, wrapped in a mystery, inside an enigma', adding that perhaps the key was Russian self-interest. The same may be applicable to Cleopatra. Named in the title, she might be expected to be regarded as the heroine. In the literary sense she is undeniably a central character; she is linked with Antony, incites action and affects the outcome of the drama. But is she to be admired, pitied or condemned? Or all three? Is she an archetypal *femme fatale* like Delilah or Jezebel? Is she a woman of towering attraction and unique qualities? Is she a clever actress who plays the part of a woman in love while performing a charade and looking all the time for her own advantage? Is she just an insecure, promiscuous neurotic whose emotional instability is frustrating to the audience and fatal to Antony? It is probable that most men watching the first performance would see her as typifying the worst characteristics of women, summing up all the traditional misogynistic prejudices and contributing significantly to the downfall of her consort. That downfall would be seen as fully deserved on the grounds of their sinfulness.

Descending to the second circle of Hell, Dante enters the realm of 'those who sin in the flesh' and 'let reason give way to their wishes'. Among a throng of spirits driven fretfully this way and that like a flock of starlings is 'the lustful Cleopatra'.³ The named historical and mythical personages inhabiting this circle (including Semiramis, Helen, Dido, Paris and Achilles) all allowed carnal passions to endanger their state and brought disaster to themselves and their people. The Egyptian queen is certainly emotionally unstable, constantly changing her mind, her feelings and her actions. Boccaccio lists Cleopatra in his 106 famous (and infamous) women and there is no doubt her name is universally known. Boccaccio admitted she 'became the subject of talk the world over'. To him she was a 'wicked woman' with 'beauty and [...] wanton eyes', 'avaricious', 'insatiable [...] for other kingdoms' and 'demanding'.⁴ One of Plutarch's modern translators summarizes her thus:

> Cleopatra is one of those women whose image the world has always preferred to fashion out of myth rather than fact. Shakespeare's 'lass unparalleled' has been the general verdict, and she lives for posterity not as a ruler with a career to be chronicled, but as a symbol of the power of woman over man. Plutarch, and to an even greater extent than Shakespeare, depicts her not merely as a queen of infinite fascination – which could scarcely be disputed – but as an enchantress and a voluptuary, a woman preoccupied above all with the life of the emotions and the senses. Historical evidence suggests that ambition rather than sex was the key to her character.⁵

Of the two traditions about her the negative one is far stronger. There are variants to her story and biased views have become 'history', but she and Antony are always accused of foolishly having let their political duties suffer through letting lust/love overrule common sense. In other words, they lost balance. A host of commentators, including Boccaccio, John Lydgate and Montaigne, regard Antony as a prince fallen through enslavement to his appetites (gluttony, avarice and lust). He was a fool and she made him more of one. Montaigne comments:

> Many examples of great public figures such as Mark Antony could be found whose lust made them forget the conduct of affairs of state; but whenever sexual love and ambition were to be evenly balanced and come to blows with similar forces, I am in no doubt whatsoever that the former would win the advantage and dominate.⁶

Commentators either emphasize the relationship as one of lust or, if it is regarded as love, they stress the infatuation and imbalance of it. John Gower (a contemporary of Chaucer) puts the pair among the constant lovers, but refers to them in Book VIII of *Confessio Amantis*, which is devoted to those who fell into excessive lechery. Excess was regarded as a dangerous sin; the Seven Deadly Sins are all forms of failure due to excess. The consensus is that Cleopatra is scheming, untrustworthy, lust-driven and self-seeking, and Antony a dupe and a fool who let his loins rule his reason. Robert Burton states that 'Lucretia stabbed herself, and so did Cleopatra, *when she saw that she was reserved for a triumph, to avoid the infamy*'.[7] He also puts a sardonic twist to the lavish gestures: 'Cleopatra hath whole boars and sheep served up to her table at once, drinks jewels dissolved, 40,000 sesterces in value; but to what end? Doth a man that is a-dry, desire to drink in gold? Doth not a cloth suit become him as well, and keep him as warm, as all their silks, satins, damasks, taffeties and tissues?'[8] It is a view expressed within a context (relevant to the original audience) that regarded all forms of ostentation (dress, action and speech) as unnecessary, wasteful, vain and sinful.

Like the earlier love tragedy *Romeo and Juliet* (1594–96), this play has a double focus and the heroine is as much the centre of attention in the story, plot and themes as the hero. Like the youthful lovers, the older couple fall victim to their own uncontrollable natures, activating external forces that help bring their own destruction upon themselves. Their excesses lead to disaster. Looked at from a Jacobean point of view their disaster is inevitable destiny, remorseless punishment for their sins. From another viewpoint their fate could have been avoided had they had the wisdom to curb their lifestyle and attend more carefully to the business of ruling. But, it may be argued, they did not have it in them to act rationally, so their catastrophes may be said to have been brought on by their characters, and that as Heraclitus said, 'Character is fate'. Their tragedy is that they are perfectly wrong for each other and are doomed to destroy themselves. They are victims of the goddess Até, who punished those who fell into delusion, folly, rash action or infatuation. She is a spirit of vengeance and mischief and can be seen at work in the blind folly of both protagonists, in Antony's rash decision to marry Octavia, in his fighting at sea (despite contrary advice), in Cleopatra's fatally misleading message of her death and the arrival of Diomedes just too late. In Aeschylus Até represents just punishment for evil and is in this sense not unlike Nemesis (retribution) and the Furies, who pursue wrongdoers. In Jacobean terms the pair have committed evil, including fornication and dereliction of the duty placed upon them by God.[9]

Unsurprisingly, opinion is divided over Cleopatra. Is she in fact a loving woman, deeply and passionately involved with Antony, albeit complex, insecure and sometimes foolish? Is she a celebrity personality, an especially charismatic woman capable of attracting all who come in contact with her? Is she a strong woman, cleverly manipulating a male-dominated world in order to survive? Or is she a scheming manipulator who uses sex as a means of keeping power and exercising control over Antony while pretending to love him? Traditionally, she is seen in a negative light, both in pagan and Christian terms. Plutarch acknowledged her allure, but condemned her as a sinful and vice-ridden woman who 'excited to the point of madness many passions which had hitherto lain concealed, or at least dormant, and it stifled or corrupted all those redeeming qualities in him which were still capable of resisting temptation'.[10] Is she evil and wrong for tempting him, or is he foolish for allowing himself to be tempted? The Jacobeans would have agreed to both views. As a woman she is subject to the usual misogynistic suspicions; any female domination was a contested concept, so as a female ruler she is suspect. She leads no armies and her presence at sea is a weakening distraction and, in the event, a liability. England had had experience with queens as sole rulers, and it had not been not entirely satisfactory (not that all male rulers had proved effective either). Elizabeth I had become accepted, partly because she could inspire military leadership in others, partly because she unsexed herself by 'marrying' the state and never taking a husband (though she was willing to use her sexuality to evoke and control loyalty and get what she wanted), partly by autocratic repression of opposition backed by punitive legislation or capricious unilateral action. Her death liberated all sorts of criticisms that fear had hushed during her life. Like Cleopatra, Elizabeth is a fine example of the differences between myth and reality. Some of the myths were self-created, some created by others, some originated from the aura that monarchy carries with it. In choosing to write about a male–female coupling for his protagonists, Shakespeare took on a pair about whom similar myths clustered. With Romeo and Juliet he created the myth. With Antony and Cleopatra he had real personages to mould into a play and the raw materials came already packaged in the messy drama of history. They are historical characters but they came with myths attached: there were the biases of the historians to take into account; there is the question whether the real Antony and Cleopatra were as portrayed in Plutarch; then there is the presentation of their characters, motives and emotions in the play. Fictional representation of real people is always risky. Is the writer giving them emotions and motives they never had? This is further complicated by Shakespeare portraying his protagonists from different angles. We get innumerable views of them from different characters within the narrative (biased for or against) and they present themselves in different ways at different times as if they cannot be consistent in their understanding of their own personality. Ultimately each individual audience member had to accept they were (for the purposes of the play) as Shakespeare presented them and were to be judged on what they said, what they did, what others said of them and whether we believe any of them.

Overall, it seems Antony is a fool and sees himself as such, entangled in the enchantments of a woman he seems to love whilst aware he is enchanted (and not therefore in full control) and dangerously entangled. Cleopatra seems to be largely presented as vacillating in her emotions, playing games all the time to achieve domination, claiming to love Antony, but showing little evidence of it. Isis was goddess of the triple moon and the moon symbolized erratic emotion. Cleopatra identified with Isis and saw herself as the earthly emanation of that universal goddess.

It seems impossible not to be critical of her manipulative, childish behaviour bearing in mind the politically detrimental effects of her actions. She seems only in her closing speeches to rise to any sort of dignity and nobility of spirit, though that too may be staged and insincere. She is admirable in having the courage to kill herself and does so with the expected theatrical awareness – dressing herself for death and staging her last great performance as a tableau of such impact it has many times been painted.[11] But there is the question whether she kills herself for love of Antony or because she refuses to accept the prospect of being a prisoner. Having failed to win over Caesar with her charms she decides death is her only option and directs it as she did the Cydnus spectacle. We must keep in mind the fact of there being two types of hero or heroine. A literary hero/heroine is simply the central character in a play/poem/novel. They do not have to be virtuous and may be, indeed usually are, imperfect, but they are the person on whom the narrative is focused. It is their story that is being told and it is about them we learn the most, though we may not sympathize or identify with them. The second hero/heroine type comes from incidents in real life, the sort who does something brave or right and is admired for their courage or their virtue. We focus simply on their heroic act and know or care little about the rest of their life or personality. Such heroism can also be an attribute of a central character in fiction. The literary hero is more complex and because the author explores more aspects of their life and thought there is more opportunity for the reader/viewer to dislike some features. Cleopatra falls into the category of fascinating real-life personality presented as a literary heroine with exceptional flaws and not entirely trustworthy or admirable.

There is, of course, an impulse in modern approaches to Cleopatra to see her as a feisty, independent, strong woman fighting for survival and therefore to be applauded for using whatever means necessary to achieve that, even when (as so often) these are dishonest. The values by which male leaders are supposed to rule should apply to a woman ruler caught in a male world. They are not. Cleopatra exhibits many of the devious ploys of politicians, plus the expected sexual wiles. In his infatuation Antony is submissive and by nature Cleopatra likes to dominate.[12] She uses her sexual influence to get what she wants and feels justified on the grounds that you do what you need and are able to do, especially if you are a woman surrounded by patriarchy. She cannot win her way by combat on the battlefield. She is not a warrior queen; the sex war is her arena and she knows that men can be tamed and subjugated by bed games. Some Jacobean women would have felt the same and supported her however sinful, petty, childish and treacherous her actions, for she subverts patriarchy. As Isis, as a serpent of the Nile, as Dido, as Omphale to Antony's Hercules, she is Egypt and its connotations of love, freedom and fertility. She is the feminine principle, but that is double-edged, for it connotes not only fertility and a life free of restraints, but also death – death of the masculine. In early Egyptian religion Isis was identified with fidelity in marriage and loving motherhood and presided over nature and magic. She gradually became an all-encompassing deity – celestial goddess of nature, protector of children and guardian of the dead. She later became synonymous with all nature and was worshipped throughout Graeco-Roman Europe as well as the East. Her brother and husband, Osiris, was killed by his jealous brother[13] and his body parts scattered. Isis collected the remains, but did not find his genitals, so in reassembling his body she substituted an artificial male member, thus creating a man but not quite a whole man. Cleopatra has similarly diminished and emasculated Antony. Egypt too is not only seen as the source of life, with the Nile's annual flood bringing silt to fertilize the fields, it also brings death (see Chapter 10). Egypt is the home of sorcery, 'cruel, superstitious, barbaric, dissolute'.[14] Egypt represents the anarchy of unrestrained will. That alone would have unsettled many in the audience, but in terms of gender role reversal, emasculation and witchcraft, Cleopatra was comprehensively demonized. Rome is supposedly more restrained, though not without its own decadence. Antony's life of debauchery, adulterous womanizing and financial corruption is little different from the sexual laxity connected with Egypt. They are a toxic pair in keeping with the jaded and cynical satire of *Troilus and Cressida* and other plays of the early 1600s. What Shakespeare does not display is that Caesar's record of promiscuity was 'quite as extensive as Antony's'.[15] He had a series of mistresses and was not at all the cold, sexless creature presented. Others in a Jacobean audience might well have seen the queen as an appalling example of what men always said about the dangers of women in general and women with power in particular. She sets a bad example and is a shameless fornicator, manipulative and spoiled by having her own way. The character Malheureux in Marston's *The Dutch Courtesan* (c. 1604) says, 'The most odious spectacle the earth can present is an immodest, vulgar woman' (I. i. 154–5). In many ways this fits Cleopatra. For all the admiration of her beauty, allure and 'infinite variety' she is at the same time, viewed from a different angle, without modesty (everything she feels is paraded in public and verbalized), without virtue (she is sexually predatory) and without the decorum expected of a royal figure. Hopping forty paces through the street, which we might think charmingly spontaneous and amusingly human, would be seen in Shakespeare's time as entirely inappropriate and vulgar for a lady and appalling in a queen. She also has a reputation for promiscuity. In moments of anger – against himself and against Cleopatra – Antony voices views of his lover that chime with the negative valuations of others. His practical wisdom speaks when he upbraids her for her colourful sexual history: 'You were half blasted ere I knew you, [...] one that looks on feeders' (III. xiii. 110, 114). It is a typical quarrel between lovers, dragging up the past ('You have been a boggler ever' [III. xiii. 115]) and airing long-suppressed niggling criticisms; Antony depicts her as a willing sex object passed from one man to another, available to all:

> I found you as a morsel, cold upon
> Dead Caesar's trencher – nay, you were a fragment
> Of Gnaeus Pompey's, besides what hotter hours,
> Unregistered in vulgar fame, you have
> Luxuriously picked out. (III. xiii. 121–5)

This is typical of the recriminations dragged up in lovers' arguments. The degree of his anger is registered in the suggestion that apart from the known affair with Julius Caesar and the rumoured one with Pompey the Great, she has been promiscuous with unnumbered other anonymous partners. 'Luxuriously' resonates with all the power of the Deadly Sins ('luxury' was another word for extreme lust). Temperance, the opposite of luxurious, was one of the Seven Cardinal Virtues, one of the key qualities rulers had to display. It signified not using absolute power to cut off the heads of all who annoyed, thwarted or disobeyed you. It signified living in a modest style so as not to offend those (the majority) who lived in poverty. It signified the control of gluttonous tendencies – whether that was gluttony or greed for food, wealth or sex. After the Egyptian fleet surrenders without a fight, Antony is incandescent: 'This foul Egyptian hath betrayed me' (IV. xii. 10) he says, and calls her a 'triple-turned whore' (13), 'this false soul of Egypt' (25) and 'a right gypsy' (28). At Actium his lieutenant Scarus describes how 'yon ribaudred nag of Egypt [...] like a cow in June,/Hoist sail and flies' (III. x. 10, 14–15). This alludes to the stereotypical male view of the instability and unreliability of women, as if they were prey to hormonal mood swings like a creature in heat.

Cleopatra had already seduced Julius Caesar and had a son by him. She is open in discussing sex, jokingly questioning the compatibility and sexual satisfaction of Antony's marriage with Fulvia ('Can Fulvia die?' – die was slang for orgasm). This would be seen as inappropriate and indecorous for a woman, let alone a queen. She is with her gentlewomen and her attendant (actually a lord and minister) Alexas, but it is still lewd and out of place when someone has just died and her husband is present. She indelicately questions the eunuch Mardian about his 'affections' because she is bored and daydreams suggestively about Antony riding his horse ('O happy horse' [I. v. 22]). Jacobeans would have seen Cleopatra as an inefficient military leader, a liability indeed, and a vulgar, immodest woman, incapable of dignity or decorous behaviour. She is a woman far adrift from 'vertuous conditions, comeley behaviours and honest entertainment toward all men'.[16] Antony admits, 'She is cunning past man's thought' and adds, 'Would I had never seen her!' (I. ii. 152, 159). But what man has not thought the same about the woman he loves when she has displayed irrational, obstinate, jealous or unsettlingly inappropriate behaviour? Enobarbus asserts that the women 'should be esteemed nothing' when compared to 'a great cause' (I. ii. 146–7) and Cleopatra as a veteran of many political manoeuvrings should admit that the survival of her state is worth some sacrifice of personal pleasure. Sending Antony out into the dangers and temptations of the wider world is necessary. She does not seem to understand that she cannot always keep him by her side as courtier, lover, slave and lapdog. Or, she knows full well, does not care and wants her own way.

Her very first words are significant and ominous. They show her demanding a statement of Antony's commitment to her: 'If it be love indeed, tell me how much.' At this early stage in the play Shakespeare is building a picture of their relationship and it looks as if she is bearing out Philo's views of her. She gets the reaction she wants when Antony declares, 'Let Rome in Tiber melt' (I. i. 34). The seriousness of what is at stake (and Antony's apparent indifference to it) shows in his following remark: 'and the wide arch/ Of the rang'd empire fall!' A little later she dislikes it when he breaks off from enjoying himself when struck by a 'Roman thought' (I. ii. 88) – a thought of Rome or a generically serious thought of the sort Romans are usually thought to have. She behaves childishly, flouncing away saying, 'We will not look upon him' (I. i. 92). It is the old problem of a woman wanting to be the sole centre of a man's attention, to be the centre of his life and for him to neglect work and duty to be with her. This evokes the old polarity of heart and head, which extends into the cultural opposition of Egypt and Rome. Egypt is a place of the heart, that uncertain, inconstant organ we connect with love. It is a place where the sensual whim of the moment counts more than circumspection or restraint. Rome is a place of the head, of rational and calm calculation. One can veer too much towards overheated emotion, disorganized impulses, the other can become cold and insensitive to people's needs. She tells Alexas to spy on Antony without saying that she sent him (I. iii. 4) and to report her mood as the opposite to his in order to provoke a reaction and make him feel upset or guilty. She ignores Charmian's common-sense advice that this is not the way to encourage his love and that the queen should not push him too far. But in her arrogance, Cleopatra claims she knows better. She pretends to faint when Antony comes in. These are the games lovers play – but not at this level.

Is this love, petty ego, women's wiles or insecurity? Men like sensible, balanced women. A constantly demanding neurotic narcissist is too wearing, too stressful. Antony foolishly declares that his business will proceed or stop 'as you shall give th'advice' (I. iii. 69), but Cleopatra will not let the matter drop and accuses him of acting ('excellent dissembling' [I. iii. 80]). He becomes angry, tries to calm her, says she is almost 'idleness itself' (I. iii. 95) and insists that he has to go to Rome. Cleopatra grudgingly concedes, 'Your honour calls you hence' (I. iii. 99), but does not believe it and adds huffily as a play for sympathy, 'Therefore be deaf to my unpitied folly' (I. iii. 99–100). Antony tries to conciliate her by saying that though he is away he is with her.

What is the audience to make of this? A Jacobean audience might be split on gender lines, but most would surely agree that Cleopatra is indecorous, undignified, overemotional, uses unbecoming tricks and is too demanding. Perhaps some would laugh. The lovers' behaviour is like the 'flyting wit' battles of Beatrice and Benedick in *Much Ado About Nothing*, with the difference that these two hold the fates of millions in their hands while behaving like squabbling teenagers. Enobarbus remarks that 'her passions are made of nothing but the finest part of pure love' (I. ii. 153) and it cannot be 'cunning'. Her 'passions' (in the plural) suggest that this current tantrum is a commonplace incident. But he undercuts what might be a serious view of Cleopatra's character; Antony says, 'Would I had never seen her!' to which Enobarbus answers that then Antony would have 'left unseen a wonderful piece of work, which not to have seen would have discredited your travel' (I. ii. 160–62). This makes the queen sound like a key sight on a gentleman's Grand Tour, not to be missed – a grand courtesan, like the famous high-class prostitutes of Venice. It is as if the writer is making the character of Cleopatra as undecipherable for the audience as she is to Antony.

This puts the pressure on the viewer to spot any definitive clues to prove whether or not the queen genuinely loves Antony. The Jacobean audience would already have decided about her moral status, but might be less certain about her affections until the end of the play – and perhaps not even then. They would judge that even if she feels genuine love for him she is still damned as a fornicator and condemned as a deserter in battle. This indeterminacy is typical of the ambiguity found in Shakespeare, particularly in his later work.

It is certainly the case that the interior profiles of Shakespeare's major tragic figures (Hamlet, Othello, Iago, Lear, Macbeth and Lady Macbeth) are all psychologically complex and ambiguous. As Kott puts it, they are 'a puzzle and a surprise to themselves' and are 'torn apart by passion'.[17] They exhibit their conflicts externally but express their inner turmoil in soliloquy. In Antony's case his feelings are often not formally expressed through long self-communing alone onstage, but spoken in dialogue. It is as if he is forced to live through his most harrowing feelings in public, surrounded by messengers and officers, courtiers and the constant presence of Cleopatra bullying, wheedling and expecting declarations corroborating his love for her and her expectations of him. He is lost among all this and has only six brief speeches when the audience has a chance to enter his mind unassailed by others and their demands upon him (I. ii. 129–37; II. iii. 31–9; IV. xii. 18–30; IV. xii. 39–49; IV. xiv. 45–55; IV. xiv. 96–105). These indicate his misery, but even his eventual death has to be shared by the persistent interruptions of his lover. Cleopatra is given no soliloquies, which suggests we are not expected to sympathize with her. She is given many speeches, however, mostly to her women, which do give insight into her restless, hyperactive personality. She lives in public and expresses her private thoughts in public. They are often trivial, inconsistent and shallow. While she is in Alexandria and he in Sicily she displays her inability to settle for very long on anything. In her boredom she calls for the 'moody food' of music, changes her mind and says she will play billiards, then decides she will go fishing and imagines a theatrical set-up with distant music playing and each fish an Antony: 'Ah, ha! You're caught!' (II. v. 15). This is an admission of sorts (unwitting or overt), suggesting she knows that she worked a trick on him, that she set a trap. The absence of her playmate forces her to address the emptiness of her life without him, but does not necessarily mean that she loves him. Because she does not busy herself with the bureaucracy of rule (as she should be doing), she is idle and bored, and wants to sleep out 'this great gap of time' (I. v. 5). Her conversation is bawdy, like that of her gentlewomen, teasing the eunuch about the ambivalent status of his sexuality.

With unwitting significance Mardian admits to thinking about 'what Venus did with Mars' (I. v. 19). He may mean that he daydreams about their sexual act, but the comment is an allusion to the image of Cleopatra and Antony as sex goddess and soldier, as illicit lovers, and as a reference to the Renaissance iconography of the emasculated male. In Botticelli's painting (c. 1483) *Venus and Mars* (National Gallery, London) Mars sleeps in post-coital exhaustion, while an impassive Venus looks past him. Satyrs, one wearing his helmet, another about to blow a shell horn into his ear, are in the process of stealing his lance. This mockery and the symbolism of the phallic lance being removed are counterbalanced by the superior, slightly contemptuous expression of the goddess. There is no hint of pleasure remembered in her look. There is the tiniest hint of a sneer on her lips. She is impassive and composed, her clothing fully adjusted, while the sleeping god, head thrown back, mouth slightly open, is naked except for a strategically draped cloth. This scenario is not the famous one where the pair are in bed trapped in a net set by Venus's angry husband and laughed at by the other gods assembled to see the pair caught in their adultery. Botticelli seems to suggest disappointment or indifference in Venus. The affair was a well-known story from Homer and was variously seen as an erotic allegory of male–female passion or a political allegory of aggression neutralized by affection (war defeated by love). Cleopatra and Antony likened themselves to the figures in this ancient story – she as one who trades in love (and all its tricks and stratagems), he as the soldier disarmed and pacified by sexual satisfaction.

Naturally enough Cleopatra wonders what Antony is doing, chatters about him as 'the demi-Atlas', as 'the arm/And burgonet of men' (I. v. 24, 25) and herself as his 'serpent of old Nile'. These comments unintentionally carry loaded, covert meanings. There is the reminder of what Antony should be (and was perhaps) as the defender of his people, holding up their world, and there is the suggestion of her as an ancient danger, the snake/woman, a killer. She is 'black/And wrinkled deep in time' (I. v. 29, 30) and admits to her life of bodily seduction ('us that trade in love' [II. v. 2]), trading sex as a means to satisfy the seductiveness of power (her past with Caesar and Pompey). She admits to sending a constant stream of letters to Antony, like a teenage girl. The thought prompts the deed as so often with her and she calls for ink and paper. This shows her to be a creature of uncontrolled impulses, reacting to whatever thoughts and whims pass through her mind. She will write every day or 'unpeople Egypt' (I. v. 81). This extravagant claim is probably not meant but is typical of her hyperbolic drama-queen style. Her response to the messenger who brings news of Antony's marriage to Octavia is particularly revealing of her lack of queenly dignity in her readiness to give way to anger and commit assault. Short temper expressed as a quickness to strike people (the Deadly Sin of wrath) is a signal weakness in King Lear, another dominant ruler. *King Lear* was performed the same year as *Antony and Cleopatra* was being written and Shakespeare was clearly absorbed by the behaviour of monarchs. The questions about her supplanter's hair, height, gait and face are typical of a jealous woman wanting to size up her rival. But the manner of her questioning suggests deep insecurity. Queen Elizabeth was not above asking visitors about the appearance of Mary Queen of Scots and she was not above striking those who brought displeasing news.

The Cleopatra we meet in Act I is a woman experienced in political manoeuvres, queen of an ancient land, but acting like a silly girl testing her lover's love and boosting her ego at the same time. The woman who beats and then questions the messenger in Act III is a spoiled, insecure, immature woman. Seventeenth-century Europe was littered with such monarchs, male and female. She also reflects both the arbitrary violence which absolute power encouraged and the cruel petulance sometimes displayed by Elizabeth I. The sequence of dialogue about Fulvia is the first of many games she plays to provoke a reaction. Her last is the message to Antony announcing her death. She is in command and mocks Antony for being under Fulvia's thumb yet expects he be under hers. The shifting premise is typical of the inconsistency of which men customarily accused women. Cleopatra tries to provoke a declaration of his attachment to her by pretending she believes Fulvia dominates him ('I have no power upon you; hers you are' [I. iii. 24]). When he finally has the chance to tell her of Fulvia's death ('At the last, best' [I. iii. 62]), that he is unconcerned by it and loves only her, Cleopatra has to quickly shift the base of her argument to accuse him of callousness and pretends to believe that is how he will react when she dies ('Now I see, I see,/In Fulvia's death how mine received shall be' [I. iii. 65–6]). This would be seen by the misogynists in the audience as a typical female ploy, wanting it both ways. It is a lose/lose situation for Antony. Those who already knew their Plutarch would see the poignant irony of this comment, for his actual reaction to news of her death is to instantly consider suicide. Her reaction to his wounded state and then death is full of grandiose declamatory poetry – but not suicide.

When the final battle was lost, the historical Antony made an offer to Caesar to kill himself if it would save Cleopatra.[18] Shakespeare omits this, but does have Caesar mockingly report that Antony had challenged him to settle their dispute by single combat. This implies that Antony has old-fashioned values compared with the new, calculating machinations of his opponent, who is too canny to risk all he has gained by pitting himself against a seasoned warrior. Goldsworthy is of the opinion she knows what Antony's reaction would be and sees in the false message of her suicide a means of achieving his removal, thus enabling her to negotiate with Caesar.[19] This would make it an act of murder through incitement to suicide. Cleopatra lacks greatness of spirit. She cannot accept that his duty calls him away and that it is to her advantage too that he conciliate Caesar. She accuses him again of playing a scene 'of excellent dissembling, and let it look/Like perfect honour' (I. iii. 80–81) in expressing sadness at leaving her. She claims his tears at parting would be for Fulvia, but that he would claim they were for herself – and this from the constant actress. It is lose/lose again for Antony. Finally she agrees he must go, but even then makes a play for sympathy, telling him not to pity her for the foolish fondness that makes her so upset at his absence. Her final words are so formulaic as to appear insincere:

> Upon your sword
> Sit laurel victory, and smooth success
> Be strewed before your feet! (I. iii. 101–3)

It is difficult not to be extremely irritated by Cleopatra's endless dramatizing and her elusive nature.

It is worth looking at her final actions and what she says. Critics from the Romantic period to the twentieth century have seen this as her apotheosis as a woman and lover, but the sequence of her speeches can be read two separate ways. In one way they are beautiful and imaginative declarations of her love for Antony and her excited, courageous anticipation of joining him in death. All the games are over and this is her genuine expression of passion for him, lifting the play to a sublime level. Another way is to see it all as beautiful trickery, speaking words of admiration and lament but doing so because it is expected and is in character. When she cannot escape her future as Caesar's curiosity by any other means, she accepts death as unavoidable and plays up her final scene. The text works best when read in this manner and it fits her two betrayals in battle and her paltering with Caesar.

The sequence that leads to her real demise begins with her fake death. It is Charmian who suggests she goes to the monument: 'There lock yourself and send him word you are dead' (IV. xiii. 4). This is an interpolation by Shakespeare. Plutarch simply says that Cleopatra 'sent messengers to tell Antony that she was dead'.[20] In handling the messy, sometimes unclear events of history, Shakespeare was not above adding little touches or omitting those incidents that did not suit his plot or themes. Shakespeare gives the idea to one of the queen's close henchwomen, suggesting the extent of female control in the state, but Cleopatra's devious mind takes up the idea immediately and embellishes it – Mardian is to report she has killed herself, speaking Antony's name as her last word. She cannot forbear to give him directorial advice: 'And word it, prithee, piteously' (IV. xiii. 9). As an actress she wants to know how the audience react: '[…] and bring me how he takes my death' (IV. xiii. 10). This is a horrific trick, but it is part of the highly charged, overemotional, extreme and theatrical life they have lived. It is also part of her manipulation of the simple Antony. It shows a remarkable degree of cruelty as well as lack of foresight and concern for how he might respond.

She met him playing a grandiose trick when she arrayed herself on her barge, setting a lavish scene, and has played tricks ever since. It is only later she begins to have suspicions his reaction might be counterproductive. Or was it part of her plan to discard Antony and realign her politics, while making it look as if she cared and had second thoughts? Antony is depressed at losing the battle, blames Cleopatra, and feels he has lost his sense of self: 'Here I am Antony/Yet cannot hold this visible shape' (IV. xiv. 13–14). He thought he had the queen's heart 'for she had mine'. If you persistently play mind games you will reach a point where you do not know what is real and what is not. While Antony is in this sensitive state Mardian arrives and takes it on him to declare, as an elaboration to the supposed suicide, 'My mistress loved thee and her fortunes mingled/With thine entirely' (IV. xiv. 24–5). Her fortunes may have been mingled with his, but not entirely or she would not seek to compromise with Caesar. Whether she loved Antony is entirely doubtful.

Antony's reaction to the false news is immediate: 'The long day's task is done […]' refers not just to the end of a day of battle and the need to unarm and rest, he is already thinking of ending his life. His heart pounding fiercely ('The sevenfold shield of Ajax cannot keep/The battery from my heart'), he is eager to overtake Cleopatra and 'weep for my pardon' (IV. xiv. 35), presumably for doubting her love. This indicates again his submissive role. He imagines them the centre of attention in Elysium:[21]

> Where souls do couch on flowers we'll hand in hand
> And with our sprightly port make the ghosts gaze.
> Dido and her Aeneas shall want troops,
> And all the haunt be ours. (IV. xiv. 52–4)

All sorts of dramatic possibilities open when his suicide is not immediately successful. It is one of those moments in history full of 'what ifs'; the difference between life and death pivots on such tiny moments. It is grimly comic that after all the mismanaged military and political moves, he cannot even accomplish what is meant to be the last great act of his life. In Plutarch he stabs himself and falls on the bed:

> But the wound did not kill him quickly. Presently, as he lay prostrate, the bleeding stopped and he came to himself and implored the bystanders to put him out of his pain. But they ran out of the room and left him writhing in agony and crying for help, until Cleopatra's secretary, Diomedes, arrived with orders from the queen to bring him to the monument.[22]

So he is manipulated to the last by Cleopatra. Not dying instantly enables him to learn that Cleopatra is in fact alive – Fate's final trick. Diomedes (yet another of the many messengers facilitating much of the action), arriving seconds too late, reports how Cleopatra began to fear the unintended consequences of her childish, thoughtless ploy. Instead of cursing the queen, Antony instantly wishes to see her one last time. Shakespeare maintains the ambiguous balance between her political cunning (designed for her survival) and her relationship with Antony. Was the message of her suicide a thoughtless, unconsidered act that backfired? Or was it a plan to get rid of a man who had become a liability? At the same time it must not be forgotten she had had three children with him, so clearly there was (or had been) some sort of bond between them. Love can die, yet people carry on pretending it is still alive.

There is some appearance of affection and anguish in her response to Antony's bleeding body being brought to the monument:

> Welcome, welcome! Die when thou hast lived;
> Quicken with kissing. Had my lips that power,
> Thus would I wear them out. [Kisses him] (IV. xv. 39–41)

> Noblest of men, woo't die?
> Hast thou no care of me? Shall I abide
> In this dull world, which in thy absence is
> No better than a sty? O see, my women,
> The crown o'th'earth doth melt. (IV. xv. 61–5)

Or is she acting to cover the unfortunate outcome of her miscalculation? There are some oddities of register, as with 'Here's sport indeed!' (IV. xv. 33). Perhaps it is a nervously inappropriate phrase uttered in the awkwardness and awfulness of the moment. Imminent death is a difficult matter to respond to, to find the right expression for, and we do not always say quite the right thing. There is also her interruption, 'No, let me speak' (IV. xv. 45). Is this again her determination to hold centre stage and have her moment of high drama as the grieving lover? Or is it a desperate need to show him how upset she is before he dies?

After Antony dies, when she no longer has to keep up appearances for his sake, there are some moving sentiments ('O withered is the garland of the war' [IV. xv. 64], 'The odds is gone' [66], 'All's but naught' [78], 'Our lamp is spent' [85]) that hint at genuine love and grief. These may, at the same time, be the clichéd rhetoric of a graveside eulogy. She appears to be contemplating suicide:

> We'll bury him, and then what's brave, what's noble,
> Let's do't after the high Roman fashion

And make death proud to take us. Come, away.
This case of that huge spirit now is cold. (IV. xv. 89–92)

The word 'brave' does not here mean courageous, but a suitably fine show. The speech again envisions a theatrical set as Cleopatra imagines her own death and funeral. She has rather swiftly decentred Antony and is planning her own send-off. Historically, after the death of Antony, Cleopatra fell ill and Caesar had her moved back to her palace. The report he was going to make a public show of her in Rome is probably untrue. He had done this with her sister and it caused great public resentment. But Shakespeare needed to concentrate the final action – her death – so she remains in the monument, and when later it is obvious she cannot compromise with the now master of the world, she sets the stage for her own exit – robed and crowned in glory. It is a cynical position, but it is difficult not to see all this as a little too self-indulgent, unless it is delivered hysterically as a genuine outpouring of emotions. It is perhaps difficult for a woman so unused to directly expressing her genuine feelings to sound entirely sincere, even if she is. There is no doubt that some of the images are graphic and evocative (Cleopatra imagining throwing her sceptre at the god; Antony imagined as a stolen jewel or an exhausted, extinguished lamp that once lit the world), but are they mere rhetoric? Is the poetry disconnected from real feeling? If your life has been lived on the ritualized, stylized stage of politics it is perhaps hard to stop acting and hard to know if your feelings are genuine or fabricated.

There are still 389 lines before Cleopatra dies. There are moves and ploys to be made before she senses that her game is up, that Caesar will humiliate her as a prisoner and public spectacle. It is then she realizes she has to choose either humiliation or death, so her last big scene is to stage her demise as her own private spectacle, but one that will ensure public impact and make her renowned. In doing this she cheats Caesar and gets to perform her last and best part – the grieving widow so bereft by loss that she prefers to die. In doing this she displays her consummate acting skills, her ability to weave words impressively, and her love of projecting herself as a work of art. Once again she wins both ways. She knows Caesar will not submit to her charms, she knows she will not be allowed to continue living with the sort of freedom, wealth and power she has enjoyed. By stage managing her suicide she keeps control of the situation (as she loves and needs to do) and does it in such a way as will make history. Throughout the play numerous messengers interrupt the action with outer-world male business and set the plot on a new course. Now the interruptions come from Caesar's negotiators as he tries to out-manoeuvre the queen. She wins the last move in their game of chess; her death defeats him.

Chapter 12

ROME VERSUS EGYPT: GENDERING THE STATE

> Suffer her never to medle with the politick government of the common-weale, but hold her at the Oeconomick rule of the house. (*Basilikon Doron*, 61)

James I's advice to his son about keeping his wife out of politics echoes the orthodox male view, reflecting a longstanding edginess about the effect women could have on the state if given any influence. History and the Bible both provided innumerable examples of the disastrous effects of direct female power and of the behind-the-scenes havoc they could wreak. This covert influence is evident in most ages, but often ignored. The consensus was that ruling a state was difficult enough with machinations and manoeuvrings by ambitious warlords, megalomaniacs, psychopaths and courtiers, without adding the insidious sorts of female manipulation. The feminist line is that men had all the power and women were excluded from it and that any form of female interference or bids for power were as unacceptable as the power plays of men.

As for females being excluded from power, history proves otherwise. Over and over women appear, leading armies, fomenting plots and coups, and subverting harmony. Gossip, false rumour mongering, flirtation, sexual favours, pillow talk and witchcraft were all part of male unease about women at court from the time of Stephen and Matilda through to James's court.[1] Traditionally, women had their domestic sphere of influence and men had their roles in the outer world. Any crossover was regarded as unnatural and dangerously undermining of order. At court women should busy themselves organizing social and cultural events like concerts, dances, masques and plays. Men's duties were with the diplomatic, political and economic arrangements of the nation. In reality there were a number of strong-minded, formidable, independent aristocratic women, running their estates, supervising the political direction of their family interests and interfering at court. Women were always involved in court manoeuvrings – the backstairs, behind-closed-bed-curtains world of covert pressure exercised over men susceptible to the sexual allure of women.

Roman history, of which most educated men would have some knowledge, was also full of women who affected the running of the state – some positively, some negatively. In *Antony and Cleopatra*, both Fulvia and the queen of Egypt penetrate a political sphere wider than their legitimate role. Octavia's role is severely reduced by Shakespeare until she becomes a virtually voiceless symbol of ideal Roman womanhood. Her brother calls her a 'piece of virtue' (III. ii. 28) and the messenger, perhaps wary of upsetting Cleopatra further, describes her as 'a body rather than a life,/A statue than a breather' (III. iii. 20–21). In reality Octavia did much to help recruit soldiers and gather ships for her husband's wars in Parthia and Media, but she did not have the aggressive will of Fulvia or Cleopatra. She does, however, provide a tragically potent contrast in her modesty – tragic because, for all her fine qualities, we know she will not focus Antony's passions as Cleopatra can. Caesar, in his reinvented self as Emperor Augustus, was partnered by the inveterate meddler, Livia, and the history of the empire is littered with women of immense power. Although they could not hold official public office, they could wield intense private influence both through their strength of personality and status and through their sexuality. Some became figures renowned for poisoning, plotting, assassination or depravity. One-person rule, as opposed to oligarchical, senatorial or parliamentary government, was more vulnerable to being swayed by whispering favourites, nagging wives and seductive mistresses. As in Rome, so at Whitehall. Elizabeth had been susceptible, for brief periods, to handsome young men – James likewise. But other political leaders at court were often manipulated by the range of baits and among them was the honey trap.

England had just had 45 years of Elizabeth I's reign in which to gauge the style and effectiveness of female rule. Obstinacy, caprice, strength of will, fortitude, humour, vindictiveness and charisma are all terms applicable to 'Gloriana'. They also fit Cleopatra and to some extent she is a reflection of the recently dead queen and an audience would inevitably make comparisons.

What is more powerfully evident is how the two diametrically opposed states of Rome and Egypt are differently gendered. There are similarities in their tendency towards decadence, as can be seen in the Alexandrian court, which seems to reel from one revel to another, and in the drunken banquet on Pompey's galley. In the last days of the Republic the wealth brought in by expanding conquests brought outbreaks of lavish display and personal misbehaviour. Just as in England in the 1600s, the old virtues – modest living, honesty in civic office and individual moral probity – were breaking down. Antony's history is full of whoring, adultery, extravagance, debt, gambling and drinking. His weakness for women expressed itself not just as a need for sexual satisfaction but as a puppyish readiness to be overwhelmed by them. He was a submissive type who never liked to upset women and was too easily drawn into worshipping them. Both the Roman and Alexandrian courts are full of hangers-on and flatterers seeking the favour of the dominant forces – i.e., Caesar and Cleopatra. The play begins with Roman disapproval of Antony's life in Egypt and then in Act I Scene ii we glimpse how decadent the Alexandrian court is, with the queen's attendants joking frivolously about sex and idly listening to a soothsayer tell their fortunes.[2] This allies them to the shadowy world of the supernatural, but it is applied to trivial matters as an indication of how petty are this court's concerns. The Romans too had their soothsayers and augurs, so once again the worlds are not so different. The Egyptians find levity in everything and licentious attitudes are prevalent, but there are darker elements secreted. In grim foreshadowing the soothsayer (who later warns Antony to beware Caesar) tells Charmian she will outlive her mistress (which she does – by fifteen lines). She delightedly responds, 'I love long life better than figs' (I. ii. 34). Those who knew their Plutarch would see the proleptic reference to the basket of figs hiding the asps at the end of the drama. Charmian jokingly wishes her fortune to be to marry three kings and be thrice a widow. Marriage and relationships are treated fairly light-heartedly throughout the play. For Charmian marriage is a temporary sexual liaison, for the Romans (as for many Jacobeans) it is a political and commercial alliance between families. Enobarbus's callously cold realism expresses the negative side of Roman marriage; of Fulvia's death he says that 'the tears live in an onion that should water this sorrow' (I. ii. 176–7). Agrippa and Enobarbus, both soldiers, express a similarly blunt view of Julius Caesar's liaison with Cleopatra: 'He ploughed her, and she cropped' (II. ii. 238). One might expect to hear these unsentimental, direct, vulgar terms from a military man expressing his view of sexual commerce. Interestingly the food image, where the phallic, thrusting sword is 'laid to bed' and transforms into a ploughshare and then into a crop, is further metamorphosed by Enobarbus describing the queen as a food that is first consumed and then consumes the consumer:

> Age cannot wither her, nor custom stale
> Her infinite variety. Other women cloy
> The appetites they feed, but she makes hungry
> Where most she satisfies […]. (II. ii. 245–8)

He predicts that Antony will never leave Cleopatra. He neither has the rational will to do so nor the sexual control to be without her. ('Will' in seventeenth-century English meant sex drive as well as rational volition.)

The language of the queen's court is looser and much more loaded with lewd innuendo than Caesar's. Both cultures have a low estimation of the relationship between lust and love. The Egyptian life is freer, less restrained and less orderly than in Rome, and blurs many of the moral boundaries. The eunuch Mardian is part of the fluid sexual profile, where the queen is no more 'womanly' than the feminized Roman general. Egypt is a world where the women run things and insist all is done according to their requirements. While Charmian and Iras play up to Cleopatra (not without some genuine affection), re-enforcing her fantasies and assisting her emasculation and manipulation of Antony, Caesar is surrounded by yes-men too. We see him a number of times ordering his go-betweens, with Maecenas and Agrippa at his elbow endorsing his judgements like parrots, saying what he wants to hear in denigration of Antony and Cleopatra. Antony seems isolated and lost. He has Enobarbus, but his Choric cynicism is often voiced to others rather than to Antony and the general's place at court seems a lonely one. He has not been fully absorbed into the Egyptian way of thinking. If Egypt was a place where the privileged and powerful had access to huge wealth, so too was Rome. Its patricians had slowly monopolized posts of power and had access to prerogatives that brought cash. The historian Sallust deplores the decaying state of the late Republic:

> As soon as wealth came to be a mark of distinction and an easy way to renown, military commands, and political power, virtue began to decline. Poverty was now looked on as a disgrace and a blameless life as a sign of ill nature. Riches made the younger generation a prey to luxury, avarice, and pride. Squandering with one hand what they grabbed with the other, they set small value on their own property, while they coveted that of others. Honour and modesty, all laws divine and human, were alike regarded in a spirit of recklessness and intemperance.[3]

His analysis could just as readily be applied to Jacobean England and its court, where a place was sought not for the honour of serving the state, but for the status and money it bestowed. Growing luxury precipitated all sorts of moral crises. Aristocratic ladies and gentlemen in London also consulted astrologers (equivalent to soothsayers) and spent their extensive leisure time in liaisons and flirtations. A foolish, drunken, weak king, extravagant himself and easily swayed, made the court a lucrative honeypot. There are similarities too in the readiness of Cleopatra and Octavius to plot secretly and undermine in a way the audience would recognize as Machiavellian. With Antony so dominated by the will of the queen, the protagonists in the political dimension are Caesar and Cleopatra, and in this respect that could be an alternative title to the play. Antony is all misdirected bluster, good intentions and muddled actions. Caesar calculates his lies in his will to power, while Cleopatra improvises her devious deceptions in response to whoever pleases or angers her or whoever has the power she needs to protect her own interests.

Despite similarities in motives and methods between the political opponents there are deep underlying differences between the two states at the cultural, philosophical and spiritual levels. One is devoted to the female principle – to Isis/Venus – and the other to the male principles of war and art – Mars and Apollo. One is ruled by the Nile, by water, by fluid change, by fertility and growth, the other by bricks, marble, steel, conquest and annexation. The triumvirs are the three pillars supporting Rome as an edifice with arches that may crack. Antony is a colossus whose 'breaking' should have made 'a greater crack' (V. i. 15). His falling out with Caesar is seen as two halves of a jaw opening to swallow up the men who will die as a result of their conflict. Octavia sees war between Antony and her brother 'as if the world should cleave, and that slain men/Should solder up the rift' (III. iv. 31–2). After Actium, Scarus declares:

> The greater cantle of the world is lost
> With very ignorance. We have kissed away
> Kingdoms and provinces. (III. x. 6–8)

This segment of the world sphere is both the Eastern provinces and Antony himself, lost for the sake of a kiss. Caesar put it similarly:

> Cleopatra hath
> Nodded him to her. He hath given his empire
> Up to a whore [...]. (III. vi. 66–8)

The metaphors used to describe Rome are redolent of masculinity, solidity and permanence, they are concrete and visualizable, while the watery imagery associated with Egypt suggests the feminine – changeable, taking the shape of whatever touches it, carrying fertility but hiding dangers. Cleopatra is consistently linked with the serpents of the Nile and it is poetically just that she dies from snake bites. She has been fertile herself – three children from Antony and one from Julius Caesar.[4] But she is as unpredictable as the Nile in its flooding and as silently devious as its snakes. The critic Camille Paglia has explored this polarity in detail from the point of view that love, freedom and the feminine are good and that the martial, restrained and controlled masculine is bad.[5] The Jacobean audience would disagree – at least those who were religious would, for they were witnessing the fall of two sinners and lived in an ethos where temperance and moderation were applauded and sin and excess were expected to be punished. Those who had any interest in political theory and matters of state would also condemn Antony and Cleopatra for their levity, the persistent pleasure-seeking and their consequent neglect of rule. They would see the protagonists as using the state's wealth for the pursuit of their own enjoyment.

Pragmatists would see the necessity of masculine military qualities in gaining and holding a country's territorial integrity, in establishing wealth-creating trade, and in keeping order among the growing population. Antony dissipates Roman rule by his failure to keep hold of the dominance of power in his relationship with Cleopatra, by his inept strategies in the Parthian campaign, and by giving away territory. In making many of the client kings independent rulers he was alienating an exceptionally valuable constituent of the Roman economy. Circumspection was a key quality in a prince and Antony has the irresponsible thoughtlessness and impulsiveness of a libertine wanton and drunk. He was never a subtle or far-sighted politician. So we may see Antony as situated between the two poles of power and passion. He was a Roman Hellenized, for Cleopatra was Greek by origin and ruled the state Alexander had conquered, based in the city he founded. Therefore Antony is regarded as weakened and feminized by contact with the East just as Alexander had been. His flaws were already clear to see before he met Cleopatra, but she played upon them and developed them to a fatal and tragic degree.

Paglia sees Egypt and Rome as the two extremes of belief and practice in classical culture – the Dionysian and the Apollonian – transformed into the tension between the natural appetites that the Christian Renaissance attempted to repress and demonize as sins on one hand and an obsessive regard for order on the other. This is a useful duality for understanding some of the complexities. Put simply, Egypt is Dionysian, Rome is Apollonian. This means Egypt stands for unrestraint, freedom, inspiration and anarchy, Rome for control, form, orderliness and repression. Cleopatra was identified with Isis, the ancient goddess of nature, with its fertility, selfish instinct and brutishness. Osiris, the emasculated consort of Isis, was seen as Dionysus, a deity of frenzy, freedom and unrestrained appetites. Caesar is connected with the orderliness, consciousness and restraint thought to be inherent in the religion of Apollo. Antony is a mix of the two, but his Roman qualities are colonized by a tendency towards the pleasure-seeking and ultimately destructive forces of unrestrained instinct. Though a Roman by origin and a conqueror by political power, he has been conquered first by Greece, then by Asiatic customs, then by Cleopatra, then by Egypt. When he met Cleopatra at Tarsus the people saw it as a meeting between Isis/Aphrodite (the Greek goddess of love, equivalent to the Roman Venus) and Dionysus. Plutarch described it thus: 'The word spread on every side that Venus had come to revel with Bacchus for the happiness of Asia.'[6] Both liked to dress up as these deities and thought of themselves as their earthly representations. It was a potent concept that the spirits of a hero or a god were in you, that you had some of their characteristics.

Another persona Antony liked to assume was as a second Alexander. He ruled a larger area of the East than anyone since Alexander, lived in the city he founded, lived with a descendent of Alexander's general and heir, Ptolemy, so the identification came naturally. The son he and Cleopatra had was named Alexander Helios, identifying him with the great ruler and the sun god. When Caesar claimed to be the son of the deified Julius Caesar, Antony had to counterbalance that and was happy when the Ephesians proclaimed him as a god (not just the son of one). 'God Manifest, son of Ares and Aphrodite [Mars and Venus], saviour of all mankind' was how he was described on some inscriptions. His arrival in Ephesus had been celebrated: 'The people hailed him as Dionysus the Benefactor and the Bringing of Joy.' But when he confiscated property from noble families, allowed property scams and imposed punitive taxes on cities in Magnesia, some called him 'Dionysus the Cruel and the Eater of Flesh'.[7] Antony asserted that his sliding scale of levies was more humane than the previous system – but he still took the money. Dionysus was a dual deity, double-edged (and dangerous) like a sword – the jovial and fun-loving god of wine, but also a savage and primitive force of unrestrained barbarism. Jacobeans, without linking this necessarily to the cult of Dionysus (probably knowing little of his cult), saw this aspect as the natural sinful outcome of not controlling the natural appetites. Hercules, another of Antony's self-created masquerades, was linked with Dionysus (known in Latin mythology as Bacchus) in that he was believed to participate in his banquets in the Bacchic paradise. In Alexandria Antony was proclaimed New Father Liber (Dionysus) and rode in a Bacchic chariot, in saffron robe, wearing an ivy wreath headdress and carrying a sacred wand – more theatricals.

Cleopatra equally enjoyed her personae as Isis/Venus (Aphrodite). At this time Aphrodite was widely worshipped as a goddess of the universe. This attribute was also accorded Isis and the two seem to have become conflated. Many votive statuettes of the period show them as one deity. Lucretius describes her thus: 'It is you who fill rich earth and buoyant sea with your presence! It is through you that every living thing achieves its life.'⁸ Similarly, Dionysus was identified with the Egyptian god Osiris. Hence Antony was also celebrated as Osiris, brother and husband of Isis. The adultery of Antony and Cleopatra thus became justified as a holy unity of Isis/Aphrodite with Osiris/Dionysus, a valuable propaganda move in a highly superstitious age. It is perhaps from this publicly authenticated and hailed alliance that the pair get their sense of being somehow above normal earthly, human status – special, elevated, divine and outside the moral restraints of ordinary life and mundane values. At a less elevated level, Antony was more attracted by the raunchy sexuality of Cleopatra than by the controlled virtue of Octavia. At both levels he was setting himself up for punishment. Gods and men did not take kindly to such arrogant, hubristic conduct.

Paglia makes the important point that 'despite his love for the glamorous personality of multiple moods and masks, Shakespeare subordinates all his characters to the public good. The great chain of being reasserts itself at the end of his plays.'[9] Antony and Cleopatra are aberrant, transgressive, wild, unstable, rogue elements, inimical to Rome's thinking, threatening its peace, and an obstacle to Caesar's ambitions. They must, like sinners, be defeated, punished and obliterated. Though engrossing as a pair, their love 'war' (a more grave version of what Shakespeare had explored in his Romantic Comedies) places them beyond what was acceptable in governors, and it is entirely expected that they will be removed from power. Had this not been a history play, and therefore limited by the facts, the couple would have still been candidates for a fall, just retribution for transgression. Apart from historical fact, the realities of politics and the judgement of morality demand it.

Egypt to Paglia is the 'fertile stamping ground of the femme fatale' who 'obeys no law but her own'.[10] She claims that 'Shakespeare, the Dionysian alchemist, is determined to rescue nature from its daemonic taint' in representing the libertinism of Cleopatra as a life-enhancing force and Shakespeare 'gives his imaginative sympathies to the Dionysian extremists'.[11] There is rather much of this mystic psycho-babble in *Sexual Personae*, but it does open up a way of discussing the self-centred energy and narcissism of the lovers and does acknowledge that 'Renaissance order must have the last word'.[12]

Fascinating as the convolutions of Cleopatra's wiles to hold Antony are, in the end their private lives will always be sacrificed to the greater good of the public communities their childish games affect. Shakespeare makes the lovers lively because they were charismatic figures and their emotions entangled. Their arguments, conflicts and games for dominance create drama. Their psychological profiles are complex and interesting, their emotional vacillations constantly fascinating (and irritating). In another dimension they would be seen as comic, like Beatrice and Benedick in *Much Ado About Nothing*, the eternal male/female sex war of love/hate. But these are people with responsibility for the security of millions and their squabbles and perpetual playtime have serious consequences. It may seriously be questioned whether they are the elevated figures Paglia and others have claimed. Coleridge believed the play to be 'the most wonderful' of Shakespeare's works because of its insight into the lovers and the 'depth and energy' of their passion.[13] Another critic from the Romantic period saw Cleopatra as a 'triumph of the voluptuous, of the love of pleasure and the power of giving it, over every other consideration'.[14] Once we see through Cleopatra, see her as a constant actress and an egotistical diva, we see that her lofty words are just overblown rhetoric. Montaigne, whose essays influenced Shakespeare, deplored the art of fine speaking because it fooled our judgement, changed the appearance of matters and created emotions falsely 'inflated with rich and magnificent words'.[15] Cleopatra may love Antony, but it is an unstable emotion, hardly ever gentle, more often provocative and egocentric. Their relationship is always volatile, always acted out at the top of their bent, always a high drama.

Nietzsche used the classical binary opposites of Dionysus and Apollo, the dark and the light, in *The Birth of Tragedy* (1872). They provide a shorthand for discussing the differences between Egypt and Rome and between the female and male forces in the play. Traditionally, the Greek and Roman cultures were thought of as rational, orderly and serenely focused on the pursuit of virtue, emotional balance, stoicism, individual probity and civic duty. The scholarly discoveries of nineteenth-century archaeologists and anthropologists revealed a darker side of the ancient world, where slavery, violence and blood sacrifice (sometimes human) were more prevalent than previously admitted, where superstition, blood cults, frenzy and alcohol/drug/dance-induced possession inspired and loosed instinctive, primitive impulses. These could lead to creative insights but also to anarchic behaviour and bloodshed. Dionysus (initially a god of wine) represents the animal drives of sexual predation and physical dominance. A combination of the positive aspects of Dionysian instinct, intuition and insight with the Apollonian concern for form, symmetry, balance and beauty can be seen as the foundation of art, government and the moral life. The extreme of either is disagreeable on the one hand and dangerous on the other. Severe form and too rigid a regulation of content and expression leads to dull, mechanical art, coldly unsympathetic but highly regimented government, and an unemotional non-empathetic life. Uncontrolled loosing of human instincts leads to sexual mayhem, the rule of might and the breakdown of the domestic and family bases of society.

A seventeenth-century audience might have been less aware of the Dionysian religion, but would certainly approve of the Apollonian approach, for it embraced order, virtue and the concept of *sophrosyne* (balance). It had its extremists in the fiercer forms of Puritanism that diminished the pleasures of life and made it a severe, ascetic battle to repress all forms of human emotion and appetite, but equally dangerous was the emerging libertinism and voluptuous life of the court. The Dionysian aspect of classical culture related to all the darker side of the human psyche: violence, superstition, witchcraft and sorcery, blood sacrifice, the rage of war, unregulated and unrestrained sexuality, and all other forms of transgression or sin. Apollo represented the humanist values of courtesy, consideration, education, virtue, order and hierarchy. That is not to say that Jacobean society, in its attempt to be orderly, humane, sympathetic to suffering and responsive to duty, did not at the same time have its dark side. Bull baiting, hunting, poisoning, stabbings, fights, murders, drunkenness, sexual libertinism, witchcraft, the Gunpowder Plot, torture and execution are all signs that mankind had not advanced very far.

Having found a neat polarity, Paglia pursues it without always seeing that a compromise between the two (*sophrosyne* in fact) is what Shakespeare seeks.

> Throughout the play, Roman personality is static and brittle, like stone. Caesar defines identity and kinship in legalistic terms. The abstract and public take precedence over the concrete, emotional, and sensuous. [...] Rome's voice is the bleak reality principle of political expediency. In Egypt, on the other hand, energy pours into self-expression. [...] Dionysian beings are playful and democratic. As queen, Cleopatra is indifferent to decorum. Her hilarity contrasts with Caesar's puritanical sobriety.[16]

What she fails to appreciate is that running a state requires that public needs take precedence over personal whim. Though Caesar is calculating, his bid for sole rule brought about a period of immense growth, luxury and power to the Roman hegemony. Indecorous hilarity, such as that shown at James I's court, with its drunkenness, its gluttony, its narcissistic love of self-display in silken finery, its promiscuity and, above all, its detachment from the needs of the people, was not only frowned upon by the Puritans but by a growing number of ordinary citizens of different ranks and different religious persuasions. Whitehall could have done with a little of Caesar's steel. The energy poured into self-expression was merely the anarchic selfishness of the privileged, the disorganized vacillation of those who did not know what to do with their lives because they did not want to shoulder responsibility, rushing from one novelty to another, satisfying one whim after another. Who would seriously want to live and serve under a ruler of such uncertain temper, such uncertainty of favour, such disregard for the job of governing as Cleopatra? Kings or queens with charisma could and had inspired loyalty and love, but only when they administered the realm thoroughly and justly. Monarchy was a full-time role. Relaxation was not ruled out, but responsibility came first.

Paglia preferences Cleopatra for her 'Dionysian multiplicity',[17] which can be interpreted as her neurotic mood swings and multiple (i.e., inconstant) personalities. Antony, by contrast, 'suffers a reduction of identity through his feminizing association with Cleopatra', which, Paglia claims, 'Shakespeare sees [...] as an aggrandizement of identity'.[18] This seems difficult to substantiate given the outcome of the narrative. Antony is diminished by association with Cleopatra – she swallows him up. He is no longer himself or in control of himself, so his identity is hardly aggrandized. Paglia suggests association with Cleopatra has enlarged Antony's vision and experience of life. Perhaps this is the case, but in doing so she destroys him. She symbolically emasculates him when she appropriates his sword and dresses him in her clothing. Paglia sees this 'exchange of clothing' as 'a paradigm for the emotional union of love', but it would be unusual to regard this humiliating joke and the de-gendering transvestism involved as a celebration of mutual love. It seems more like contempt than caring; Cleopatra is colonizing Antony's gender and role. Paglia further claims Cleopatra 'absorbs Antony's identity' and is herself 'psychically immersed in the irrational and barbaric'.[19] She is using Antony, subverting his self for the sake of her own self. It is an assertion of female dominance, a humiliation and destruction of the male's identity by a voracious female intent upon her own survival and maintenance of power.

Those female insects that eat the male after mating are not the only species to act thus. Cleopatra is both destroyer and life enhancer. If this is so, the killer cancels out all life-enhancing qualities. It is open to question whether the audience is expected to sympathize with the lovers and see them as innocent victims. It is seriously open to question whether the audience is expected to sympathize with Cleopatra as a woman in a man's world fighting for survival. It is very seriously open to question whether the deaths of the couple are meant to transfigure them in the eyes of a Jacobean audience. A Christian assessment would damn Cleopatra for denigrating and emasculating Antony and she rightly dies as a requirement of tragedy, morality and hierarchy. If they were private citizens she might be fun and life enhancing in small doses, but she is unreliable and unstable, and potentially dangerous if you tried to leave her.

Paglia claims, on the grounds of her cradling the asp like 'my baby at my breast' (V. ii. 309), that 'the mother is one of Cleopatra's many personae'.[20] On the contrary, this aspect of her life is omitted totally; she displays no maternal characteristics. Why miss the opportunity to show her softer, nurturing side? Perhaps because Shakespeare wished to highlight her personal and political destructiveness. Equally we see no aspect of her rule that demonstrates progressive, constructive engagement with her state. Cleopatra is never shown running her realm. Antony briefly reconnects with Rome and its political needs, but Cleopatra seems only to access the leisure, wealth and deference available to her privileged position. Not only does she not govern, but she shows no interest either in her people. They are merely curiosities that she and Antony observe as an occasional recreation as they sneak around the streets at night.

There is tragic, poetic justice in Cleopatra seeing the asp as a suckling child, for it reverses normality. She subverts governorship by being an uncontrolled sybarite and control freak and is then finally subverted herself by one of the lowliest creatures, one Shakespeare's audience associated with evil. She deals death in her demand that her self-absorption be replicated by those around her, for she shrinks the selfhood of her entourage. She is the main event. If Cleopatra is a maternal figure she is a fatal one, the mother as death and as false mother. Nothing of her mothering or of her family life is portrayed or mentioned. The action is a reversal of normality, where the nursing mother, instead of providing life-giving milk to the suckling child, is killed by the baby envenoming her breast.

This subversion of nurturing is justice, as Cleopatra is a killer. Apart from the false and misleading message of her own death causing Antony to commit suicide, her conduct has 'killed' his reputation and destroyed his power. He has helped achieve this himself, but is ably pushed to it by her alluring lifestyle and betrayals. She is physically and verbally violent, is full of bravado but runs away from Actium, and then has her fleet surrender at the second naval encounter. She threatens a maid, assaults a messenger and is generally aggressive in her language. Ultimately she kills her own state, for the pair's military defeat leads to Egypt being swallowed up into the Roman polity. Paglia regards such conduct as offensive 'by modern middle-class standards'. It would be transgressive to Jacobean aristocrats and bourgeoisie too and indefensible by any humanist, cultured, civilized measure throughout the period. Paglia seems unwilling to admit that a queen who 'breaks through social restraints to plunge into the sensual, orgiastic pleasure of pure feeling' should be soundly condemned.[21] But then, 'Her body is the earth mother torn by the strife of the elements of the cycle of birth and death. Ugliness, pain, abortion, and decay are nature's reality.' The first claim is emotional nonsense. The brutality of nature might aptly describe the context of the late-republican Roman world, and the Jacobean world too, but the seventeenth century would condemn Cleopatra as yet another spoiled, destructive, childish product of the monarchical system. The Jacobeans would admire the quiet virtues of Octavia. Younger than Cleopatra, beautiful, intellectual, of impeccable reputation and sociable, she was patroness of the work of Vitruvius and supported Maecenas's literary circle. Very different from Fulvia and diametrically opposite to Cleopatra, the Renaissance would see in her the courtly qualities promulgated by Castiglione. Compared to her Cleopatra is one of a long line of demi-courtesan whores shimmying through Renaissance history and drama, dangerous to morality, a threat to society and fatal to those who love and serve them.

'For Cleopatra, life is theatre. She is a master of propagandists. Truth is inconsequential; dramatic values are supreme. Cleopatra shamelessly manipulates others' emotions [...]. She scripts her suicide' and 'has a sensational flair for improvisation and melodrama'.[22] On the Jacobean stage, the audience would be watching a young man acting as a female, pretending to be a queen who acts all the time. Politics is theatre and monarchs have to act, but there is expected to be a solid basis of truth and honesty under the show. The Puritans had issues with the whole matter of representation in the playhouse, but some accepted that pretence was a way to show greater realities and truths. The 'amoral dissimulations'[23] of Cleopatra would be condemned while the actor of them might be applauded for his skill in representing them. Dante condemned liars and counterfeiters to Nether Hell. Just above those who betrayed family, guests, overlords or country were those who practised fraud: panders and seducers, flatterers, hypocrites, fraudsters and falsifiers. Actors are professional falsifiers, counterfeiting someone else. But their aim is not to cheat, for audiences know they impersonate another in order to project some moral lesson. The Cleopatra represented in the play is constantly counterfeiting her emotions, mixing real feelings with assumed ones in order to play tricks, to the point where no one knows which statements or actions are intended and genuine and which are misleading lies. Caesar too is an actor, hiding his motives and intentions like any politician. But while Caesar keeps his own counsel and is calm and restrained, Cleopatra is noisy, obvious at times, unstable and volatile. With benevolence Caesar would make the better ruler. Cleopatra is too unreliable and erratic. Her Egypt is too much focused round her court and her whims. It is a playground for the privileged, unwary of political realities in the wider world, led militarily by two commanders who are more bound up with each other than concerned with the business at hand, dangerous children playing with fire.

Along with the mystical undercurrents of Dionysus and Apollo, Paglia promotes astrological allusions as part of the meaning of the characters. Cleopatra clearly is a creature of fire and air: 'Fire is will, originality, boldness, the amoral life force. Air is language, wit, balance, humane perspective.'[24] She certainly uses language effectively and fluently (part of her skill as an actress) and has wit, meaning both amusing skill in manipulating ideas and words, but also in its sense as acute intelligence. However, 'balance' and 'humane perspective' are not among her characteristics. The third element, water, represents 'intuition, sympathy, deep feeling, mystical oneness and prophecy'.[25] Her suspicious intuitions about the danger of Antony being drawn back into the circle of Rome's influence prove true. She has little time for sympathy as she is largely motivated by her own needs. Whatever 'mystical oneness' is supposed to mean, one could say that she has absorbed into her behaviour some of the features of Isis, with whom she affected identification, and she correctly intuits what Caesar plans to do with her. The final element, earth, 'is order, method, precision, realism, materialism'.[26] This pragmatic, down-to-earth profile clearly suits Caesar, who, Paglia claims, is associated with 'patience, pragmatism, emotional reserve, discipline, application'.[27]

Because Caesar's general in charge of his land forces at Actium is named Taurus, and Taurus the Bull is the first of the three earth signs in the zodiac, Paglia sees this as enforcing the astrological underpinning. That might be convincing if Shakespeare had made up the name and encrypted it into the text as some mystical message, but there really was a celebrated soldier of that name and Shakespeare merely uses this fact of history. Taurus only says two words and leads the army across the stage, a standard incidental character such as we find often in the history plays. Many in the audience believed in predictive reading of their stars and in zodiac signs as markers of personality, but the stars as fate seem a peripheral element in the text. Clearly there are substantial personality differences between Caesar and Cleopatra, but Paglia goes too far in detecting alchemical and astrological meanings hidden in the lexis. The most ludicrous example of this overlaying of an idea relates to Antony's depressive weariness (mental and physical) after the lost Battle of Actium: 'At his darkest moment, Antony says to Cleopatra, "Love, I am full of lead" (III. xi. 72). This is the play's nadir, before the transformation into spiritual gold.'[28] This seems like delusional word spinning considering the disaster of the following sea battle, Cleopatra's foolish lie about her death, Antony's absurd attempt at honourable Roman-style suicide, being hoisted into the monument, and their verbal attempts to resurrect their relationship through poetic rhetoric, particularly when it is clear Cleopatra would have lived on if she could have seduced her captor or made a suitable compromise for her future. Paglia seems intent on decoding the play as an alchemical process by which the protagonists are turned into something splendid through suffering and resurrection. If they are redeemed the audience would more readily see this in terms of Christian ideology and the process of tragedy than as a spiritual alchemy. Kott too sees them transformed at the last: 'Antony and Cleopatra become the great lovers only in acts four and five. And not just great lovers. They pronounce judgement on the world.'[29] A Jacobean audience would view their judgement, their *contemptu mundi* (contempt for the world), as a Christian deathbed epiphany of the vanity of the world's baubles ('this dull world [...]/No better than a sty' [IV. xv. 63–4]), that ''Tis paltry to be Caesar' (V. ii. 2), and that all life is but fortune nurturing us for death.

Paglia's conclusions are more realistic and more viably tied to what the play is doing:

> The symbolic marriage of Antony and Cleopatra, enacted at the moment of death, removes the lovers from the social order. Their hedonism and self-involvement have damaged their nations and their cause. [...] *Antony and Cleopatra* demonstrates that life cannot be lived as a series of perpetual self-transformations without violating social and ethical principles. [...] Social order and stability were primary English Renaissance values.[30]

The return to strong, directed government under an emotionally stable ruler is something the audience could applaud.

Chapter 13

LITERARY CONTEXT

Genre

Obviously *Antony and Cleopatra* is a history play and a Roman history play at that, whose narrative was widely known from Plutarch's *Lives of the Noble Greeks and Romans*. In its themes it is no different from the English history cycle that Shakespeare began early in his career and completed in the period just before the Roman Plays. The politics and personalities explored in the play resonate with the early 1600s in Jacobean England. The lead characters are grand figures and this was an age when politics was dominated by personalities – strong (sometimes ruthless) individuals rather than parties or principles. Very few of the lower sort appear or have voices. There is the servant on Pompey's galley who remarks on how having great place but failing to live up to it is like a face without eyes. There is the clown (rustic) who brings the asps to Cleopatra, his demotic lexis contrasting sharply and ironically with the high-flown poetry of the queen preparing her suicide. But apart from these two and the messengers bringing news, all the rest of the servants servicing the courts in Rome and Alexandria are silent. This is a high-end drama of the makers and shakers, the privileged powerbrokers, but it is one that shows their manifest and multiple weaknesses both as leaders and as human beings. They are not only inefficient in the practical matters related to the administering of their state, but severely faulty ethically. Caesar is a 'white devil' (a hypocrite), adopting the moral high ground while actually plotting deviously to undermine his political partners. We see this before and after the meeting at Misenum which brings together the four political heavyweights of the time and shows them as just as capable of making drunken fools of themselves as the common tavern regular. Pompey is a rebel threatening the peace of his native land and when offered an opportunity to have his rival murdered rejects it not on moral grounds, but because his honour is compromised by knowing Menas's plan. He rebukes the would-be assassin for not doing the deed first without alerting him – another 'white devil'. Kott sees Menas's offer to kill the triumvirs (II. vii.) as 'one of the greatest scenes [...]; another scene not found in Plutarch, but taken straight from the experience of the Renaissance; a scene strikingly modern'.[1] What he means is that it is a truly Machiavellian offer, a piece of underhand, visionary *realpolitik*, wiping out his enemies with one blow and taking power instantly without moral qualms. Lepidus is a non-entity, a weak follower of the other two triumvirs, who lacks gravitas and becomes incapably drunk at a crucial meeting when the dignity of Rome needed to be upheld. Ventidius, a successful warrior, holds back from pursuing his military victories for fear of arousing the jealousy of Antony. He puts Antony's and Caesar's military reputations into an interesting light when he asserts they have always won 'more in their officer than person' (III. i. 17). Maecenas and Agrippa (though the latter was in reality a talented soldier) are represented simply as yes-men poodles playing up to Caesar. They are 'courtiers' hanging on to the rising man. Enobarbus speaks his mind, sees clearly the strengths and weaknesses of Antony, but ultimately betrays him. And then there are the title characters – flawed, flawed and flawed again. Politically they are inept, naive and neglectful of their duties. Morally they are deeply sinful.

So, it is a history play and a highly political one. But it is also a love story and morality play. Despite his angry outbursts against her, there is little doubt that Antony loves Cleopatra, or thinks he does. Her feelings are less certain, even at the end of the play. Most of the tradition sees Cleopatra as promiscuous, unreliable and a self-obsessed politician seeking to ensure her own survival. Antony is largely seen as a fool, a playboy and a hopeless voluptuary who lost his world for the sake of a lust-driven strumpet. Nevertheless, their story is renowned as one of the world's great love stories. It can be argued that Shakespeare's play is a realignment of this dynamic, which portrays the pair as charismatic but imperfect figures and their love as a mix of self-deceiving folly, self-interest and self-preservation (on Cleopatra's part). It is a messy relationship that is technically immoral but has some aspects of genuine feeling, though they are often masked by quarrels and sulks and obscured by the events of the outer world. So, it is a love story of sorts – a love story of erratic mood changes, but always underpinned by a deep need for each other. Is that love or desperation? Though she is more politically skilled and he a blunt, unsubtle soldier, both are needy individuals, insecure and incomplete as personalities. This may seem a bizarre thing to suggest, considering what strong selves they seem to project in public. The biographies of both betray them as often less than in full control of their fortunes, forced by circumstances and making bad decisions. It is a love story then that is waylaid by the world.

Would they have been uniformly happy had they been private citizens? Probably not. Cleopatra seems to thrive on dramas, usually those she has fabricated herself and which focus on her. Antony needed a strong woman who could satisfy him sexually, but he does have doubts about her sincerity.

Antony and Cleopatra is a history play and love story, but is it also a tragedy? It features the fall of a prince – in fact the fall of two – falling from a state of prosperity into misery. Thus far it conforms to the medieval concept of tragedy. What the Renaissance brought to the genre was the exploration of the hero's psychological complexities – his strengths and good qualities that, because he undergoes suffering, make him a figure to be pitied, and his failings and unwise actions, for which he deserves punishment. These are evident in the play, doubly so with the two protagonists, but the presentation of both is incomplete and confused to some extent by the lack of insight into their inner thoughts. Shakespeare has made it impossible for the audience to reach definitive conclusions. Motives, reactions and intentions can all be expressed for the audience through soliloquy, but these are absent. There are a few short speeches by Antony alone onstage, but they do not develop sufficiently to help the audience understand his inner turmoil. Cleopatra is always seen from outside. Her comments and actions tell us much – little of which is good – but she is never given the opportunity to speak to the spectators on a personal basis.

Not being able to access the inner turmoil of the protagonists does not preclude them from the audience's sympathy, though it does diminish its scope. Both central figures have their *hamartia* (tragic flaw), both experience reversal of fortune (*peripeteia*). Antony has some sense of recognizing his failings (*anagnorisis*), his mistake in becoming embroiled in the 'Egyptian fetters' of 'this enchanting queen' and his military-naval misjudgements. But he seems not to see (though others do) the marriage with Octavia as a foolish move, committing himself to a family alliance he cannot and probably never could maintain. Cleopatra fits less neatly the Aristotelian mould. She shows no awareness of having made mistakes. Her tragedy is more the tragedy of her people in having such a weak and detached leader.

Though the play is essentially a historical love tragedy, following closely the facts of the events, Shakespeare (as he does in *Hamlet*, *King Lear* and *Macbeth*) interpolates elements of comedy to offset the tragedy and remind the audience that life is a mixture of both. Even in the pomp and ceremony with which powerful people attempt to give weight, dignity and authority to their acts, they are still human, still makes fools of themselves, and even the most well-organized rituals can go wrong or can be unintentionally ridiculous. The play can be seen as a piece of grim, dry humour mocking the pretensions of the great. The levity of Charmian, Iras and Alexas with their lewd jokes, the drunken scenes on board Pompey's galley, and the repetitious clowning of the death-bearing rustic are examples of fairly obvious broad humour. But there is a dimension of black or ironic humour. The ease with which Antony allows himself to be lured into marriage with Octavia is laughable. It is a foolish and ridiculous act that might make one smile and shake one's head in anticipation of disaster. Cleopatra's pathetic, schoolgirl manoeuvrings with Antony, her wildly vacillating mood swings, her suddenly remembering it is her birthday after the emotional fallout of Actium, her beating of the messenger, and her silencing of the dying Antony so that she can lament are all grimly comic. Antony too has his absurd moments. His overstated declarations of love would be better suited to an 18 year old. His furious outbursts, particularly with Thidias, and his readiness to placate Cleopatra when she is angry or jealous show his lack of self-control and betray his stupidity. Displacing anger onto others when you are to blame for the situation is amusing to the spectator. Angry outbursts are funny in general – they make us red-faced, we splutter to get our words out, make mistakes over our words and say silly things. The botched suicide, the difficulty the women have hauling the dying Antony into the monument, and his pathetic gasps of 'I am dying, Egypt, dying' and 'O quick or I am gone!' (IV. xv. 19, 43, 32) could be grimly comic if not delivered with careful pathos. They all darkly remind us of the vulnerability of man, the vanity of human pretensions, the absurdity of trying to endow our lives with dignity at moving moments and failing to do so. The vanity of all human pretensions was a given in this highly religious age. It has to be said that seeing humour in any of the scenes or phrases mentioned above depends crucially on the individual viewpoint and personal value system of the viewer. One member of the audience might grin to themselves or snort in derision, another might be moved to tears or silence. Comedy or tragedy is in the eyes, mind, heart and ethics of the beholder.

The Text Alone

Taken out of context the play is still comprehensible as a story of two lovers whose involvement with each other distracts them from their duties, leads them into conflict with a political rival and ends with their losing their states and their lives. Told thus the storyline is relatively simple and straightforward, but the Plutarch source is, even as a historical document, enriched by the moral context – i.e., the author's comments on Antony's behaviour and to a lesser extent that of Cleopatra. Plutarch makes judgements and sets the narrative within the values of his time. Written just over a hundred years after the events, the Greek text reflects the Roman values of an age that had seen the first ten or so emperors (including those instructive specimens Tiberius, Caligula and Nero) with all the accompanying power plays, court plots, sexual decadence, poisonings and assassinations. Despite the context of his own time, the historian still measures Antony's conduct against the expectations and virtues of the Republic, reflecting politics then as just as much of a precarious labyrinth and bloodbath as it was in imperial times. Two further contexts inform the assessments a Jacobean audience would make. While endorsing many of the Roman values, they would be influenced by the massive body of political writing about the requirements of ideal leadership appearing during the Renaissance (associated with the obvious comparisons that would be made with their current monarch) and the powerful Christian values of sin and virtue that formed the shared background of those viewing the piece in whichever venue it first appeared. Though the story works without its contexts, they add value and deepen and broaden the possible responses to the actions of the three lead characters, especially Antony and his mistress. The fascination of the text is in the complex and ambivalent presentation of the title characters and the constant giving and withdrawal of the audience's sympathy. It also lies in the resonances with contemporary political and court life. The play is diminished without its contexts.

Antony and Cleopatra in Shakespeare's Oeuvre

Stories from history were common sources for drama in the whole Elizabethan-Jacobean period. Chronicle Plays focusing on English history were immensely popular and continued to be so with the ordinary audiences at the public theatres. They had an intermittent interest too for individual writers as a means of commenting on contemporary society and politics via the mask of the past. The history play was seriously rivalled in the 1600s by much more topical satirical dramas, the City Comedies, focused on London and its problems. Other history plays drew from recent European historical incidents (like the story of Vittoria Accoramboni which provided the plot for John Webster's 1612 play *The White Devil* or the religious conflicts of France which provided the plot of Marlowe's 1593 *Massacre at Paris*). Yet others went back to pre-Christian pseudo-historical events such as those which feature in *Gorboduc* (1561), *Locrine* (c. 1580–1595), *King Lear* (1606). Classical subjects figure too, especially as Seneca's plays became available in Latin and then English editions. Jonson attempted two plays from Roman history: *Sejanus, His Fall* (1603) and *Catiline, His Conspiracy* (1611). That they did not please the public has more to do with Jonson's severely classical, Senecan style of writing dialogue than with the subjects, both of which in themselves would have been very much to the taste of the time.

Shakespeare first forayed into a Roman setting with his early drama *Titus Andronicus* (possibly 1588). As with his English history cycle, the Roman Plays seem only marginally intended to instruct the audience in history. They are not period drama,[2] but are more focused on the discussion of Elizabethan-Jacobean political/social problems disguised by the mask of the past. They also raise, of course, universal and perennial questions relating to the human condition. *Titus Andronicus*, influenced by Seneca's *Thyestes* (based on a very bloody myth), is concerned with revenge (later to be a popular subgenre), power, politics and the savagery men (and women) are capable of wreaking on their own kind.

Later in his career Shakespeare turned to classical history again with *Julius Caesar* (1599), *Antony and Cleopatra* (1606–07) and *Coriolanus* (1607–09). He also used ancient Athens as the setting for his satirical study of society *Timon of Athens* (1605–08).[3] Why should he have turned to these distant periods? Thomas North's translation of Plutarch (the source for the three Roman Plays) had been available since 1579. The contents and the handling of the stories are the clue. These are political plays, largely concerned with the nature of good and bad leadership, loyalty and betrayal, and the tension between the public and the private. Self-interest, ambition, intrigue and plotting are natural associations with such concerns, but too clear a reference to the Jacobean court was risky. Imprisonment, fines and censorship all played their part in deterring dramatists from being too person or event specific. Above all there was an ongoing, neurotic discourse about the flattery, that 'filthy vice',[4] that surrounds anyone in a governing role. Time and again writers refer to flattery as the most dangerous element in court life. The crucial need of monarchs to discriminate between those who told them the truth (however unpalatable) and those who smiled and lied to mislead or please, was ever present in the English court, indeed it was a recurrent staple of all politics. Richard Martin's welcome speech to James in 1603 warned: 'Curiosity of wit and affected straines of Oratory I leave to those, who more delight to tickle the princes eare, then satisfie his deeper judgement.' He advises the new king to 'practise your temperance and moderations for here flattery will essay to undermine, or force your Majesties strong constancie and integrity'.[5] Antony was lured by Cleopatra's flattery of his ego. As Plutarch puts it, 'Plato speaks of four kinds of flattery, but Cleopatra knew a thousand.'[6] Though *Julius Caesar* is the immediate historical predecessor of Antony's story, the second work is not a sequel. It stands alone despite similarities relating to the political power conflicts they both involve. The Antony of *Antony and Cleopatra* is a different character – older, weaker personally, though now extremely powerful as a triumvir. He is a man at the peak of his civic and political power, but deeply entangled with the Egyptian queen. He is no longer the youthful playboy hero of the first play who saves the Roman polity and earns the love of the people. He is situated at just the point Aristotle identified as suitable for a tragic hero's fall. What all four Roman pieces share is the atmosphere of plotting and ambition; lies and self-interest of coterie rule. The central characters are all from the privileged, power-holding and power-seeking rank and the plays all set off echoes of English court life. It is noticeable that all the Great Tragedies, Problem Plays and Roman Plays have a focus on politics and leadership and a cynical, negative view of humanity.

The Literature of the Time

It was once believed that Shakespeare was not topical or satirical, that the works of Jonson, Marston, Middleton, Dekker, Beaumont and Fletcher were more grounded in specific critiques of their times, while Shakespeare, though including some references to contemporary events, tended to be more concerned with the broad, universal problems of humanity divorced from the particularities of here and now. This view has changed. Between 1600 and 1606, Shakespeare became more engaged with contemporary social decadence, moral decline, and political questions connected to kingship, rule, power and punishment. This reflects a moralism evident in many playwrights, pamphleteers, polemicists and priests. The view that the time was out of joint is evident in *Troilus and Cressida* (1601–02), *All's Well That Ends Well* (1602–04), *Measure for Measure* (1604) and *King Lear* (1605–06). Like *Antony and Cleopatra*, the last two particularly deal with similar problems of imperfect leadership, the nature of government, authority and the complex ambiguities of both princely and personal morality. It is as if the plays originate from a common strand of thought and feeling, expressing a black melancholy about the nature of human beings. Yet within this period Shakespeare also wrote *Much Ado About Nothing, As You Like It* and *Twelfth Night*. No biographical evidence explains the bitterness of the author, but both *Measure for Measure* and *King Lear* share an extreme sense of darkness about humanity. Perhaps the more he saw of political life as a King's Player, the more cynicism bit. Ends of centuries tend to provoke ominous fears in people. Add to that a prevailing sense that the world (and society) is in decline and might end, and there is a potent recipe for gloom and pessimism about human kind. It was not only the drama that reflected this melancholy. In 1606 alone (the year Shakespeare was probably writing *Antony and Cleopatra*) *King Lear* was performed and *Macbeth* probably written. Both are very dark plays, both explore complex psychologies, both have strong political dimensions focused on governorship, both show the catastrophic outcomes of choosing the path of evil. The same year saw not only Tourneur/Middleton's disturbingly vicious portrait of court cunning, malice and violence, *The Revenger's Tragedy*,[7] but Jonson's virulent attack on greed and deception, *Volpone*. 1606 also saw Thomas Dekker's pamphlet *The Seven Deadly Sins of London* (an excoriating picture of his times), Barnabe Rich's pamphlet *Faults, Faults, and Nothing but Faults*, along with Dr Samuel Gardiner's *Doomsday Book* (a warning to Christians about the iniquity of the times and a wake-up call to those who had set their faces against piety).

Shakespeare was immersed in the world of theatre and the writers who inhabited it. Whatever he read or saw on the stage left traces in his own work. That process of acquiring impressions, images, words and phrases, storing them for later use, is common to all writers. He was also immersed in the outer world of Bankside, where theatres were interspersed with brothels, cheap taverns and crowded rickety tenements. Humanity teemed here, from rich to poor and everything in between: a world where cutpurses and conmen, silken courtiers going to the Globe (or a brothel) rubbed up against prentices on an afternoon jolly which might end in the pit of the theatre – after a suitably liquid lunch. There was the world north of the river where he lodged in Silver Street from at least 1603–05. Nearby was Cheapside, the City's commercial and civic artery, heaving with market traders and shopkeepers, the bustle, stink, emotions and dramas of everyday life. Cheapside was a wide thoroughfare used ceremonially for mayors and kings to process from the City to Westminster or the reverse, but chiefly functioning as the money, food and general goods hub of London, with stalls and shops and all the noisy activity associated with buying, selling and haggling. There were tallow chandlers, drapers, tailors, haberdashers, general mercers, timber sellers, butchers and above all goldsmiths. The luxury goods shops had a Continent-wide reputation. Silver Street housed a number of silversmiths' workshops.[8] Nearby Wood Street, Milk Street and Poultry indicate the products they chiefly sold. On Bread Street, running off the south side of Cheapside, was the Mermaid Tavern, where Shakespeare met to eat, drink and talk, talk, talk with Jonson, Middleton, Marston and other writers working for the King's Men. Though writing a play was usually a solitary activity, there was collaboration and much interchange of ideas and gossip. The Mermaid sessions probably generated many ideas that became interwoven in subsequent plays. In an age before newspapers, tavern chat circulated news and rumour, not always distinguishing between them.

Shakespeare was also intermittently part of another world – the court. A leading member of the King's Men, he was frequently involved in command performances at whatever palace the king happened to be in, for he and the other senior members of the company were made grooms of the chamber and, as members of the royal household, wore the royal livery.[9] This locus too had its dramas, its passions and emotional tangles. Literary influence, everyday life and the closed world of the court all intermix in his work.

The dominant literary genre of the time is the play, though pamphlets, poetry, sermons and other written polemic forms abounded and could be influential. The *Essayes* of Michel Montaigne (translated by John Florio and published in 1603) make a vital contribution to the issues Shakespeare deals with at this time and there are the more immediate influences of his historical source, Plutarch, and the literary borrowings from his recent and past reading. The vibrant tensions of the real world are mixed into the text too. These came from Shakespeare's own observations and ever-alert ears and re-emerge in the background figures – Mardian, Alexas, Charmian, Iras and the many servants and messengers – who bring the mundane world and the political world into the private domestic locus of Antony and his lover.

There is also a literary context relating to the topicality of the plays of the 1600s. The general tone of the theatre and theatre people naturally had an effect upon *Antony and Cleopatra*. Shakespeare spent much of his working, money-earning time in the Globe or at Blackfriars, as actor, writer, director and co-sharer in the business. Leisure time was spent with writers, discussing ideas, works in progress, what rival theatres were producing, what the company was about to present, what was popular with audiences, what pieces had failed, the mood of London and the state of the world, much as any group of work colleagues might. Fashions in the styles of plays reflected authors' tastes and educational backgrounds but also the demands of theatregoers. They constantly changed. Comedy was always a good bet for pleasing the public. Tragedy or serious topics were less certain, as Jonson discovered when his Senecan-style political tragedy *Sejanus His Fall* (1603) was rejected by the Globe audience. Chronicle histories (popularized by Marlowe's *Tamburlaine*, performed 1587), using the exotic foreign past or recent British history, were always likely to succeed. These introduced political themes not always possible to handle if they were too contemporary, but the King's Men also began to develop interest in stories of the fall of powerful men. This opened a market for tragedy focusing and sublimating current fascination with courtiers and favourites who rose, flourished magnificently, then fell spectacularly. The current political firmament was replete with falling stars not directly portrayed on stage, for the story of their eclipse raised questions about the rule of the monarch. The conduct of historical or fictional figures could represent *hubris* humbled and the audience could be left to make the contemporary identification. Increasingly there were city men whose rise to power and fall into infamy could be used as subject matter for tragedy or tragicomedy. Undercapitalized merchants overspeculating and civic politicians overreaching themselves attempting to move into the landowning nobility made apt subjects for didactic examples on the stage. Court corruption added to the popularity of Revenge Tragedy that continued into the late Stuart period of Charles II. Marlowe and Shakespeare combined chronicle history and tragedy, but also refined plays that focused on the personal downfall of charismatic fictional individuals, as in *Faustus* (performed 25 times between 1594 and 1597), *The Jew of Malta* (first performed in 1592) and Shakespeare's four Great Tragedies.

By the 1600s two subgenres were in fashion – the Revenge Tragedy and the City Comedy. The first type was triggered by Thomas Kyd's immensely popular *The Spanish Tragedy* (first performed c. 1582), followed by a flood of court-centred bloodthirsty stories of revenge carefully planned and cruelly executed. After *Hamlet* (1600), among the most well known are Marston's *Antonio's Revenge* (1601) and *The Malcontent* (c. 1603), Tourneur/Middleton's *The Revenger's Tragedy* (1606), Webster's *The Duchess of Malfi* (1612) and *The White Devil* (1612), and Middleton/Rowley's *The Changeling* (1622). Varying degrees of revenge form part of many dramas. In *Antony and Cleopatra*, the ostensible reason for Caesar's move against Antony is revenge. His family's honour has been insulted by the rejection of Octavia. This is only the official excuse for the inevitable political conflict. Caesar is not driven by deep-seated embitterment or a need to administer the 'wild justice'[10] of deserved punishment that generally motivates the malcontents in Revenge Tragedies. His discontent is only the excuse he was looking for. He has removed Lepidus from power and now needs to defeat Antony if he is to annexe Egypt's corn wealth for Rome and make himself autocrat. He may be seen as making a typical manoeuvre to gain political mastery, but also as an instrument of the gods' punishment of those who have grown too big, climbed too high, and become too arrogant and too remiss. In seeing themselves as gods, Antony and Cleopatra have offended and deserve retribution. To a Christian audience their behaviour offends not only the Seventh Commandment ('Thou shalt not commit adultery'), but the first and second ('Thou shalt have no other gods before me' and 'Thou shalt not make unto thee any graven image'), for they have made their love and lifestyle into an idol. They are just another example of negligent leadership, wantonness and extravagance.

City Comedy grew in response to the increasing importance of commerce in London and its emergence as a mercantile, financial, trading and transport centre rivalling Antwerp, Amsterdam and Venice. The expansion of its population and the flood of money running through it precipitated numerous social tensions. London became a decadent showcase for luxury consumerism, therefore attracting shallow wannabes and shady swindlers. At all social levels there were people who affected style and fashion, were ambitious for notoriety, celebrity and power. At all social levels there were parasites and tricksters scrounging and scamming money out of the foolish or unwary, providing playwrights with immense opportunities for comedy and satire. While would-be courtiers, dressed à la mode but without a penny in their purse, were mocked according to longstanding satiric tradition, humorous treatment of ambitious citizens and their snobbish wives and children, proliferated too. This reflected the rising profile and power of this relatively new force in urban society. The fabulous wealth of some provoked traditional complaints about luxury, vanity, avarice, envy and pride. These in turn triggered discussion, comment and judgement about materialism, loss of spiritual values, and questions of charity, poverty and crime. The old binary opposition of the industrious and the idle apprentice reappears in City Comedies to focus attention on conduct and misconduct. The status, definition and behaviour of gentlemen are also scrutinized.

Plays had become the 'brief chronicles of the time', reflecting growing tensions between the ranks as they began to change, blur and separate more widely. Satire is a tricky style, not always understood but often offensive. The 1597 satire *The Isle of Dogs* by Jonson and Thomas Nashe aggravated the authorities and was closed for being a 'lewd plaie' full of 'slanderous matter'. If it satirized the queen that was sedition. In 1559, very soon after her accession, Elizabeth I had issued a proclamation forbidding plays to discuss 'matters of religion or of the governance of the estate of the Commonwealth'. Such concerns were the province of 'grave and discreet persons', 'men of authority, learning and wisdom', not to be aired before or by the general public.[11] From 1581 until his death in 1610, as master of the revels Edmund Tilney demanded he or a deputy should see all plays before they could be performed in the theatre. No copy of the text of *The Isle of Dogs* exists, but its content was enough to have Jonson and two actors arrested and imprisoned. Tilney's sensitivity (or concern for the nation's moral health) was matched in 1605 by the king's own irritability when *Eastward Ho!* mocked the Scottish accent and the Scots' greedy depredations in London. The authors were imprisoned briefly. Jonson's persistent echoing of updated Juvenalian satirical targets in *Every Man out of His Humour* (1598), *Volpone* (1606) and *The Alchemist* (1612) created a lively atmosphere of criticism of contemporary mores.

In May 1606 an increasingly touchy king and increasingly defensive Commons passed the Act to Restrain Abuses of Players, with fines of £10 for each profane usage of the name of God or Jesus Christ during a performance – a blunt form of censorship that typically missed the point. It was society that needed cleansing. Shakespeare, as a keen observer of human greed, vanity, cruelty and selfishness, was drawn to offer his own satirical comments. By choosing a story set in the past, Shakespeare can make political and satirical points without fear of censorship, banning or imprisonment. He can also handle political matters (as part of genuine history) without fear of reprisal. *Antony and Cleopatra* has a degree of social criticism, suggestive of a wider corruption that expressed the split between the hypocrisy, venality and veniality of those in comfortable authority and the mass of servants and slaves on which the ancient world ran, a world where a small number of immensely rich and influential families held all the power and the rest obeyed. They are the rowers of the galleys, the legionaries in the armies and the servants in the palaces. The distant, pre-Christian settings of the Roman Plays, with their references to the Olympian panoply of deities, avoids the danger of blasphemy. Shakespeare never quite sits square in any of the subgenres. His history plays carry more than history in them, his love romances have cynical undertones, his satirical Problem Plays address more than the normal targets. Equally, his tragedy of Antony and his paramour, while telling the tragic, true history of their fall, is full of satirical comments on the nature of governance.

Sources

All the key features of the story derive from Sir Thomas North's 1579 translation of Plutarch's *Lives of the Noble Greeks and Romans*. There are some minor influences from other writings that contributed little more than details, words and phrases. Appian's *Roman History* provided some facts not present in Plutarch, but the 'Life of Antony' is by far and away the main source and, though largely about Antony, has significant and largely negative judgements of Cleopatra. Shakespeare's portrayal of Antony follows North very closely from the winter of 41–40 BC, which the lovers spent in Alexandria, to their deaths in 30 BC. Prior events are reported within the narrative, like the meeting on the Cydnus.

The play proper begins a little after the meeting at Tarsus, when Caesar needed to deal with Antony. The immediate problem is the military threat to security in Italy posed by Fulvia, Antony's brother and Pompey. The broader problem is that Antony, revelling in Alexandria, is not administering the restless Eastern provinces. That winter various deputations (mostly ex-soldiers) tried to persuade Antony to address the growing crisis in Parthia and Media. This is where the play begins and Shakespeare has Fulvia's death reported in Alexandria, as it neatly coalesces the personal and the political. Historically, when news of Fulvia's death arrived Antony was in Italy negotiating the treaty of Brundisium, which gave him suzerainty of the East. Therefore he was not with Cleopatra. By having it happen in Cleopatra's court, Shakespeare can create considerable drama out of the queen's reactions.

Plutarch showed Shakespeare that the age of Antony and the political struggles of the late Republic were not dissimilar to the Wars of the Roses and the Tudor-Stuart period, with continual outbursts of bloody violence, a perpetual atmosphere of political rivalry, plots, suspicion, assassinations and the rising and falling of figures of power. In *Antony and Cleopatra* he wrestles with the messy succession of events of actual history, discarding and condensing them in order to provide a clear, strong storyline. Plutarch's biased portrayal covers all of Antony's life (83–30 BC), indeed commencing with the family background and military and political experiences of his father and paternal grandfather. The play only covers the last ten years of Antony and Cleopatra's lives, condensed radically (he dying at 47 or 50, she at 39).

Shakespeare had considerable experience of manipulating multiple characters and varied narrative strands, choosing which incidents to represent, which to report, which to discard. Early in his career he had marshalled the mass of details, encounters and personages of the Wars of the Roses sequence of *Henry VI* (three parts, 1590–92) and *Richard III* (1593), then *Richard II* (1595), *King John* (1596–97), *Henry IV* (two parts, 1597–98) and *Henry V* (1599). These were sourced mostly from Holinshed's *Chronicles*, but there were multiple other historical and poetical sources in which the writer could find useful details. With this play Plutarch is the only source for the base narrative, but a few verbal borrowings are evident from a poem and play by Samuel Daniel (*Letter from Octavia* and *Cleopatra*) and a French play translated by the Countess of Pembroke.[12] There is an interesting version too in Chaucer's *Legend of Good Women*, which Shakespeare must have known. The Pyramus and Thisbe story (*A Midsummer Night's Dream*) came from it and the Cleopatra story immediately precedes it.[13]

By the time he began *Antony and Cleopatra* Shakespeare was well used to giving coherence and meaning to the sometimes inchoate and awkward events of history, collapsing long time scales and multiple locations. History's underlying story is often littered with details that distract from and diffuse the narrative. Antony's life is full of digressive incidents and Shakespeare strips away much of Plutarch to streamline the narrative, discarding or concentrating details in order for the impelling action to emerge and focus the power collision between the lovers and the 'scarce-bearded' up-and-coming Caesar. Whether handling the seismic political struggles for mastery of England or the Roman world, the themes addressed are the same: leadership, loyalty, betrayal, plotting and the brutality and cunning of man. Such concerns, particularly portraits of leaders, were of intense interest to Shakespeare's audiences – whether the broad social range of the Globe, the narrower niche market of the private Blackfriars theatre or the even more restricted court clientele. Plutarch's 'Life of Antony' is full of betrayals, changing alliances, inter-family plots, senatorial intrigues, short-term rises to high-profile government and catastrophic falls, power plays and bloodshed.

All such incidents would be seen as less instructive of Roman history than illustrative of English court politics. Antony's grandfather had been executed in the Sullan Civil War. His father had unsuccessfully fought a sea battle and lost much of his fleet, but was renowned for his benevolence, honesty and generosity. These are personal qualities Antony shared and political experiences he would come to share. Plutarch acknowledges his subject's good characteristics, but unsparingly and persistently traces his failures in living up to the heroic image he cultivated. He highlights that his passion for Cleopatra was 'the fatal influence' lying 'dormant' while 'wiser counsels' prevailed, how it 'blazed once more into life' and Antony 'flung away all those nobler considerations of restraint that might have saved him'.[14] This is virtually a definition of *hamartia*, and thus Shakespeare situates his hero.

The tension between show and substance was something the audience would consciously connect with particular characters at court. The youthful Antony – a heavy drinker, womanizer and spendthrift, living a libertine existence – is also the adult Antony. He was 'boastful, insolent, and full of empty bravado and misguided aspirations',[15] as displayed in his desperate third and fourth act optimism. London was full of such 'Roaring Boy' wasters. Some were probably in the audience, the by-product of a hierarchy topped by wealthy, titled families, bred to do nothing. Rome was not dissimilar. Several examples are given of Antony's physical courage and his ability to lead and inspire loyalty, but his moral decadence and political naiveté are plentifully evident. Appearance-wise he had a 'bold and masculine look', a thick beard, aquiline nose and broad forehead. He cultivated this Herculean look, believing he was descended from the hero, but it also chimes in with his projected showman image. When he had to address large crowds he would often dress with tunic belted low down on his hips, a voluminous, heavy cloak and an impressively large sword at his side. Plutarch describes how Antony used to eat with his troops, joining in and enjoying their vulgar conversation. So rough and lewd was his style of conversation that Cleopatra adjusted her own style to join him. The play's several allusions to Hercules are triggered by Plutarch. Like Cleopatra, Antony had a penchant for staging large-scale theatrical events that had him and his mistress at the focal point. He liked to think of himself as Mars or Hercules or Dionysus. Specific references, and some allusions, are made to the pair masquerading as Mars and Venus, Dionysus and Isis, Hercules and Omphale. He had a 'weakness for the opposite sex',[16] and was given to cultivating a theatrical appearance, making extravagant (often hollow) gestures and ostentatiously displaying his wealth and power.[17] The 'Life' reflects a continual flow of interchanging positives and negatives, greatness of heart countered by petty jealousies and spiteful, sometimes unchivalrous and ignoble behaviour. For all his aspiring to a heroic, great-hearted image, Antony seemed constantly mired in degradations. Overall Plutarch has a poor opinion of Antony.

Shakespeare deviates from Plutarch in virtually omitting the long, complex and disastrous Parthian campaign. In Plutarch the Parthian war occupies many pages. Shakespeare also excises Antony's married life with Octavia. This lasted from 40 to 37 BC, when the pregnant Octavia was sent away and Antony returned to the East to renew his affair with Cleopatra. He divorced Octavia five years later (32 BC). The years spent with Octavia (and their two children) are cut to speed the plot, to give the sense of a brief politically motivated union and to use her unexpected return to Rome as Caesar's excuse to push towards an official rupture between the two men. In fact, after the pact made at Misenum with Pompey (39 BC) Antony made Athens his headquarters and he and Octavia lived there for a year and a half. He had coins issued with himself and various Dionysian emblems on them; by 42 BC the people of Ephesus had come to identify him with the god. The couple lived in Athens as happy leaders of society and patrons of various cultural events. Excising this leaves the marriage as nothing but a cynical political move (on Antony's and Caesar's part), in line with many Roman (and Jacobean) marriages – a political peace-making alliance only. It also strengthens the sense of Cleopatra's hold on Antony that he cannot keep away for very long. In the play there is the feeling that very little time elapses between the arrangement of the alliance and Antony's dismissing Octavia to Rome. Agrippa proposes the union in Act II Scene ii and seven scenes later, in Act III Scene ii, Octavia returns to Rome. (Onstage this takes minutes. In real time it was three years.)

Enobarbus confirms Cleopatra's hold by his comments when the marriage is first arranged: 'He will to his Egyptian dish again' and 'He married but his occasion here' (II. vi. 128, 133). This tragic prolepsis adds to the feeling of the inevitability of the clash between Caesar and Antony as well as enforcing the sense of Antony being spellbound by love (or lust). Scarus talks of his general as 'the noble ruin of her magic' (III. x. 19) and other references hint that Cleopatra has bewitched Antony. Plutarch talks of the 'spell and enchantment' Cleopatra's physical presence could create.[18] Shakespeare builds up the character of Enobarbus (minimally present in Plutarch), and makes him into a vocal, cynical chorus, loyal to his leader but commenting on him too with clear sight and common sense. He is a constant counterbalance to the hyperbole and theatrics of the protagonists, representing a down-to-earth soldier's view, rather vulgar at times, but direct and grounded in the realities of life. He is the non-flattering, sincere friend political theorists thought essential as a companion to rulers, and maintains, for the audience, a rational voice among the simmering, overblown, unreal, insincere emotions both of Alexandria and of Rome. In Plutarch's history Enobarbus deserts before Actium, whereas Shakespeare has him remain loyal for much longer. This demonstrates Antony's capacity for generating loyalty, but also shows how even the most supportive man will eventually leave as a fool falls, deaf to advice and blind to his own safety. It was a relationship developed in detail between the Fool and Lear in the same period. At the point when Enobarbus leaves Antony's entourage his general's military decisions have become a fatal joke. Shakespeare and his contemporaries portray many different courts and their hangers-on. The loyalty of honest men and disloyalty of flattering feeders is staged time and again and must always have set off resonant echoes of the London court merry-go-round.

Shakespeare's story follows Plutarch's Antony from the peak of his political power (one of the triumvirs ruling his third of the empire) through to his defeat and demise. The progress of the play is from confident (and therefore hubristic) prosperity to ridiculous, pathetic misery. Many critics see the catastrophe stage as bringing out the nobility of the characters through the poetical sentiments they express. These sentiments may also be seen as baseless expressions of courage in the face of adversity, fine words signifying nothing as their lives collapse in confusion, doubtful motives, and the petty machinations and countermoves of politics.

Shakespeare only uses the last two-thirds of Plutarch's narrative to fill out the details of the play. Plutarch devotes space to dealing with Antony's clashes with the politician Dolabella and his irrational, automatic opposition to anything Dolabella proposed, spurred on by the jealousy of a rival for Julius Caesar's ear. Dolabella's role in the play is minor and the antagonism between the two is given little traction in the narrative. Plutarch also traces in detail the instinctive dislike between Antony and Octavius that began at their first meeting. The scene with the soothsayer introduces the idea that Octavius Caesar is Antony's nemesis, rival and constant victor, setting up a classic opposition like that of the Macbeth/Malcolm and Othello/Iago pairings. It is not just an opposition of good and bad but of a fated pair with one the destined destructor of the other. The triumvirate was born in blood and proceeds in blood. Caesar, Lepidus and Antony's betrayal of their friends as they traded for power is only partially reflected in the play, but the shadow of its polluted beginnings mars its continuation, and marks the inevitable conflict of the two masters of the universe.

The play is so streamlined and fast-paced as to feel in performance as if it takes only a few days. The timescale is unimportant; it is the action and outcome that hold attention. This was suited to the open, uncluttered stage with no sets, only easily moved thrones, tables and benches.

Characters enter, speak, exit and the next group follows immediately. Navies and armies are implied, reported by spectators (as are the battles) or represented onstage by small groups acting as the visible front men (as in Act III Scene i where Ventidius enters 'as it were in triumph' with 'Silius and other Romans, Officers and Soldiers, the dead body of Pacorus borne before him'). The onstage cast is often large. Many of them, speakers and non-speakers, will be doubling up parts and making multiple and speedy costume changes. There are 36 individually named characters, plus servants, messengers, sentries, the dead body of Pacorus, Roman officers, and the massed soldiers and mariners to be imagined in the background. The pace of succeeding scenes, many of them short, is typical of all the history plays. It also gives the sense of a rush to disaster, slow to start but speeding up and becoming unstoppable. This is typical of the tragic dénouement.

Historically (and within the play's scope) Antony's best days were behind him and though he had enjoyed the high points of popular reputation and military success, his life was scattered with scandalous events and multiple indications of his personality flaws. Some features of Antony's past, recounted in Plutarch, are reported in Shakespeare's dialogue, some by friends, others by those ill-disposed towards him. The prurient curiosity of Rome-based characters is a way to describe the excesses of his life in Egypt and advance the persistent opposition of Roman, male, militaristic values to Egyptian, female, feminizing attitudes. Antony's handling of the volatile situation after Julius Caesar's murder saved the Republic from prolonged civil war, but he later mismanaged his own affairs so foolishly as to provoke conflict. This is Shakespeare's starting point.

In keeping with Aristotelian expectations, the drama charts his fall from prosperity (with some reports of his past glories). It has him at the height of his official power, but already in the trammels of his fatal involvement with Cleopatra. His *hamartic* weaknesses are already in place: libertinism, a tendency towards a luxurious and extravagant lifestyle, and an absurd, besotted attraction to a double-dealing and unreliable queen, an obsession he is incapable of controlling. In discussing the effects of dalliance and kissing, Robert Burton asserts: 'It was Cleopatra's sweet voice, and pleasant speech, which inveigled Antony, above the rest of her enticements. As a bull's horns are bound with ropes, so are men's hearts with pleasant words. Her words burn as fire.'[19] In discussing the tricks and potions used by bawds, he claims she 'used Philters to inveigle Antony, amongst other allurements'.[20] The play too makes suggestions of some sort of witchcraft being worked upon Antony. That alone would have damned Cleopatra in the eyes of most Jacobeans, though love had always been linked to magic, spells, potions and an uncontrollable state where the soundness of the mind was lost – a means to explain the psychological fixation and emotional bonding experienced in love. It would, however, be wrong to see this play as celebrating great love. There is no doubt Romeo loves Juliet and vice versa. The matter is more open to question here. Plutarch makes clear his mistrust of Cleopatra. A contemporary audience would largely see it as an instructive morality play demonstrating the consequences of folly and lust at a personal and public level. There is no question the lovers are charismatic, larger-than-life characters, but they are not to be applauded. Antony's failings in the political sphere were evident early on. As a tribune (spokesman for the people) he won the admiration of the soldiery by joining them in their exercises, eating with them and giving gifts. But the civilian population found him lazy in dealing with complaints, unwilling to spend time listening to problems, and all too ready to pursue sexual intrigues. His lifestyle, similar to that of many at Whitehall, caused offence, scandalized many and 'earned him the contempt of all men of principle'.[21] Plutarch seems largely to agree with Cicero's 'drink-sodden, sex-ridden' view of Antony. Shakespeare projects his hero as a very similar character, but the question remains whether Antony has any redeemable features that make him a man whom the audience can pity.

Minor elements are contributed by other writers. Appian of Alexandria (AD c. 95–c. 165) may have provided the details of the separate wars waged against Italy and Caesar by Antony's brother Lucius and Sextus Pompey. The latter is mentioned only very briefly by Plutarch and the former not at all. Some verbal echoes come from the Countess of Pembroke's play *Antonius*, translated from the French of Robert Garnier's play *Marc Antoine*. Her English version was printed in London in 1592. It seems clear Shakespeare had read the book, for in addition to the eight or so close verbal echoes in evidence,[22] thematically it prioritizes rational control and duty over the senses and personal relationships. These echoes hardly warrant Muir's claim that 'the verbal links are substantial', but they appear to have stuck in Shakespeare's memory and reappear in the writing of his play.[23] This is how poets work, gathering ideas, phrases and words, storing them, then using them later as needed. Such identical verbal or phrasal borrowings are just that – not sources, but borrowings and influences only. Much of the ethical underpinning in *Antonius* is angled towards that traditional view that those born to public position had a duty to care for the community, which is how many audiences would assess the Antony situation anyway. The countess's translation may have lain dormant in Shakespeare's mind and then been triggered when he began to contemplate Antony's history. Other possible influences are Samuel Daniel's poem *Letter to Octavia* (1599) and his play *Cleopatra*.

LITERARY CONTEXT 217

In the prose argument that introduces the poem, Daniel describes the Octavia marriage:

> *Antonie* hauing yet vpon him the fetters of *Ægypt*, layd on by the power of a more incomparable beauty, could admit no new Lawes into the state of his affection, or dispose of himself, being not himself, but as hauing his heart turned Eastward, whither the poynt of his desires were directed, touched with the strongest allurements that ambition, and a licentious soueraignty could draw a man vnto.[24]

The word 'fetters' appears too in Shakespeare ('These strong Egyptian fetters I must break' [I. ii. 122]). Daniel also refers to Octavia's 'modesty', a word picked up by Maecenas (II. ii. 251). There are numerous other comments suggesting Antony will be drawn back to the East to his 'Egyptian dish'. Again, these are lexical influences that may have further triggered interest in looking at Antony in the period after that covered in *Julius Caesar*. The representation of his character in the second play is very different from that of the first. Antony emerges as a deeply and variously tainted man, a massive wreck. Almost every new step he takes in his life expresses his inner weaknesses. Even his previous marriage had unforeseen consequences; his relationship with Fulvia foreshadows that with Cleopatra, for Fulvia was, in Plutarch's words,

> not so basely minded to spend her time in spinning and housewivery, and was not contented to master her husband at home, but would also rule him in his office abroad, and commaund him that commanded legions and great armies: so that Cleopatra was to give Fulvia thankes for that she had taught Antonius this obedience to women, that learned so well to be at their commaundment.[25]

Here is a basic and grave gender role reversal. The transgression is made worse by Antony's apparent compliance with such a subversion of hierarchy. His authority was further subverted by his underlings taking or forcing bribes in the realms of the Eastern empire: 'He over-simply trusted his men in all things. For he was a plaine man, without subtletie.'[26] Plutarch's comments on Antony's strength in adversity set him up as an ideal subject for a tragedy: 'It was characteristic of Antony to show his finest qualities in the hour of trial, and indeed it was always when his fortunes were at their lowest that he came nearest to being a good man.' He also makes a significant point: 'Many people become so discouraged by adversity that they give way to their habits all the more and allow their judgement to collapse.'[27] Bacon asserted that while 'prosperity doth best discover vice, [...] adversity doth best discover virtue'.²⁸ Antony's vices certainly emerged through the privileged life he was born into, but it may be questioned whether the adversities he faces bring out his virtues. They seem simply to re-emphasize his weaknesses and encourage hollow bluster.

A further source may have influenced that aspect of Shakespeare's treatment of Cleopatra that presents her as a martyr for love. This is an alternative to the traditional view of her as a Delilah figure. Shakespeare's ambivalent handling of Cleopatra as not only devious and dominant but as also possibly truly loving Antony may well have been suggested by Chaucer's presentation of her in *The Legend of Good Women*. This poem, in the common medieval form of a dream vision, was previously used by Shakespeare for his Pyramus and Thisbe story for the mechanicals' play in *A Midsummer Night's Dream*. 'The Legend of Thisbe of Babylon' follows the very first story, 'The Legend of Cleopatra'. The prologue has Queen Alceste demanding the poet recount the lives of virtuous women to counter his misogynistic treatment of them in *The Canterbury Tales* and *Troilus and Criseyde* (a subject Shakespeare used in 1601–02). She commands him to begin with Cleopatra, as a challenge to men, showing a woman who had 'doon so strong a peyne for love' (undergone such suffering for love). The legend begins with Antonius 'fallen in prosperitee' and having become 'rebel unto the toun of Rome', leaving his wife ('suster of Cesar') to 'han [have] another'. This caused 'with Rome and Cesar stryf'. This account puts the Octavia marriage before Antony met Cleopatra. Antony is a 'worthy gentil werreyour' (sensitive and chivalrous warrior), 'but love had broght this man in swich a rage' (love had become such a passion) that he was 'narwe bounden in his las' (tightly entangled in his love's snare). In the Courtly Love manner Antonius does not wish to die in battle but 'to love and serve'. He is described as being a man of 'persone' (presence), 'gentilesse' (sensitivity), 'discrecioun' and 'hardinesse', as well as of 'desert' (merit) and 'chivalrye', so he has both the qualities of a knight and of a sensitive lover. The queen is described as 'noble' and 'fair as is the rose in May'. The couple perform a wedding ceremony and have a wedding feast, but indulge in none of the decadent, frivolous living of Shakespeare's couple. They are projected as being high ranking, of noble qualities, suitable icons of the medieval concept of love. The legend moves on to describe the sea battle. Antony is defeated and escapes, and 'fleeth eke the queen' (the queen flees also). In this version Cleopatra's flight comes after Antony's and does not trigger her lover's desertion. Antony defeated laments he was ever born, laments his loss of honour:

> And for dispeyr out of his witte he sterte,
> And roof [pierced] him-self anoon through-out the herte
> Er that he ferther wente out of the place.

The story is considerably foreshortened compared with the Plutarch and Shakespeare versions; there is only one day-long sea battle, followed by Antony's immediate suicide. Shakespeare diminishes the suicide by drawing out the death, and reduces its dignity and effect further by having Antony call upon his servant, Eros, to do the deed, and having Eros shame him by efficiently killing himself rather than kill his master. While Chaucer seeks to present the couple as noble and admirable examples of aristocratic values, Shakespeare, at nearly every opportunity, displays his protagonists as petty, bumbling, undignified and ineffective.

Cleopatra, 'that coude of Cesar have no grace' (who could elicit no sympathetic treatment – 'grace' being the quality of mercy and graciousness expected from a leader), flees to Egypt, making such lamentation it cannot be described, and has her workmen build a shrine of all the rubies and 'stones fyne' she can find, fills the place with spices and has Antony's body embalmed and shut into the tomb. She then has a pit dug alongside his shrine, fills it with 'alle the serpents that she might have', leaps into it and is bitten to death, 'naked, with ful good herte' – a very different end to Shakespeare, despite Chaucer's avowal 'this is storial sooth [historical truth], hit is no fable'. There is some doubt about the truth of the death by snake venom. Horace and Virgil speak of death by snake bite, though some historians relate that Cleopatra had studied various poisons and their effects, implying she poisons herself. Before lying in her fatal bed she delivers a speech to Antony as her 'love', her 'knight' who was nere [never] out of myn hertes remembraunce'. She reminds his spirit that she swore that whatever happened to him (good or bad), she would share the same 'lyf or deeth'. She will keep that covenant and prove there was 'never unto hir love a trewer queen'. (Chaucer omits, or did not know of, her ritualized dressing for death and lying on a golden couch.) This vignette (only 125 lines) owes nothing to Plutarch and is different in significant ways. It clearly typifies a powerful love and sacrifice.

The legend finishes with the words 'Explicit Legenda Cleopatrie, Martiris' (Thus ends the legend of Cleopatra the martyr). Her final speech too highlights her love, her complete identification with Antony in 'wele or wo' and in 'lyf or deeth'. Plunging naked into a pit of snakes is more dramatically spectacular and horrific than in Shakespeare, but the later writer handles her death more effectively and practically for a stage performance and it is more dignified and quietly managed. Noticeably, Chaucer's queen reacts immediately to her lover's suicide and there is no hint of her provoking it. Finally, and most importantly, there is no doubt that Chaucer's Cleopatra deeply loves Antonius. There is no devious paltering with Caesar and the sincerity of her love is not in doubt. Shakespeare presents a more complex character whose true feelings and motives are unclear. She is altogether more political.

At the end she perhaps discovers and expresses a sort of love for Antony precipitated by the sense of her own hopelessness. She has to valorize her life with him and declaring love for him and horror at his loss, whether she feels it or not, at least appears to justify her past and present actions. But not entirely.

Chapter 14

POLITICAL CONTEXT

The Eyeless Face

> To be called into a huge sphere and not to be seen to move in't, are the holes where eyes should be, which pitifully disaster the cheeks.
> (II. vii. 14–16)

It is ironic that one of the most telling political judgements should be made by a servant. It is a reminder that the acts of the great are always judged at the bar of the common people and that disregard for their views is a dangerous policy. This was certainly so in the increasingly critical atmosphere of Jacobean England, where the lavishness, drunkenness and general decadence of the gentry and the court were becoming an all-too-common topic of discussion and escalating anger. The servant is referring to Lepidus's inebriation and the growing boisterous booziness of the political leaders of Rome on board Pompey's galley. It is a scene reminiscent of the revels in Alexandria and a sign that Rome was equally capable of unrestrained, undignified behaviour. What makes this more serious, however, is that these are men making decisions about the state's security and have put themselves in a vulnerable situation. It is only the skewed sense of honour shown by Pompey that saves them from being assassinated and the whole history of Rome lurching in another direction. A few scenes previously Antony had spoken gravely of 'the world and my great office' (II. iii. 1). By Act III Scene vi he has cast Octavia aside, returned to his pleasure, and set his downfall in motion for failing to move in his 'huge sphere' and 'great office'.

The Roman Plays, like the Great Tragedies and Problem Plays, are suffused with political matters. They are full of dissimulation, flattery, ambition, rivalry, scheming, strategic murders and political takeovers. Shakespeare seems, at this period, to be preoccupied by the nature, extent and style of governing states.

It would be wrong to assume this is an abstract and theoretical exploration of political philosophy. Few in the original audience would not see similarities, however distant, to the conduct of their own courtiers and politicians. It would be equally wrong to see references to specific issues or persons; all the settings are masked by period or place. Nevertheless, the image of the eyeless face of the leader of men is potent and would reverberate loudly in an age beginning to raise voices against the traditional monopoly of power held by kings and nobles who regarded the state as their property to do with as they liked. The blind-eye image is also used in *King Lear* where the king advises the blinded Gloucester: 'Get thee glass eyes;/And like a scurvy politician, seem/To see the things thou dost not' (IV. vi.). The incompetence of politicians (and schemers, for 'politician' could mean a shyster) was increasingly portrayed onstage and visible in everyday life as James I's regime revealed its continuing corruption and increasing corruptibility. The long-standing complaints of the public against untrustworthy lawyers, the judiciary biased in favour of the upper ranks, tax farmers, monopolists, enclosers and all the rest of the tainted governing elite continued to gain relevance. The problems proliferated as James allowed favourites to hold increasing sway and as the court turned in on itself, secured more of a hold on power and purse (royal and public), and lived as a self-perpetuating, self-sufficient society-within-society. The promise that bubbled in 1603 had burst by 1606.

The view of the great too is voiced. Antony's reference to 'our slippery people/Whose love is never linked to the deserver/Till his deserts are past' (I. ii. 192–4) and Caesar's remark that 'he that is was wished for until he were' (I. iv. 42) are a reminder of the reality of politics. Leaders may be blind but the led are fickle. The 'common body' is like a reed in water going whichever way the current drifts (I. iv. 44–7).

Examined closely, *Antony and Cleopatra*, rather than a love tragedy, may appear more obviously a play about political demands and political realities within a known historical context. It demonstrates that 'dignity and love cannot be reconciled with the struggle for power which forms the matter of history'.[1] It employs a love affair between two highly placed leaders of the world as the means of triggering a conflict with and a power play by Caesar. His move to take sole power was probably inevitable, and Antony's failure to co-operate in dealing with the problems that affected the security of Italy, his neglect of his corporate responsibilities and his ill-planned handling of Rome's interests in the East simply made that clash happen sooner. The Octavia alliance gave Antony a second chance to establish a means of keeping the peace between himself and Caesar, but his inevitable mishandling of the opportunity gave his rival the excuse he needed. It also enabled Rome to invade and take over a vital grain source. Up until then Egypt had been a *de facto* client state but still officially independent. Rome needed its corn, its wealth and for it to no longer be a faraway state of uncertain loyalty with considerable influence in the region and the potential for heading up a disaffected alliance of Eastern kingdoms.

The large proportion of the play is concerned with politics. Philo's opening comments set the theme and the dominant concern – the negligent running of Rome's Eastern empire. This is outer world, overt politics. The love story – domestic and gender politics – is intertwined, the underlying driver of decisions and actions on Antony's part, always serving to enhance or inhibit the political development. The majority of the scenes incorporate either wholly or partially matters of state and power. There are many short scenes that move the action back and forth widely throughout the Roman world and each involves reports of battles fought, marches made and political moves executed. There are meetings to discuss policy, to conciliate partners in the triumvirate, and a number of messengers bring news or take information to other parties. Many are nameless minions, but others are named ambassadors and negotiators. Underlying all this busy to-ing and fro-ing is Antony's slow collapse and Cleopatra's contribution to it.

Much of the factual element, taken from Plutarch, is reported rather than represented. In this Shakespeare uses the practice of the classical Greek drama to assist him in handling the multiple incidents of history. Battles, murders and other key events were reported by messengers or the chorus because they could not be staged. In this story the actual train of events was exceptionally complex and stretched over many years.[2] Shakespeare streamlines and simplifies these in order to keep the narrative flowing, omits some features and condenses the timeline. The free-running performance common to Elizabethan historical drama facilitates this. Scenes run from one to the other without having to change scenery, for none is used.[3] Locations are given in the dialogue, events are discussed in order to bring the audience up to date with developments, and the passage of years is omitted, so that the whole process seems to take place within weeks or days. The outer world of plotting, rumour and intrigue is still a dominant aspect of what is supposed to be a love story, one of the great romances. In fact romance is in short supply, while deviousness and hidden motives abound. The protagonists are drawn into, submerged and eventually swamped by the politics they thought they could ignore. The duty they neglected catches up with them. Shakespeare puts the relationship firmly in its public dimension and displays how ill the human and the personal sit within politics. In tune with his other plays of this period, he is more concerned with exposing bad government than elevating love. The play concurs with William of Malmesbury: 'Majesty and love do not go together.'[4] Kott, discussing history and power, asserts that 'generals and rulers are good or bad, wise or stupid, prudent or mad. Antony was mad, and he lost.'[5] History is cruel because having power or seeking it makes people do cruel things and love makes people do mad things. Put the two together and you have an exciting fatal mixture. Paglia links the two in saying of Antony: 'A leader cannot live by love alone. Antony betrays his men, and he betrays himself.'[6]

It has recently become more fully recognized that there is a good deal more politics in Shakespeare's writing than was traditionally perceived. This is most true of the works from *Hamlet* (1599–1602) onwards. There are some topical connections with the English scene, but much more relating to current discourses about political theories. The petty games of love do not allow majesty to show through, they reduce it to the degraded jealousies, misperceptions and madnesses of love. In *A Midsummer Night's Dream* the mistakes and mayhem that love causes are a source of amusement. In *Othello* and *Antony and Cleopatra* love and jealousy cause disaster on a larger scale, for when the demands of neglected public duty have increased to crisis point, disaster strikes. The fall of a public figure has more collateral consequences. Shakespeare conforms to the values of his time in showing how unrestrained passion is dangerous, how female freedom within the public domain is dangerous, and how male libertinism does not accord with morality or civic duty. All these features resonate with the tone and manner of English politics, court life and the mores of the time. In addition to the current interest in matters to do with government and governors, there was a contemporary concern with stories in which princes were brought low by allowing sexual desire to occupy too dominant a place in their lives. The Revenge Tragedies are full of such plotlines.

The play presents not just the central powerbrokers – Antony and Caesar – but brings in subsidiary forces seeking power. There are Pompey and the pirates, Menas and Menecrates, there is brief mention of Fulvia's wars, and in the background the Parthian rebels defeated by Ventidius. Reported also are all 'the kings o' th' earth' (III. vi. 69) Antony levies as allies in the fight against Rome. In an act of political theatre (known as the Donations of Alexandria), calculated to alarm and irritate Rome, Antony, with Cleopatra dressed as Isis, staged a formal, public gifting of the key provinces of the East.

> I' th' market-place, on a tribunal silvered,
> Cleopatra and himself in chairs of gold
> Were publicly enthroned. At the feet sat
> Caesarion, whom they call my father's son,
> And all the unlawful issue that their lust
> Since then hath made between them. Unto her

> He gave the stablishment of Egypt; made her
> Of lower Syria, Cyprus, Lydia,
> Absolute Queen. (III. vi. 3–11)

To consolidate his dynasty further, Antony then gave away to his sons Media, Parthia, Armenia, Syria, Cilicia and Phoenicia. These gifts of the hard-won East mark Antony breaking free of alliance with Rome and setting up an independent empire. It is not without significance that one of his and Cleopatra's sons was called Alexander Helios, while Cleopatra's family, the Ptolemies, were descended from one of Alexander the Great's Macedonian generals and the Eastern kingdoms were once part of the Hellenic Empire. Antony, disposing of this region, sees himself as the new Alexander. Caesar, Maecenas and Agrippa are suitably horrified at this dismantling of Rome's power. They express themselves in such a way as to hint at blasphemous *hubris* in the staging of this event, in the masquerade of the queen as the chief female goddess of Egyptian mythology, and in Antony's public largesse of what would be seen in Rome as not his to give away. As triumvir he is a steward, not an owner. Tensions escalate at this news, but lurch closer to catastrophe when Octavia returns as a cast-off wife. Before listing the kings Antony is recruiting to oppose Rome, Caesar comments, 'Cleopatra hath/ Nodded him to her. He hath given his empire/Up to a whore' (III. vi. 66–8).

All these aspects tie in to the theme of the inappropriate conduct of a ruler (and its consequences) and would provoke thoughts in the audience relative to how those concerns resonated in English political life. An inescapable feature of this is Antony's status as a privileged Roman of patrician background. In both Rome and England it was automatically assumed that a young man of rank and established ancestry had access to power and the money that power gave access to. The gates were open regardless of whether a young man of such background was fitted for any of the roles of power. Family contacts, influence and money – in other words, nepotism and bribery – could gain you a place whether you were suitable or not. It was clear from early on that Antony did not entirely possess the requisites for rule. (The same could be said of King James.) Antony's mother was noble and virtuous. She was the archetype of those Roman matrons who, excluded from public life themselves, prepared their sons, through a severely disciplined and virtue-led upbringing, to assume power and achieve high honour, and then lived in the reflected glory of their success, sometimes even influencing affairs via their offspring. The youthful promise of Antony soon went awry. His friend Curio was a voluptuary, 'wholly enslaved to the demands of pleasure'. To make Antony more pliable he inducted him into 'a life of drinking bouts, love affairs, and reckless spending'.[7] By the time this friendship had ended it was too late. The pattern of Antony's lifestyle was fixed; always living well beyond his means, believing civic posts would come his way simply because of his background and that the public purse would supply his needs. (The Whitehall court contained many like-minded young men.) Dishonestly grabbed from the late Pompey the Great's property, Antony's town house and country villas were renowned for lavish banquets and orgies. The Alexandrian Antony is simply following his established life pattern but at a higher level. He had achieved celebrity status by his persistent attention-seeking hedonism, by the right contacts and by being in the right place at the right time. Whatever his abilities, his conduct and immoral proclivities made him a less than admirable figure – how like many of the rich, witling courtiers of James I's court, where the political system was little different from the late Republic's ongoing transition into one-man rule under Caesar and the subsequent excesses of ruthless absolutism experienced under the emperors. As with Vienna (*Measure for Measure*) and pagan Britain (*King Lear*), the Roman past becomes a correlative for the Jacobean present.

The central political plot strand concerns Antony's relationship with Caesar. A subsidiary of this is how the triumvirs negotiate with Pompey. This outer-world politics is the subject of Act I Scene iv, Act II Scenes i, ii, iv, vi, vii, and Act III Scene ii, v and vi, the last of which involves the return of Octavia alone from Athens and is followed by a scene on the headland of Actium before battle. These scenes involve firstly the arbitration and conciliation meeting of Antony and Caesar, with the marriage alliance proposed to cement their pact (though it proves the means of severing it), then the peace negotiations with Pompey. These are the main drivers of the political strand until the Caesar–Antony war breaks out. The subsequent scenes are politics by military means, where manoeuvring is carried out with weapons rather than weasel words. The first sea battle scenes and the aftermath take up Act III Scenes vii–xiii. Act IV Scenes i–xiv are concerned with the land battle and the second sea battle and takes the plot to Antony's suicide. Act IV Scene xv concerns the final meeting of Antony and Cleopatra. Then the whole of Act V (two scenes) is concerned with the political manoeuvrings of Caesar and Cleopatra, her suicide and the closing moments with Caesar triumphant but muted by the deaths of his defeated rivals. Of the 42 scenes in the play, 32 are thus focused on matters of power politics. It is difficult to argue that this is dominantly a love tragedy. It is a play about politics on a world stage, with love as the victim.

The insincerity and deceitfulness of people as they haggle and negotiate for position and policy is the unchanging feature of politics. It is evident in every scene that focuses on politics and character after character is revealed as a cheat and a hypocrite. Time and again King James promised support or gave the impression he would do this or that, but then reneged on his word; he only did it to please petitioners and get rid of them. Active, effective courtiers had to be careful not to do too well in accomplishing whatever they had been set to do, for to succeed too well might evoke the prince's jealousy. Flattering the governor and playing to his moods are part of all of Shakespeare's works in the 1600s. They create a consistent picture of the venality, ambition and deception at work in high-level society. Ventidius shows his understanding of this when he tells Silius he will do no more militarily for fear of rousing Antony's jealousy. He knows that the glories of politicians, for which they take the plaudits, are often the achievements of their underlings:

> Caesar and Antony have ever won
> More in their officer than in person. (III. i. 16–17)

He backs this up by mentioning Sossius, who was so successful in Syria that he lost Antony's favour. This shows the pettiness of great men, a common mean-minded human weakness and one of the negative qualities a true king would not have. A readiness to acknowledge what others have done for you betokens a sense of justice and displays a benevolent generosity of spirit.

Pompey behaves honourably in refusing Menas's offer to murder their enemies while they are on board the galley, but he nevertheless dishonours himself:

> Ah, this thou shouldst have done
> And not have spoken on't. In me 'tis villainy;
> In thee't had been good service. (II. vii. 74–6)

This caveat shows his flexible concept of morality. Menas responds in an aside to the audience, 'For this/I'll never follow thy palled fortunes more' (II. vii. 82–3). Loyalty is on a sliding scale too. Both Pompey and Menas are motivated by self-interest and profit. The lack of honour among politicians shows again in Pompey's hope that 'Salt Cleopatra' and her 'witchcraft', beauty and lust will 'tie up the libertine in a field of feasts [...] that sleep and feeding may prorogue his honour' (II. i. 21–6). Historically, Antony's return to Egypt enabled Pompey's forces to return to pillaging Italian, Adriatic and Illyrian coastal towns. Peace talks and pacts are little more than smiles and empty promises. Lepidus counsels Enobarbus to tell Antony to placate Caesar rather than be aggressive and reproachful. The weak appeaser wants a quiet life. Though Enobarbus declares he will encourage

Antony 'to answer like himself' (II. ii. 4), in the outcome Antony, with some difficulty, steers a course between anger and surrender. This is laudable, but is ruined by his weakness in agreeing to marry Octavia. The meeting with Pompey shows how men settle their differences (though it is all a bluff and blind, masking brutal intentions). Cleopatra's method for dealing with problems and getting what she wants is to tease and wheedle, to cry, pretend to faint, make accusations, scream and screech. She is a spoiled child, self-involved, self-indulgent, impulsive and reactionary. She achieves nothing, palters with a big political beast and is crushed. But in the end, the male method is no more successful for it too is founded on froth. Caesar fails to disarm the problem of Antony and has to resort to arms. He fails to solve the Pompey threat, only postpone it. He fails to control Cleopatra and is cheated of his planned triumph. The world of politics is shown up as smiles and lies and devious hypocrisy. Towards the end of their drunken evening on Pompey's galley, Antony jokingly warns the totally inebriated Lepidus (who is probably being held up by Antony): 'These quicksands, Lepidus,/ Keep off them, for you sink' (II. vii. 60–61). It is a dramatic irony for Antony himself is sinking in his own metaphorical quicksand. A little later, leaving the galley and descending into the boat that will take them away, Enobarbus offers a similar warning with a covert irony hidden in it: 'Take heed you fall not' (II. vii. 131). These two comments foreshadow the outcome of the play, but like the minutiae of politics their surface covers other meanings and other motives. They add to the growing tension as the audience watches helplessly as Antony sleepwalks into disaster.

Another feature of the political world is the moveable loyalty of courtiers. The rising man at Whitehall, Windsor or Hampton Court was always flattered by the silken flies buzzing round anyone who had power and access to jobs and money. Genuine loyalty out of love features in a number of the plays preceding and succeeding *Antony and Cleopatra*. In an age when most households had servants, their honesty and trustworthy service was vital. The good master or mistress nurtured (consciously or unconsciously) love and commitment in a servant that outlasted any difficulties the family might face. Some servants became like members of the family and would be looked after in old age. The faithfulness and reliability of servants is a recurring theme in many plays. The loyalty of Kent in *King Lear* and the disloyalty of Iago in *Othello* are crucial. Kings had hundreds of servants, from the humblest under-gardener to the King's Secretary, his prime minister. Betrayal by scheming servants is a common feature of Revenge Tragedies – a sharp reminder of how much governors rely on the honesty of those around them. In Scarus and Dercetus we see two men prepared to serve Antony to the last. At Antony's death, Dercetus (described by North as one of Antony's guards and presumably close to him) immediately switches sides. His announcement to Caesar tells us all we need to know:

> Mark Antony I served, who best was worthy
> Best to be served. Whilst he stood up and spoke
> He was my master, and I wore my life
> To spend upon my haters. If thou please
> To take me to thee, as I was to him
> I'll be to Caesar. If thou please not,
> I yield thee up my life. (V. i. 6–12)

It is a simple case of survival. Scarus's loyalty outlasts the fiasco at Actium though his comments make clear his anger: 'We have kissed away/Kingdoms and provinces' (III. x. 7–8) and 'Yon ribaudred nag of Egypt – /Whom leprosy overtake!/[…] like a cow in June,/Hoists sails and flies' (III. x. 10–15). He fights bravely in the land battle outside Alexandria and is singled out for mention by Antony. In Plutarch, the queen, whom he had earlier cursed heartily, gives him a golden breastplate and helmet as a reward. He then deserts that night. This shameful ingratitude is omitted by Shakespeare. Cleopatra gives him gold armour and he stays with Antony and watches the final stage of the war as Cleopatra's ships 'yielded to the foe' and 'carouse together' with the enemy (IV. xii. 11–12). Scarus exits when ordered by Antony to tell the army to disperse (IV. xii. 17), and we see him no more. Like Enobarbus, he stayed faithful almost until the last. Like Enobarbus he saw clearly the mistakes Antony was making and is deeply, angrily frustrated by it. Enobarbus saw how at Actium Antony has made his 'will/Lord of his reason' (III. xiii. 3). His sexual enslavement overruled common sense. Though Cleopatra fled, Antony should not have followed: 'The itch of his affection should not then/Have nicked his captainship' (III. xiii. 7–8). Both these soldiers see how Antony's actions are led by his being sexually besotted. The word 'will' was a common quibble on sexual desire and 'itch' suggests he sees Antony's so-called love as little more than a base sexual need. These servants stay with Antony as long as they can, but then the practical and primal call of survival forces them to desert.

Putting aside the question of loyalty, a matter of great concern to the Jacobeans, there is another matter here that would disturb the original audience. A usurping queen (she has assumed time and again superiority over the Roman governor) holding a man captive (like Omphale did with Hercules) subverted what they regarded as the proper hierarchy. Antony is captive because of her hold over his affections and his appetites. He even suggests, in his anger after her fleet betrayed him, that she holds him captive by witchcraft. She is 'this grave charm', 'a right gypsy', a 'spell', a 'witch' (IV. xii. 25, 28, 30, 47). One of the basic beliefs about sorcery was that under a spell you no longer had control of yourself, but were manipulated by the spell caster. Her lover's abusive, understandable anger drives her away, and at Charmian's suggestion she goes to her monument and sends news of her suicide. In the end Antony is left alone with just his servant Eros. His calling Eros (though this was the servant's real name and is given in Plutarch) sounds felicitously like he is calling out to 'love'. Love has brought him to this and love is all he has left.

When Antony, in desperation, challenges Caesar to single combat, Enobarbus knows Caesar will not risk all he has gained in the possible mischance of a duel. Enobarbus thinks that when men's fortunes go ill their judgement follows: 'Caesar, thou hast subdued/His judgement too' (III. xiii. 36–7). As Euripides is credited with saying: 'Whom the gods would destroy they first make mad.' Enobarbus sees it as folly to stick by a foolish fallen lord, but he who remains loyal gains a place in history. Antony is aware that his failures and fall have consequences for others: 'Oh, my fortunes/Have corrupted honest men!' (IV. v. 16–17). Part of the pity and fear the audience experience is in response to seeing Antony losing the trust and presence of the men about him. To the Romans about him the battlefield is a male gendered space. It is not a place for a woman (physically or spiritually), especially not when the general is in an intense relationship with that woman. His attention should be completely focused on tactical decisions. Enobarbus puts it bluntly in a lewd but appropriate analogy:

> If we should serve with horse and mares together,
> The horse were merely lost. The mares would bear
> A soldier and his horse. (III. vi. 7–9)

His last comment references gender reversal again, specifically female dominance. He is even more direct and says her 'presence needs must puzzle Antony'; she distracts his 'heart', his 'brain' and his 'time'. The conflict between the oppositely gendered states is also neatly drawn in his report that in Rome people believe 'that Photinus, an eunuch and your maids/Manage this war' (III. vi. 14–15). Cleopatra is furious: 'Sink Rome, and their tongues rot.' She asserts, 'A charge we bear i' th' war' and that 'as the president of my kingdom, will/Appear there for a man' (III. vi. 17–18). In Plutarch, Canidius points out to Antony that Cleopatra was paying for part of the expense of the hostilities and should not be sent away. Antony had not wanted her there. By giving Enobarbus the role of mouthpiece for what many of Antony's forces felt and transferring Canidius's point to Cleopatra,

Shakespeare adds another factor to the audience's probable dislike of her. It also more strongly attaches blame to her as the cause of the disaster when she flees from the battle. Antony's rushing after her like a 'doting mallard' simply proves what Enobarbus had feared. The retreat of the Egyptian fleet sets up or confirms suspicions of Egyptian unreliability, adding to the ambiguous loyalty of Cleopatra. Is she acting on the instinct of natural law that entitles every human being to prioritize their own survival? Is it just womanly fear? Is she ready to betray Antony in order to secure her own life? Who gave the order for the Egyptian fleet to surrender at the second sea battle? Was Antony acting on secret orders from the queen? Was it the spontaneous action of sailors who did not believe they could win anyway? Antony believes that 'this foul Egyptian hath betrayed me' (IV. xii. 10.). He expresses this view in Plutarch too.

Cleopatra's delayed suicide looks like an attempt to see if she can negotiate a compromise with Caesar. Is this understandable and/or forgivable? To the Roman way of thinking, suicide was an honourable act that wiped out dishonour – whether it was Lucrece's suicide after being raped or a commander's suicide after losing a battle. To the Jacobeans, suicide was a sin whatever its cause. It was no longer seen as an honourable act after military or naval defeat, it only added to the state of sinfulness of both protagonists. Yet at the same time, like Othello's self-inflicted death and like that of Romeo and Juliet, there is dramatic and emotional impact attached to such acts seen onstage.

Slipping into further degradation, Antony sends an ambassador to Caesar begging to be allowed to live in Egypt or to live as a private citizen in Athens – from ruler of the East to a nothing. Cleopatra sues to be allowed to pass her crown to her heirs. Caesar's answer is naked politics. He perhaps senses a split between the pair and tries to drive a wedge between them, the standard divide and defeat ploy. The ambassador is told to tell Cleopatra she will have her desire if she drives Antony out of the country or has him killed. Then, in a private conversation with one of his own men, he gives Thidias a mission to promise anything to the queen as long as she rejects her lover. He believes women are weak at the best of times 'but want will perjure/The ne'er touch'd vestal (III. xii. 30–31). Like Cleopatra wanting to know how Antony responds to her being merry or sad or ill, Caesar wants Thidias to 'observe how Antony becomes his flaw/And what thou think'st his very action speaks' (III. xii. 34–5). There is something of the victor gloating in this, a demeaning thing for a ruler to do. There is also something of circumspection, wanting rightly and sensibly to gauge the reactions of enemies. Antony's defiance and challenge to single combat is equally ambivalent. It is both brave and foolish. Foolish to think Caesar will risk his security 'against a sworder [a skilled swordsman]' (III. xiii. 31). In sneering at 'the boy Caesar', Antony abuses him as a coward and asserts his 'ministers would prevail/Under the service of a child as soon/As i' th' command of Caesar' (III. xiii. 23–5). This suggests that the courtiers who administer Caesar's government would serve anyone – child, youth or man – as long as they kept their power. It is a hit at the super-serviceable sycophants who buzz around the court. Enobarbus, in a sharp aside, recognizes the folly of Antony thinking 'the full' Caesar will 'answer his emptiness' in a duel. Plutarch asserts of Antony: 'His character was, in fact, essentially simple and he was slow to perceive the truth.'[8] Clearly here, Antony shows little understanding of how political matters stand.

For all her charisma and theatrical glamour Cleopatra had little experience of wielding military power and needed Antony's legions and his strength. But she had money and ships and more money for more ships. These were indispensable for Antony to move his troops about the Mediterranean. So she needed his muscle and he needed her money. But his military skill and political understanding are now highly doubtful. Abandoning his land troops at Actium, leaving their escape to be led by his subordinates, was a dishonourable act contrary to all Roman values and particularly the military code of his class. Though there was some degree of love between Antony and Cleopatra, it is rarely shown in the play. What we see onstage are numerous arguments and a few more affable moments. After Actium Antony is reproachful but not condemnatory. After the second naval defeat, when the Egyptian fleet surrenders without a fight, the meeting between the pair is charged with vicious recrimination. It is not loving support they show each other but bared teeth. After the Alexandrian battles, Antony is incandescent with rage, believing the queen has betrayed him. Only in his dying moments does he soften. Both seem most to express need of each other when they are apart. Antony enjoys her company and revels in the display of themselves as he had earlier in his life in Italy, ostentatiously progressing around the country with a train of actors and actresses, with himself and his courtesan/actress/mistress at the head of the lavishly dressed circus entourage. Will she switch allegiance? She is now in a more positive position than Antony, for Caesar needs Egyptian corn, Egyptian wealth and Egyptian loyalty. He does not need Antony, who is unpredictable and impulsive. In trying to split the allies Caesar is only using the situation pragmatically (as any Machiavellian politician would).

NOTES

Introduction

1 *The Prince*, XV, 90–91.
2 John Dryden, preface to *All for Love, or the World Well Lost* (1677).
3 A vamp uses her sexual attractiveness to seduce and control men.

Prologue. The Setting

1 William of Malmesbury, *De Gestis Regum Anglorum*, III, 257.
2 Gurr gives 1608 as the date for performance at the Globe (233). He provides no source for the claim, but a large cast might work better on an open, thrust stage.
3 Quoted in Gurr (*The Shakespearean Stage, 1574–1642*, 218), from Henry Fitzgeoffrey's book of verse. See also Susan Shapiro, '"Yon Plumed Dandeprat": Male "Effeminacy" in English Satire and Criticism', *Review of English Studies*, n.s., 39 (1988): 400–412. A dandeprat was a silver coin of little value (about 2p).
4 Daniel was part of the Countess of Pembroke's literary circle. She was a Sidney, married William Herbert, and published a closet drama, *Antonie*, in 1592. Shakespeare knew the Herbert and Sidney families. Antony seemed to be a subject of common interest. See the section 'Sources' in Chapter 13.
5 Wilders (74) points out that paintings of the subject had, since the mid-sixteenth century, portrayed Cleopatra setting the asps to her breasts. Thus Barnes may have acquired the image from an early pictorial source.
6 Brathwait, *The English Gentlewoman*, 197.
7 Anton, *The Philosophers Satyrs*, 46.
8 General observations from his edition of the play.
9 The following references are from John Russell Brown, *Casebook*.
10 A suitable allusion to the story of Hercules expiating an accidental murder by being made slave to the Queen of Lydia. His humiliation, the gender reversal and cross-dressing parallel the degraded antics of Antony.

Chapter 1. The Historical Context

1 Throughout the book Octavius Caesar is generally referred to as Caesar. Whenever Julius Caesar is referenced his full name is used.
2 Goldsworthy, *Antony and Cleopatra*, 83.

3 Goldsworthy, *Antony and Cleopatra*, 87.
4 Weldon, *The Court and Character of James I* (1651). Sir Anthony Weldon, a courtier and politician, was banished from court for criticizing the Scots.
5 Davies, *The Early Stuarts*, 7.
6 Machiavelli had referred to 'the great changes and variations, beyond human imagining, which we have experienced and experience every day' (*The Prince*, 130; written 1513, published 1532). In 1606 the European world was still morphing from its medieval past.
7 Historical Manuscripts Commission, *Calendar of the Manuscripts of the Most Honourable the Marquess of Salisbury*, vol. 12, 272.
8 Anouilh, *Antigone*, 34.

Chapter 2. The Elizabethan World Order: From Divinity to Dust

1 The Catholic Church had imagined another level: Purgatory, an escape route for avoiding Hell. Venial sinners, after death, could purge their souls of sin and make themselves suitable for Heaven. Masses paid for by money left in wills were believed to assist in cleansing the soul of the departed. Protestantism saw Purgatory as a doctrinally suspect, corrupt moneymaking scheme and dropped it from Anglican teachings.
2 Uranus was not discovered until 1781.
3 Elyot, *The Boke Named the Governour* (1531).
4 See Revelation 21.
5 *A Defence of Iudiciall Astrologie* (quoted in Thomas, *Religion and the Decline of Magic*, 414).
6 A court comprising privy councillors and judges, instituted to try cases of suspected treason by powerful lords whom the ordinary courts were unable to bring to book. Under the Stuarts it became a means of curbing the Crown's political opponents, most of whom belonged to the dissenting religions.
7 A tribe with eyes in their shoulders and a mouth in their chest was reported by Sir Walter Raleigh after his 1595 trip to Guiana and recorded in Hakluyt's *Voyages* (viii).
8 *Psychomachia* is the struggle between good and evil for the mind/soul of man. Often portrayed on stage as a good and a bad angel – advising or tempting the protagonist (as in *Faustus*), by the 1600s they lost their allegorical state and metamorphosed into secularized characters, like a good friend and a false friend or a wise, disinterested adviser and a flattering self-seeker.
9 For revisionist analyses of the times see Bouwsma, *The Waning of the Renaissance*.
10 Literacy was accelerating and cheap books and pamphlets increasingly numerous. By 1600, 25 per cent of males and 10 per cent of women could read (Mortimer, *The Time Traveller's Guide to Elizabethan England*, 102). In London male literacy was 80 per cent.
11 Its reliance upon mind, reason and will marks the Renaissance's divergence from medievalism.
12 The church tried to keep track of unlicensed presses producing heretical or treasonable matter, but smuggled imports from Holland and the mobility of printers made it very difficult to police thought.
13 Augustine, *City of God*, 548.
14 Revelation has Hell underground. Milton (*Paradise Lost*, 1667) has Hell specially created by God from the materials of Chaos to receive the falling angels after their defeat and expulsion from Heaven.
15 Beier, *Masterless Men*, 125.

16 Formalized by St Thomas Aquinas, seminal medieval Christian thinker. Hell's hierarchy is variously organized by different writers. Matthew (12:24) calls Beelzebub 'the prince of the devils'.
17 Incubi were male demons thought to have sex with sleeping women. Succubi were female demons coupling with men.
18 *Nichomachean Ethics*, X. 9. 199.
19 See Chaucer, *The Wife of Bath's Tale*, 1109–32.
20 Castiglione, *The Book of the Courtier*, 55.
21 Increasingly, successful merchants like Cranfield, Ingram and Swinnerton were drawn into government advisory groups. Some inevitably took advantage of the opportunities for jobbery. See Peck, *Northampton*, ch. 7.
22 See Peck's two works listed in the Bibliography.
23 Nichols, *The Progresses, Processions, and Magnificent Festivities of James the First*, 128–32. A benefice was a parish post for a priest. 'Placemen' were those who held court or government posts, often through family influence.
24 *Basilikon Doron* (*A King's Gift*), a conduct book for kings, justifies the principles of divine right.
25 British Library, shelf mark 1103.f.29.
26 British Library, shelf mark 695.a.b. (from the 1603 printed version of the sermon).
27 Many gained military experience fighting the Spanish in the Netherlands.
28 Quoted in Mortimer, *The Time Traveller's Guide to Elizabethan England*, 49.
29 See Peck, *Northampton: Patronage and Policy at the Court of James I* and *Court Patronage and Corruption in Early Stuart England*.
30 As plantations in Virginia and New England became settled and Newfoundland and Nova Scotia were exploited, importation of materials (timber, beaver fur, minerals, fish, tobacco, etc.) became valuable commercial investments.
31 Five 'young gentlemen' were imprisoned for 'ill beseeming' drunkenness for three weeks in November 1606. They were brought before the Star Chamber and fined as well 'for example's sake' (Harrison, *A Jacobean Journal*, 346).
32 Many aristo-gentry families put younger sons to professions and trades so they should have an income, since land and fortune were bequeathed to the eldest male alone.
33 I. i. 114–16, 138 (New Mermaid edition, 1994).
34 Cited in Stone, *The Crisis of the Aristocracy*, 27.
35 Ashley, *England in the Seventeenth Century*, 18.
36 Ashley, *England in the Seventeenth Century*, 18.
37 Thomas Wilson, *State of England* (quoted in *Camden Miscellany*, vol. 16, 43).
38 Kishlansky (*A Monarchy Transformed*, 44), describing the huge network of family members given posts under the influence of the Duke of Buckingham, James's favourite.
39 Edmund Bolton, antiquarian, refers to 'the vent of Virginia' as used by the government to resettle the idle multitude (Peck, *Northampton*, 119).
40 See Beier, *Masterless Men*, 14, 16.
41 Recently discovered legal documents show Shakespeare being fined for hoarding food, presumably to sell at inflated prices (*Sunday Times*, 31 March 2013). His role as a moneylender puts a hypocritical slant on his comments about usurers and tarnishes his stance as someone concerned for the poor.
42 Burton's *The Anatomy of Melancholy* (1621) explores this multiplicity of psycho-emotional types.
43 Campbell (*Shakespeare's Tragic Heroes*) interprets heroic flaws from physiological diagnoses.

44 'No animal fawns so much as a dog, and none is so faithful' (Erasmus, *Praise of Folly*, 134).
45 'Those who have deliberately preferred a life of irresponsible lawlessness and violence become wolves and hawks and kites' (Plato, *Phaedo*, 134). See also Leviticus 11:14, where kites are listed with many other birds that are 'an abomination'.
46 Plato regarded bees, wasps and ants as 'social and disciplined creatures' (*Phaedo*, 134).
47 In Webster's *The White Devil*, the corrupt Duke Brachiano is described as a yew tree. This tree was traditionally associated with graveyards. Brachiano causes deaths and dies horribly as punishment for his failure to give virtuous shelter.
48 *The White Devil* (1612), III. iii. 49–50.
49 After his visit he built Guiana into a fabulous treasure resource to encourage James to support his colonization of the place. His *Discovery of Guiana* (1591) refers to 'the great and golden city of MANOA, which the Spaniards call EL DORADO' and laid out his plans to colonize 'for return or profit' but also as a 'let or impeachment' to the Spanish (cited in Christopher Hill, 159). He fell foul of James's pro-Spanish policy.
50 'The Order for the Burial of the Dead' (*Book of Common Prayer*, 86).
51 Gawdy, *Letters*, 132. A sewer seated you at table and might also serve you.
52 Quoted in De Lisle, *After Elizabeth*, 205. Scaramelli revealed to the signory that English politicians, aristocrats and courtiers blamed the government for 'having sold England to the Scots'.
53 Gawdy, *Letters*, 131.
54 Quoted in De Lisle, 210, from *The Calendar of State Papers Relating to English Affairs, Existing in the Archives and Collections of Venice* (London, 1900), vol. 10, 1603–7.
55 Montaigne, 'On Anger', 810.
56 'Of Anger', 226. The translation is Bacon's.
57 By 1604 eight hundred and thirty-eight new £30 knights had been created.
58 Aristotle, *The Politics*, 67. See Castiglione, 298.
59 *Basilikon Doron*, 4. All quotes from the EEBO Editions reprint of the 1682 edition.
60 Beier, *Masterless Men*, 43.
61 Nichols, *The Progresses, Processions, and Magnificent Festivities of James the First*, 327 (emphasis added).
62 Daunton, *Progress and Poverty*, 137.
63 Historical Manuscripts Commission, *Calendar of the Manuscripts of the Most Honourable the Marquess of Salisbury*, vol. 12, 272.
64 Clapham, *Elizabeth of England*, 98.
65 Peck, *Northampton*, 156.
66 Strype, *Memorials of Thomas Cranmer* (1690), rec. 114.
67 'Homily against Disobedience', from David Wootten, *Divine Right and Democracy*, 94–8.
68 For confrontations between congregants and clergy see Cressy, *Agnes Bowker's Cat*, ch. 9.
69 See Bunker, *Making Haste from Babylon*, 103. Some Mayflower separatists came from this area of Nottinghamshire, West Riding and Lincolnshire. John Cotton, Puritan minister of St Botolph's, Boston, also gathered followers round him.
70 *Basilikon Doron*, 18, 19, 18.
71 Brathwait, *The English Gentleman* (1631), 115.
72 Brathwait, *The English Gentleman*, 115.
73 Webster, *The White Devil*, III. ii. 64–6.
74 *The Seuen Deadly Sinnes of London* (1606), 46.
75 Henry Percy, *Advice to His Son*, 119.

Chapter 3. Sin, Death and the Prince of Darkness

1. Wycliffe, Prologue to the Apocalypse, 493.
2. After fornication (prohibited sex), nonattendance was the second most common offence.
3. Prenuptial sex, adultery and bastard birth were increasingly prosecuted. See Dabhoiwala, *The Origins of Sex*, 41.
4. Her views are discussed in Chapter 11.
5. Castiglione, *Book of the Courtier* (Hoby's translation), bk. 1.
6. Lucifer was a prince of light before he fell. The testaments call the Devil a prince, and as darkness denotes sin joining the two terms is natural. Edgar's phrase, 'The Prince of Darkness is a gentleman; Modo he's called, and Mahu' (*King Lear*, III. iv.) takes these names from an anti-papist pamphlet by Samuel Harsnett and links evil with the sham politeness of gentlemen that masks devious intent.
7. *Basilikon Doron*, 12–13. See *Two Elizabethan Puritan Diaries*, ed. M. M. Knappen.
8. Dabhoiwala, *The Origins of Sex*, 41. Family dysfunctionality of different sorts was also worryingly increasing (see Beier, *Masterless Men*, 56), not only among the homeless, but in settled communities and in the governing classes.
9. The anonymous *Memorial* (addressed to James on his accession) demanded the reintroduction of the Edwardian reforms, more practising preaching ministers, strict observance of the Sabbath and the banishment of the ring exchange in marriage and other 'superstitious' remnants of popery. Cited in De Lisle, *After Elizabeth*, 192.
10. 'To Philosophize Is to Learn How to Die', *The Complete Essays*, 96.
11. *Basilikon Doron*, 13.
12. Dollimore, *Radical Tragedy*, 189.
13. *History of the World* (1603–13), II, 214 (1820 edition). Cooper, *Certaine Sermons* (1580), cited in Thomas, *Religion and the Decline of Magic*, 91.
14. *The Prince*, XXV, 130.
15. Bacon, *The Advancement of Learning* (1605), 157.
16. See Botticelli's painting *The Abyss of Hell* (1480).
17. Orgel and Strong, *Inigo Jones*, I, 282.
18. *Confessions*, VIII, 7.
19. Dabhoiwala, *The Origins of Sex*, 42.
20. 'If they cannot contain, let them marry: for it is better to marry than to burn' (I Corinthians 7:9).
21. 'Superflux' is the excess money or food the rich were supposed to give to the poor.
22. *On the Good of Marriage*, ch. 21.

Chapter 4. The Seven Cardinal Virtues

1. *The Book of the Courtier* (1528), 87–88.
2. This takes place before the narrative begins; it was a scandalous piece of trickery by which Pompey the Great's house in Rome was put up for auction, but then simply occupied by Antony.

Chapter 5. Kingship

1. Goldsworthy, *Antony and Cleopatra*, 3.
2. One-fifth of all plays from 1588–1608 were histories (Harbage, *Shakespeare and the Rival Traditions*, 85, 260).

3 Goldsworthy, *Antony and Cleopatra*, 265.
4 City-state (Greek). In theology, morality and political theory a person was seen as a state, governed well or ill.
5 Plato's *Republic* is the starting point (much referenced in James's *Basilikon*), but others took up the theme: Xenophon (*Cyropaedia*), Isocrates (*Oration to Nicocles*), Cicero (*De Officiis*), Seneca (*De Clementia*), John of Salisbury (*Policraticus*, 1159), St. Thomas Aquinas (*De Regimine Principum*, c. 1265), Erasmus (*Education of a Christian Prince*, 1516), Machiavelli (*Il Principe*, 1532).
6 All Elyot quotes from the 1970 Scolar Press unpaginated facsimile reprint.
7 Written (44 BC) as a guide to behaviour in public life after the murder of Julius Caesar.
8 Cf. Castiglione, *The Book of the Courtier*, bks I–III.
9 It was not, at this time, usual for sons of the nobility to go to university. This had begun to change by the end of the sixteenth century, but for reasons of social prestige rather than concern for education (see Secor, *Richard Hooker*, 76).
10 Stone, *The Crisis of the Aristocracy*, 617.
11 Republicanism or anti-monarchism were not yet discernible movements, but Buchanan's *Law of Kings* (1579) and Raleigh's *Prerogative of Parliaments* (1603) were beginning to question absolutism and suggest ways of controlling it.
12 Speech to Parliament (1610). See Wootten, *Divine Right and Democracy*, 107.
13 Goldsworthy, *Antony and Cleopatra*, 156.
14 Goldsworthy, *Antony and Cleopatra*, 393.
15 *A History of England*, cited in *Basilikon Doron*, 62.
16 *Anatomy of Melancholy*, pt 3, sect. 2, memb. 4, 763.
17 'Of all the responsibilities that fall to a prince, the most important is justice. And to maintain this, there should be appointed to hold office men of wisdom and probity, who must be good as well as judicious' (Castiglione, *The Book of the Courtier*, 307).
18 'On the Vanity of Words', 343.
19 The authors of *Eastward Ho!* were briefly jailed for mocking the Scots.
20 This note must have been added for the 1603 edition as the plot postdates the 1598 first edition.
21 According to Winwood's *Memorials* it was 'twice represented by the King's Players, with exceeding concourse of all sorts of people; but whether the matter or manner be not well handled, or that it be thought unfit that Princes should be played on the stage in their life-time, I hear that some great Councellors are much displeased with it, and so 'tis thought shall be forbidden' (Harrison, *A Jacobean Journal*, 172).
22 Buchanan also taught Montaigne at the Collège de Guyenne in Bordeaux.
23 Nichols, *The Progresses, Processions, and Magnificent Festivities of James the First*, 327. Ben Jonson wrote part of the address. He criticized the political state in *Sejanus* (1603), then became involved with court masque production as a covert means of instruction.
24 Castiglione, *The Book of the Courtier*, 300.

Chapter 6. Patriarchy, Family Authority and Gender Relationships

1 Ephesians 5:22–3. See also I Corinthians 11:3.
2 Genesis 3:16.
3 *Hallelujah* (1641).
4 *Basilikon Doron*, 54.
5 *Basilikon Doron*, 58.

6 *Basilikon Doron*, 60–61.
7 Education in the classics informed Jacobean men about devious, lecherous and homicidal Roman women, particularly patrician ladies and empresses.
8 From *De Cultu Feminarum*. Cited in Ellerbe, *The Dark Side of Christian History*, 115.
9 Homily XV to the People of Antioch.
10 Cited in Starr, *The 'Natural Inferiority' of Women*, 45. Clement also advocated equality of the sexes and women being admitted to leading roles in the church.
11 *Malleus Maleficarum*, sec. 1.
12 The comment is from the incestuously obsessed Duke Ferdinand in *The Duchess of Malfi*, II. v. 6.
13 Castiglione, *The Book of the Courtier*, 43.
14 A similarly orthodox view is voiced by the unmarried Luciana in *The Comedy of Errors* (1588–93), II. i.
15 A gull was a fool, someone gullible.
16 Cited in Stone, *The Crisis of the Aristocracy*, 615.
17 Stone, *The Crisis of the Aristocracy*, 614.
18 See Dusinberre, *Shakespeare and the Nature of Women*, 2–4.
19 *Seuen Deadly Sinnes of London*, 44.
20 For further detail on female writings, see Mortimer, *The Time Traveller's Guide to Elizabethan England*, 68–71.
21 *Norton Anthology of English Literature*, vol. 1. (1962), 1553–5.
22 The letters between the gentry couple Sir John and Margaret Winthrop in the second decade of the seventeenth century testify to both a loving marriage and a highly articulate woman. Similarly, Lovell recounts the affection Bess of Hardwick achieved with her several husbands.
23 *Basilikon Doron*, 61–62. The marginal note indicates James knew these pseudo-historical characters from Polydore Vergil's *Anglica Historia* (1532).
24 See, for example, Elizabeth Hoby (Laoutaris, *Shakespeare and the Countess*) and Elizabeth Talbot (Lovell, *Bess of Hardwick*) – both formidable and not always pleasant women.
25 'Almost half of all babies died within twelve months of birth' (Lovell, *Bess of Hardwick*, 1) and the teenage deaths of longed-for heirs litter the records. Elizabethan and Jacobean family monuments in churches display sad little sculpted groups of dead children.
26 Stone, *The Family, Sex and Marriage in England, 1500–1800*, 37.
27 See Dusinberre, *Shakespeare and the Nature of Woman*.
28 Mothers often bequeathed money or property to a younger son to ensure he was not left destitute when his father died and the eldest inherited all.
29 See Lovell, *Bess of Hardwick*, 302.
30 See Schleiner, *Tudor and Stuart Women Writers*.
31 The early 1600s was a time of punitive action by various authorities against fornication, adultery, incest, homosexuality and prostitution. See Dabhoiwala, *The Origins of Sex*, ch. 1.
32 Berry and Foyster, *The Family in Early Modern England*, 3.
33 Berry and Foyster, *The Family in Early Modern England*, 3.
34 Berry and Foyster, *The Family in Early Modern England*, 3.
35 William Gouge, *Of Domesticall Duties* (1622).
36 *The First Blast of the Trumpet against the Monstrous Regiment of Women* (1558).

37 'On the Affection of Fathers for Their Children', 448.
38 Stone, *The Family, Sex and Marriage*, 136.
39 Behn's first play was *The Forced Marriage* (1670). Before this, masques and dramas for private reading were female authored.
40 Mulcaster citations in the *Norton Anthology*.
41 *Norton Anthology*.
42 Stone, *The Family, Sex and Marriage*, 143.
43 'The Epystle of the Translatour' from Hoby's translation.
44 See Campion in *Norton Anthology*.
45 *Norton Anthology*, 1036–9. For the texts of Speght, Swetnam and others see Butler, *Female Replies to Swetnam the Woman-Hater*.
46 Castiglione, *Book of the Courtier*, 47, 108.
47 Sermon, 1 September 1522.
48 'The word and works of God is quite clear, that women were made either to be wives or prostitutes' (*Works* XII, 94). 'God created Adam master and lord of living creatures, but Eve spoilt all, when she persuaded him to set himself above God's will. 'Tis you women, with your tricks and artifices, that lead men into error' (*Table Talk*).
49 See Rubin, *Mother of God*, pt VI.
50 There was a subgenre of books on famous and virtuous women. Christine of Pizan's *The Book of the City of Ladies* and Boccaccio's *De Mulieribus* were most influential.
51 Castiglione, *Book of the Courtier*, 198.
52 Resentful, beaten servants could not legally run away and leave the parish. That was to become a masterless man/woman and carried a prison sentence. This implication that the servant was the property of the master was yet another of the ancient practices that restricted the liberties of the English.
53 Stone, *The Family, Sex and Marriage*, 137.
54 Stone, *The Family, Sex and Marriage*, 137.
55 Stone, *The Family, Sex and Marriage*, 136.

Chapter 7. Man in His Place

1 Robert Crowley, *Voice of the Last Trumpet* (1550).
2 For attitudes to commercial enterprise Weber (*The Protestant Ethic and the Spirit of Capitalism*, 1904–05) and Tawney (*Religion and the Rise of Capitalism*, 1926) are still relevant. So too is L. C. Knights, *Drama and Society in the Age of Jonson* (1937), chs 1–4.
3 Goldsworthy, *Antony and Cleopatra*, 7.
4 See Peck, *Northampton*, ch. 7.
5 Quoted in De Lisle, *After Elizabeth*, 195.
6 Stubbes, *Anatomie of Abuses*, sig. C. 11v.
7 From 'King Edward's Remains: A Discourse about the Reformation of Many Abuses', *History of the Reformation*, Bishop Burnet.
8 *Ben Jonson: Works*, VII, 735.
9 *Ars Poetica* (*The Art of Poetry*), I, 351.

Chapter 8. Images of Disorder: The Religious Context

1 Cressy, *Agnes Bowker's Cat*, 139.
2 Thomas, *Religion and the Decline of Magic*, 179.

3 Cressy, *Agnes Bowker's Cat*, ch. 9.
4 1606–07 was the period when separatists exiled themselves to Leiden before sailing to America, fleeing increasing persecution. See Bunker, *Making Haste from Babylon*, pt 2.
5 Falling asleep during the sermon and disrespecting the vicar were fineable offences.
6 The play compresses the time we assume Antony and Octavia are together before he returns to Cleopatra. It appears to be very brief (thus exacerbating Caesar's anger). In reality he married her in 40 BC (the year Cleopatra bore him twins), parted from her in 37 BC and divorced her in 32 BC. They had two daughters.
7 *On Obligation*, I, 11.
8 Gawdy, *Letters*, 148.

Chapter 9. The Context of Tragedy

1 John Lydgate published *The Fall of Princes* (1439), partially derived from Boccaccio.
2 Part of this was translated into English in the early 1500s.
3 Scott-Kilvert, *Makers of Rome*, 341.
4 Scott-Kilvert, *Makers of Rome*, 341, 342.
5 Scott-Kilvert, *Makers of Rome*, 346–47.
6 Lear carries his daughter's dead body onstage, laments and then dies himself.
7 *Palladis Tamia* (1598).
8 *Troas* (1559), *Thyestes* and *Hercules Furens* by Jasper Heywood, *Oedipus* (1563) by Alexander Nevyle, *Agamemnon*, *Medea*, *Hercules Oetaeus* and *Hippolytus* (c. 1567) by John Studley, *Octavia* by Thomas Nuce, and Newton's adaptation of *Thebais*.
9 Quoted in Thomas, *Religion and the Decline of Magic*, 91, 92.
10 Thomas, *Religion and the Decline of Magic*, 91.
11 *Antigone*, 34.

Chapter 10. 'O'erflowing the Measure': Restraint and Excess

1 Hughes-Hallett, *Cleopatra: Histories, Dreams and Distortions*, 220. This excellent study considers the many differing interpretations of Cleopatra's character and motives.
2 Hughes-Hallett, *Cleopatra*, 28.
3 Hughes-Hallett, *Cleopatra*, 136.
4 *Sermons*, 2:100.
5 Nashe, *The Unfortunate Traveller*, 267.
6 Kott, *Shakespeare: Our Contemporary*, 139.
7 *De Officiis (On Duty or On Obligation)*, 4.
8 Ovid, *Metamorphoses*, 98.
9 See Davidson in the 'Further Reading' list.
10 This has been attributed to Euripides.
11 Bevington, *Antony and Cleopatra*, 13.
12 Preface to *All for Love*, 11.
13 Cicero, *Selected Works*, 105.
14 North's translation (in Bullough, *Narrative and Dramatic Sources of Shakespeare*, 319).
15 Scott-Kilvert, *Makers of Rome*, 325.
16 North's translation (Arden edition, 1956, 258).
17 Green, *Alexander to Actium*, 664.
18 *Famous Women*, 175, 180–81, 185.

Chapter 11. Infinite Variety: Isis or Strumpet?

1. Machiavelli, *The Prince*, 101.
2. Mrs Jameson, *Characteristics of Women* (1833). Cited in John Russell Brown, *Casebook*.
3. *Inferno*, V, 38–39, 63.
4. *Famous Women*, 178, 180–82.
5. Scott-Kilvert, *Makers of Rome*, Appendix, 352.
6. Montaigne, 'The Tale of Spurina', 830.
7. *The Anatomy of Melancholy*, pt 1, sect. 2, memb. 3, subs. 6, 228.
8. *The Anatomy of Melancholy*, pt 2, sect. 3, memb. 3, 512.
9. The Jacobeans would have seen little difference between the pagan gods and the Christian God (except in the supposed beneficence of their deity), as both ordered and monitored the world and punished offenders.
10. Scott-Kilvert, *Makers of Rome*, 292.
11. English, German and French writers too, particularly in the sixteenth–eighteenth centuries, were fascinated by her. They commonly emphasized her sirenical and sinful side as temptress and femme fatale (see Hughes- Hallett, *Cleopatra: Histories, Dreams and Distortions*, 223).
12. Antony made poor choices in women. Fulvia did not conform to Roman (certainly not Jacobean) expectations of a woman. Plutarch described her as 'a woman who took no interest in spinning or managing a household, nor could she be content to rule a husband who had no ambition for public life: her desire was to govern those who governed [...]. In fact Cleopatra was indebted to Fulvia for teaching Antony to obey a wife's authority, for by the time he met her, he had already been broken in and schooled to accept the sway of women' (Scott-Kilvert, *Makers of Rome*, 280).
13. This sibling rivalry is reflected in the jealousy between Caesar and Antony, both seen as 'pseudo-sons' of Julius Caesar by themselves and others.
14. Frye, *Fools of Time*, 71.
15. Grant, *Cleopatra*, 276.
16. Hoby, 'The Epystle of the Translatour', from *The Courtyer of Baldessar Castilio*.
17. Kott, *Shakespeare: Our Contemporary*, 138.
18. Grant, *Cleopatra*, 327.
19. Goldsworthy, *Antony and Cleopatra*, 380.
20. Scott-Kilvert, *Makers of Rome*, 341.
21. The Elysian Fields where the happy dead wandered. In Homer's time it was thought to be an island in the West. By Virgil's day it was thought to be a part of Hades, the Underworld, where heroes and other special personages 'lived' as happy spirits.
22. Scott-Kilvert, *Makers of Rome*, 341.

Chapter 12. Rome versus Egypt: Gendering the State

1. For the problems caused by female rule and male unease, see Helen Castor's *She-Wolves*.
2. Historically, the soothsayer was sent by Cleopatra to accompany Antony on his trip to Italy to deal with Sextus Pompeius. His secret mission was to report proceedings to the queen and keep hinting to Antony the need to detach himself from Caesar. See Grant, *Cleopatra*, 193.
3. Sallust, *The Jugurthine War: The Conspiracy of Catiline*, 182–83.

4 When the play starts, in the winter of 41–40 BC, Cleopatra was pregnant for the first time by Antony. Her and Octavia's childbearing is omitted as being a distraction from the condensed intensity of the decline and fall of the pair.
5 Paglia, *Sexual Personae*, ch. 7.
6 Scott-Kilvert, *Makers of Rome*, 293.
7 Scott-Kilvert, *Makers of Rome*, 291.
8 Lucretius, *De Rerum Natura*, I, 3f.
9 Paglia, *Sexual Personae*, 212.
10 Paglia, *Sexual Personae*, 213.
11 Paglia, *Sexual Personae*, 214.
12 Paglia, *Sexual Personae*, 213.
13 *Coleridge's Shakespeare Criticism*, I, 76–79.
14 Hazlitt, *Characters of Shakespeare's Plays*, 74–75.
15 'On the Vanity of Words', 343.
16 Paglia, *Sexual Personae*, 214.
17 Paglia, *Sexual Personae*, 215.
18 Paglia, *Sexual Personae*, 216.
19 Paglia, *Sexual Personae*, 216.
20 Paglia, *Sexual Personae*, 217.
21 Paglia, *Sexual Personae*, 219
22 Paglia, *Sexual Personae*, 219.
23 Paglia, *Sexual Personae*, 221
24 Paglia, *Sexual Personae*, 223.
25 Paglia, *Sexual Personae*, 223.
26 Paglia, *Sexual Personae*, 223.
27 Paglia, *Sexual Personae*, 224.
28 Paglia, *Sexual Personae*, 226.
29 Kott, *Shakespeare: Our Contemporary*, 139.
30 Paglia, *Sexual Personae*, 226–27.

Chapter 13. Literary Context

1 Kott, *Shakespeare: Our Contemporary*, 128.
2 Elizabethan-Jacobean drama made little attempt to replicate period costume. Jacobean actors playing Romans wore doublet and hose, perhaps only making a token gesture in the direction of verisimilitude by throwing a cloth over the shoulder as a version of the toga. Their armour would have been such as soldiers wore in the Tudor-Stuart era.
3 Timon was a subject found in Plutarch.
4 James's view in *Basilikon Doron* (51).
5 British Library, shelf mark 1103.f.29.
6 Scott-Kilvert, *Makers of Rome*, 296.
7 Once ascribed to Tourneur, then as a collaboration, it is often now thought to be by Middleton.
8 See Stow, *The Survey of London* (1598).
9 Orgel, *Inigo Jones*, 45.
10 'Revenge is a kind of wild justice, which the more man's nature runs to, the more ought law to weed it out' (Bacon, 'Of Revenge').
11 Wickham et al., *English Professional Theatre, 1530–1660*, 51.

12 See Muir, *The Sources of Shakespeare's Plays*, 220–37.
13 A number of sixteenth-century Chaucer editions were published: William Thynne's (1532 and 1532), John Stow's (1561) and Thomas Speght's (1598 and 1602).
14 Scott-Kilvert, *Makers of Rome*, 303.
15 Scott-Kilvert, *Makers of Rome*, 272.
16 Scott-Kilvert, *Makers of Rome*, 274.
17 As his retinue left the city of Rome he had his servants lead holding up his golden drinking cups. Whenever he stopped on a journey pavilions were set up and lavish meals spread.
18 Scott-Kilvert, *Makers of Rome*, 293.
19 *Anatomy of Melancholy*, pt 3, sect. 2, memb. 2, subs. 4, 700.
20 *Anatomy of Melancholy*, pt 3, sect. 2, memb. 2, subs. 5, 719.
21 Scott-Kilvert, *Makers of Rome*, 279.
22 See Muir, *The Sources of Shakespeare's Plays*, 225–27; and J. D. Wilson (ed.), *Antony and Cleopatra*, x, note 2.
23 Shakespeare knew the Herbert family, the Earls of Pembroke.
24 Quoted in Muir, *The Sources of Shakespeare's Plays*, 227.
25 North's translation, Arden edition (ed. M. R. Ridley), Appendix 5, 258–59.
26 North, 261.
27 *Makers of Rome*, 285–86.
28 'Of Adversity', 75.

Chapter 14. Political Context

1 Kott, *Shakespeare: Our Contemporary*, 128.
2 The play begins in 41–40 BC when Antony and Cleopatra are in Alexandria and Fulvia took up arms. It ends in 30 BC.
3 The separation and numbering of scenes and acts did not happen until Nicholas Rowe edited the play in 1709.
4 *De Gestis Regum Anglorum*, III, 257.
5 Kott, *Shakespeare: Our Contemporary*, 137.
6 Paglia, *Sexual Personae*, 225.
7 Scott-Kilvert, *Makers of Rome*, 272.
8 Scott-Kilvert, *Makers of Rome*, 291.

BIBLIOGRAPHY

Anouilh, Jean. *Antigone*. London: Methuen, 1964.
Aristotle. *The Nichomachean Ethics*, trans. David Ross. Oxford: Oxford World's Classics, 2009.
_____. *The Politics*, trans. T. A. Sinclair. London: Penguin Classics, 1981.
Augustine, St. *City of God*, trans. Henry Bettinson. London: Penguin Classics, 2003.
_____. *Confessions*, trans. R. S. Pine-Coffin. London: Penguin Classics, 1964.
_____. *On the Good of Marriage (De Bono Coniugiali)*, ed. P. G. Walsh. Oxford: Clarendon Press, 2001.
Bacon, Sir Francis. *The Advancement of Learning*, ed. Arthur Johnston. Oxford: Clarendon Press, 1980.
_____. *The Essays*, ed. John Pitcher. London: Penguin, 1985.
Beier, A. L. *Masterless Men: The Vagrancy Problem in England, 1560–1640*. London: Methuen, 1985.
Berry, Helen, and Elizabeth Foyster. *The Family in Early Modern England*. Cambridge: Cambridge University Press, 2007.
Bevington, David, ed. *Antony and Cleopatra*. Cambridge: Cambridge University Press, 2005.
Boccaccio, Giovanni. *Famous Women*, trans. Virginia Brown. Harvard University Press, I Tatti Renaissance Library, 2003.
Book of Common Prayer, ed. Brian Cummings. Oxford: Oxford World's Classics, 2013.
Bouwsma, William J. *The Waning of the Renaissance*. New Haven: Yale University Press, 2000.
Brathwait, Richard. *The English Gentleman*. London [1631].
_____. *The English Gentlewoman*. London [1631].
Brown, John Russell. *Shakespeare: Antony and Cleopatra, a Casebook*. London: Macmillan, 1984.
Bullough, Geoffrey. *Narrative and Dramatic Sources of Shakespeare*. London: Routledge and Kegan Paul, 1964.
Bunker, Nick. *Making Haste from Babylon*. London: Pimlico, 2011.
Burnet, Bishop. *History of the Reformation*. London [1682].
Burton, Robert. *The Anatomy of Melancholy*, ed. Floyd Dell and Paul Jordan-Smith. New York: Tudor, 1938.
Butler, Charles. *Female Replies to Swetnam the Woman-Hater*. Bristol: Thoemmes Press, 1995.

Campbell, Lily B. *Shakespeare's Tragic Heroes*. London: Methuen, 1930.
_____, ed. *Parts Added to the Mirrour for Magistrates by John Higgins and Thomas Blennerhasset*. Cambridge: Cambridge University Press, 1946.
Castiglione, Baldassare. *The Book of the Courtier*, trans. George Bull. Harmondsworth: Penguin Classics, 1981.
Castor, Helen. *She-Wolves*. London: Faber, 2010.
Cicero. *On Obligation*, trans. P. Walsh. Oxford World's Classics, 2008.
_____. *Selected Works*, trans. M. Grant. London: Penguin Classics, 1971.
Clapham, John. *Elizabeth of England*, ed. E. Plummer Read and C. Read. Pennsylvania: University of Pennsylvania Press, 1951.
Coleridge, Samuel Taylor. *Samuel Taylor Coleridge: Shakespeare Criticism*, ed. T. M. Raysor. London: Dent, 1960.
Cressy, David. *Agnes Bowker's Cat: Travesties and Transgressions in Tudor and Stuart England*. Oxford: Oxford University Press, 2001.
Crowley, Robert. *Voice of the Last Trumpet*. London [1550].
Dabhoiwala, Faramerz. *The Origins of Sex: A History of the First Sexual Revolution*. London: Penguin, 2013.
Dante. *The Divine Comedy*, trans. C. H. Sisson. Oxford: Oxford World's Classics, 2008.
Daunton, M. J. *Progress and Poverty*. Oxford: Oxford University Press, 1995.
Davies, Godfrey. *The Early Stuarts*. Oxford: Clarendon Press, 1976.
Dekker, Thomas. *The Seven Deadly Sins of London* [1606]. Whitefish, MT: Kessinger, 2013.
De Lisle, Leanda. *After Elizabeth*. London: Harper Collins, 2005.
Dollimore, Jonathan. *Radical Tragedy: Religion, Ideology, and Power in the Drama of Shakespeare and His Contemporaries*. New York: Harvester Wheatsheaf, 1984.
Donne, John. *Sermons*.
Drakakis, John, ed. *Antony and Cleopatra*. London: Macmillan New Casebooks, 1994.
Dryden, John. *All For Love*, ed. Bonamy Dobrée. Oxford: Oxford University Press, World's Classics, 1928.
Dusinberre, Juliet. *Shakespeare and the Nature of Woman*. London: Macmillan, 1979.
Ellerbe, Helen. *The Dark Side of Christian History*. Orlando, FL: Morningstar & Lark, 2001.
Elyot, Sir Thomas. *The Boke Named the Governour*. Menston: Scolar Press, 1970.
Erasmus, Desiderius. *Praise of Folly*, trans. Betty Radice. London: Penguin Classics, 1971.
Ford, John. *'Tis Pity She's a Whore*, New Mermaid edition, ed. M. Wiggins. London: A. & C. Black, 2007.
Frye, Northrop. *Fools of Time*. Toronto: University of Toronto Press, 1967.
Gawdy, Sir Philip. *The Letters of Sir Philip Gawdy*, ed. Isaac H. Geaves. London: J. Nichols, 1906.
Goldsworthy, Adrian. *Antony and Cleopatra*. London: Weidenfeld & Nicolson, 2010.
Gouge, William. *Of Domesticall Duties*. London [1622].
Grant, Michael. *Cleopatra*. St Albans: Panther Books, 1974.
Green, P. *Alexander to Actium: The Historical Evolution of the Hellenistic Age*. London: Thames and Hudson, 1990.
Gurr, Andrew. *The Shakespearean Stage, 1574–1642*. Cambridge: Cambridge University Press, 1992.
Harrison, G. B. *A Jacobean Journal*. London: Routledge, 1946.
Hazlitt, William. *Characters of Shakespeare's Plays*. London: J. M. Dent, 1906.

Hill, Christopher. *Intellectual Origins of the English Revolution*. Oxford: Oxford University Press, 1965.
Historical Manuscripts Commission. *Calendar of the Manuscripts of the Most Honourable the Marquess of Salisbury*. London [1883].
Hoby, Lady Margaret. *The Private Life of an Elizabethan Lady: The Diary of Lady Margaret Hoby*, ed. Joanna Moody. Stroud: Sutton, 1998.
Hoby, Thomas. *The Courtyer of Baldessar Castilio* [1561].
Horace. *Ars Poetica* (*The Art of Poetry*).
Hughes-Hallett, Lucy. *Cleopatra: Histories, Dreams and Distortions*. New York: Harper & Row, 1990.
James I, King. *Basilikon Doron*. EEBO Editions reprint of the 1682 edition.
Jonson, Ben, George Chapman and John Marston. *Ben Jonson: Works* [1925–52], ed. C. H. Herford and Percy Simpson. Oxford: Clarendon Press, 1997.
———. *Eastward Ho!* New Mermaid edition. London: Ernest Benn, 1994.
Kishlansky, Mark. *A Monarchy Transformed: Britain 1603–1714*. London: Penguin, 1996.
Knights, L. C. *Drama and Society in the Age of Jonson* [1937]. London: Penguin, 1962.
Knox, John. *The First Blast of the Trumpet against the Monstrous Regiment of Women*. Geneva [1558].
Kott, Jan. *Shakespeare: Our Contemporary*. London: Methuen, 1972.
Leggatt, Alexander. *Shakespeare's Political Drama*. London: Routledge, 1989.
Lovell, Mary S. *Bess of Hardwick*. London: Little, Brown, 2005.
Lucretius. *De Rerum Naturae*.
Machiavelli, Niccolo. *The Prince*, trans. George Bull. Harmondsworth: Penguin Classics, 1961.
Malmesbury, William of. *De Gestis Regum Anglorum* [1125].
Marston, John. *The Dutch Courtesan* [1604], ed. M. Wine. London: Edward Arnold, 1965.
Mason, H. A. *Shakespeare's Tragedies of Love*. London: Chatto & Windus, 1970.
Middleton, Thomas. *A Mad World My Masters* [1605], ed. M. Taylor. Oxford: World's Classics, 1995.
Miola, Robert. *Shakespeare's Rome*. Cambridge: Cambridge University Press, 1983.
Montaigne, Michel. *The Complete Essays*, ed. M. A. Screech. London: Penguin Classics, 2003.
Mortimer, Ian. *The Time Traveller's Guide to Elizabethan England*. London: Vintage Books, 2013.
Muir, Kenneth. *The Sources of Shakespeare's Plays*. London: Methuen, 1977.
Nashe, Thomas. *The Unfortunate Traveller* [1594]. In *Shorter Elizabethan Novels*, ed. George Saintsbury. London: Dent, 1966.
Nichols, John. *The Progresses, Processions, and Magnificent Festivities of James the First*. London [1828].
Norton Anthology of English Literature, vol. 1. London: W. W. Norton, 1962.
Orgel, Stephen. *The Illusion of Power*. Berkeley: University of California Press, 1991.
Orgel, Stephen, and Roy Strong. *Inigo Jones: The Theatre of the Stuart Court*. Berkeley: University of California Press, 1973.
Ovid. *Metamorphoses*, trans. Mary M. Innes. London: Penguin Classics, 1955.
Paglia, Camille. *Sexual Personae*. London: Penguin, 1991.
Peck, Linda Levy. *Court Patronage and Corruption in Early Stuart England*. London: Routledge, 1993.

_____. *Northampton: Patronage and Policy at the Court of James I*. London: Allen & Unwin, 1982.
Percy, Henry. *Advice to His Son*, ed. G. B. Harrison. London: Ernest Benn, 1930.
Plato. *The Last Days of Socrates*, trans. Hugh Tredennick. London: Penguin Classics, 1971.
Plutarch. *Makers of Rome*, trans. Ian Scott-Kilvert. London: Penguin Classics, 1965.
Rackin, Phyllis. *Shakespeare and Women*. Oxford: Oxford University Press, 2005.
Ridley, M. R. *Antony and Cleopatra*, Arden edition. Cambridge, MA: Harvard University Press, 1956.
Sallust. *The Jugurthine War: The Conspiracy of Catiline*, trans. S. A. Handford. London: Penguin Classics, 1982.
Schleiner, Louise. *Tudor and Stuart Women Writers*. Indianapolis: Indiana University Press, 1994.
Secor, Philip B. *Richard Hooker: Prophet of Anglicanism*. Tunbridge Wells: Burns & Oates, 1999.
Seneca. 'On Mercy' in *Dialogues and Essays*, trans. John Davie. Oxford: Oxford World's Classics, 2008.
Starr, Tama. *The 'Natural Inferiority' of Women*. New York: Poseidon Press, 1991.
Stone, Lawrence. *The Crisis of the Aristocracy*. Oxford: Clarendon Press, 1966.
_____. *The Family, Sex and Marriage in England, 1500–1800*. London: Penguin Books, 1979.
Stow, John. *The Survey of London*. London: Dent (Everyman's Library), 1970.
Strype, John. *Memorials of Thomas Cranmer*. London [1690].
Stubbes, Philip. *Anatomie of Abuses*. London [1583].
Tawney, R. H. *Religion and the Rise of Capitalism* [1926]. London: Penguin, 1990.
Thomas, Keith. *Religion and the Decline of Magic*. London: Penguin, 1991.
Traversi, Derek. *Shakespeare: The Roman Plays*. London: Hollis & Carter, 1963.
Weber, Max. *The Protestant Ethic and the Spirit of Capitalism* [1904–05]. London: Unwin University Books, 1968.
Webster, John. *The Duchess of Malfi* [1612–13].
_____. *The White Devil*, New Mermaid edition, ed. Christina Luckyj. London: A & C Black, 1996.
Weldon, Sir Anthony. *The Court and Character of James I*. London [1651].
Wickham, Glynne, Herbert Berry and William Ingram, eds. *English Professional Theatre, 1530–1660*. Cambridge: Cambridge University Press, 2000.
Wilders, John, ed. *Antony and Cleopatra*. Arden Shakespeare, 2004.
Wilson, John Dover, ed. *Antony and Cleopatra*. Cambridge: Cambridge University Press, 1950.
Wootten, David. *Divine Right and Democracy: An Anthology of Political Writings in Stuart England*. Indianapolis: University of Indiana, 2006.
Wycliffe, John. *The Wycliffe New Testament*. London: British Library, 2002.

INDEX

Aeschylus 143, 169
Alchemist, The (Jonson) 42, 209
All's Well That Ends Well (Shakespeare) 22, 205
Ambrose, St 73
A Mad World My Masters (Middleton) 99, 130
A Midsummer Night's Dream (Shakespeare) 20, 23, 116, 211, 218, 224
A Mouzell for Melastomus (Speght) 113
anagnorisis 72, 137, 158, 201
Anatomie of Abuses (Stubbes) 240
Anglica historia (Polydore Vergil) 88, 239
Anouilh, Jean 15, 150, 234
Anton, Robert 5, 233
Antonie (Countess of Pembroke) 217, 233
Antonio's Revenge (Marston) 208
Antony and Cleopatra (Shakespeare) characters: Agrippa 185, 186, 200, 213, 225; Alexas 26, 174, 201, 207; Caesar (Octavius) 1–3, 9–11, 15–16, 24–25, 30, 37–38, 50, 57, 62, 65, 67, 75, 77, 80–82, 85, 92, 96, 101, 120, 129, 134–35, 138–45, 147–49, 152, 154, 159–61, 163, 165–66, 171, 173, 177–80, 182, 184–89, 192, 195–97, 199–200, 204, 208, 210–11, 213–14, 216–17, 219, 222, 224–33, 238, 242; Canidius 159, 161, 230; Charmian 26, 137, 140, 164, 179, 185–86, 201, 207; Dercetus 228; Dolabella 25, 145, 214; Enobarbus 6, 15, 25, 79–80, 135, 137, 158, 161–62, 174–75, 185–86, 200, 213–14, 227–32; Eros 137, 139, 144, 219, 230; Fulvia 16, 81, 101, 138, 143, 159–60, 173, 178, 184, 195, 210, 217, 242, 244; Iras 26, 137, 140, 159, 186, 201, 207; Lepidus 9, 65, 152, 200, 208, 214, 227–28; Maecenas 25, 79, 159, 186, 200, 217, 225; Menas 64, 224, 227; Octavia 13, 15, 68, 77, 82, 101, 106, 129, 134–35, 138, 153, 155, 159, 169, 177, 184, 187, 190, 195, 201–2, 208, 211, 213, 216–18, 221–22, 225–26, 228, 241; Philo 97, 153, 157; Pompey 9, 16, 26, 64, 73, 145, 162, 173, 177, 184, 199, 202, 210, 213, 216, 221, 224, 226–28, 237; Scarus 161, 173, 187, 213, 228–29; Thidias 25, 28, 73, 81, 84, 202, 231; Ventidius 79, 200, 215, 224, 227
Apollo 68–69, 159, 187–88, 191–92, 195 (see also Delphi)
Appian 210, 216
Aquinas, St Thomas 73, 235, 238
Araignment of Lewde, Idle, Froward, and Unconstant Women (Swetnam) 114
Aristotle 22, 72, 145, 205, 236
Ars Poetica (*The Art of Poetry*) (Horace) 240
As You Like It (Shakespeare) 67, 205
Augustine, St 22, 66, 69, 73, 234
Aylmer, Bishop 117

Bacon, Sir Francis 25, 44, 103, 217, 236–37, 243
Bankside 206

Barnes, Barnaby 4, 233
Basilikon Doron (James I) 46, 73, 82–83, 85, 89–90, 183, 235–39, 243
Beaumont, Francis 205
Becon, Thomas 101
Behn, Aphra 96, 109, 240
Beier, A. L. 234–37
Berry, Helen (and Elizabeth Foyster) 239
better sort, the 4, 18, 23–24, 29, 35, 37, 47, 79, 105
Blackfriars Theatre 211
Blount, Edward 5
Boccaccio, Giovanni 116, 135, 141, 166, 168, 240–41
Bosch, Hieronymous 58
Boke Named the Governour, The (Elyot) 32, 46, 78, 234
Book of Common Prayer, The 12, 236
Book of Homilies, The 48, 97, 116, 125
Botticelli, Sandro 176–77, 237
Bouwsma, William J. 234
Brathwait, Richard 5, 50, 233, 236
Brown, John Russell 233, 242
Buchanan, George 91, 238
Bullough, Geoffrey 241
Burnet, Bishop 240
Burton, Robert 88, 169, 215, 235
Busino, Orazio 65

Caesar, Julius 1–3, 9–11, 15–16, 25–26, 30, 37–38, 40, 50, 57, 62, 65, 67, 72, 75, 77, 80–82, 85, 92, 96, 101, 114, 120, 129, 135, 138–45, 147–49, 151–52, 154, 159–63, 165–66, 171–73, 177–80, 182, 184–90, 192, 195–97, 199–200, 204, 208, 210–11, 213–17, 219, 222, 224–33, 238, 241–42
Caesar, Octavius (*see* Octavius)
Calvin, John (*see* Calvinists)
Calvinists 12, 113
Camden Miscellany 235
Campbell, Lily Bess 235
Campion, Thomas 113, 240
Carey, Elizabeth 113
Castiglione, Baldassare 24, 57, 73, 75, 78, 96, 112–14, 116, 195, 235–40
Castor, Helen 242
catharsis 137, 149

Catiline (Jonson) 203, 242
Cecil, Robert 25, 121
Chain of Being, The Great 17, 20, 21
Changeling, The (Middleton/Rowley) 208
Chaucer, Geoffrey 115, 141, 143, 168, 211, 218–19, 235, 244
Cheapside 4, 206
Cicero 3, 37, 72, 79, 81, 83, 92, 118, 120, 129, 135, 155–56, 164, 216, 238, 241
City Comedies 4, 22, 29, 46, 120, 203, 209
Clapham, John 236
Clement of Alexandria 95
Cleopatra (Daniel) 4, 139, 211, 216
Coleridge, Samuel Taylor 5, 6, 191, 243
Comedy of Errors, The (Shakespeare) 114, 239
Commandments, The Ten 53, 63
Confessio Amantis (Gower) 169
Conway, Viscount 32
Cooper, Bishop Thomas 62, 148, 237
Copernicus, Nicholas 19
Coriolanus (Shakespeare) 36, 204
Corporal Works of Mercy, The 74
Cranmer, Thomas 48, 236
Cressy, David 236, 240–41
Crowley, Robert 240
Cymbeline (Shakespeare) 22, 91, 115

Dhabiowala, Faramerz 237, 239
Daniel, Samuel 4, 139, 211, 216–17, 233
Dante 22, 24, 57, 63, 64, 137, 141, 167, 195
Daunton, Martin James 236
Davies, Godfrey 234
De Casibus Virorum Illustrium (Boccaccio) 135
Defence of Good Women, The (Elyot) 116
De Ira (Seneca) 44, 72, 143
De Jure Regni (Buchanan) 91
Dekker, Thomas 29, 51, 101, 205–6
De Lisle, Leanda 236–37, 240
Delphi 69, 159
De Mulieribus Claris (Boccaccio) 116, 135
dénouement 137–38, 146, 215
De Officiis (Cicero) 72, 79, 83, 118, 155, 238, 241
Devil's Charter (Barnes) 4
Dido 168, 172, 180

Dionysus 16, 65, 135, 152–53, 165, 188–91, 195, 212
Dissenters 11–12, 49, 109, 125–26 (see also Calvinists, Puritans)
Divine Right 28, 84, 91, 235–36, 238
Dollimore, Jonathan 62, 237
Donne, John 128, 153
dowry 64, 105–6
Drake, Sir Francis 20
Dryden, John 5, 163, 166, 233
Dusinberre, Juliet 239
Duchess of Malfi, The (Webster) 98, 208, 239
Dutch Courtesan, The (Marston) 117–18, 172

Eastward Ho! (Chapman, Jonson, Marston) 31, 34, 70, 120, 209, 238
Elizabeth I 10–12, 42, 108, 122, 170, 178, 184, 209
Ellerbe, Helen 239
Elyot, Sir Thomas 19, 32, 46, 73, 78–83, 87, 89, 92, 116, 120, 135, 234, 238
English Gentleman, The (Brathwait) 236
Erasmus, Desiderius 75, 112, 236, 238
Every Man Out of His Humour (Jonson) 209

Faerie Queen, The (Spenser) 12, 116
Fall of Princes, The (Lydgate) 135, 241
Faustus (Marlowe) 58–59, 61, 208, 234
Filmer, Robert 84
First Blast of the Trumpet, The (Knox) 239
Fletcher, John 100, 205
Florio, John 106, 207
Ford, John 55–56
Fortune, Wheel of (see *Rota Fortunae*)
Free Monarchies, The True Law of (James I) 46, 91
Freytag's Pyramid 138
Frye, Northrop 242

Gardiner, Samuel 206
Garnier, Robert 216
Gawdy, Sir Philip 43–44, 130, 236, 241
gender relationships 93
Globe Theatre x, 4, 16, 206–7, 211, 233
Goldsworthy, Adrian 76–77, 86, 120, 178, 233–34, 237–38, 240, 242

Gorboduc (Sackville and Norton) 67, 203
Gouge, William 239
governor / governorship 3, 14, 42, 46, 57, 73, 76–78, 80–82, 87, 124, 190, 194, 205, 224, 227–29
Gower, John 168
Grant, Michael 242
Green, Peter 241
Gregory I (pope) 63
Gunpowder Plot 58, 192
Gurr, Andrew 233

Hallelujah (Wither) 238
hamartia 79, 135–36, 201, 212
Hamlet (Shakespeare) 67, 96, 98, 141, 143–44, 176, 201, 208, 224
Harrison, George Bagshawe 235, 238
Hazlitt, William 6, 243
Heaven 17–23, 59, 62, 65, 81, 108, 234
Hell 17–18, 20, 22–23, 50, 57–59, 61–62, 64–65, 137, 167, 195, 234, 237
Henry IV, Part I (Shakespeare) 211
Henry VI (Shakespeare) 46, 115, 211
Henry VIII 11, 48, 113, 122
Henry, Prince of Wales 82
Hercules 6, 123, 129, 141, 143, 152–53, 164–65, 172, 189, 212, 229, 233, 241
Heydon, Sir Christopher 19
Heywood, Thomas 29, 241
hierarchy 3, 17–18, 22–23, 26–27, 35, 37, 39–40, 42, 47–48, 94, 108, 122, 128, 156, 192–93, 212, 217, 229, 235 (see also Pyramid, the Social)
Hilton, Walter 21
Hoby, Lady Margaret 109, 239–40
Hoby, Sir Thomas 112, 242
Holinshed, Raphael 129, 144, 211
Horace 30, 124, 219
hubris 31, 54, 57, 65, 81, 87, 92, 136, 146, 152, 161, 207, 225
Hughes-Hallett, Lucy 152, 241–42
humours, theory of the 37

Institution of Marriage, The (Erasmus) 112
Instruction of a Christian Woman (Vives) 112
Isle of Dogs, The (Jonson and Nashe) 209

Isis 3, 16, 65, 123, 135, 171–72, 187–90, 196, 212, 224, 242
Isocrates 238

James I: general 10, 14, 58, 62, 67–68, 90, 94, 121, 154, 234, 235; works: *An Apologie for the Oath of Allegiance* 76; *A Premonition to All Most Mightie Monarchs* 76; *Basilikon Doron* 46, 73, 82–83, 85, 89–90, 183, 235–39, 243; *Demonologie* 58; *The True Law of Free Monarchies* 46, 91
Jameson, Mrs 242
Jew of Malta, The (Marlowe) 208
John Chrysostom, St 95
John of Salisbury 238
Johnson, Samuel 5
jointure 105
Jonson, Ben 25, 29, 39, 41–42, 47, 78, 118, 124, 203, 205–7, 209, 238, 240
Julius Caesar (Shakespeare) 2, 204, 217
Juvenal 30

kingship ix, 12, 22, 26, 37–38, 46, 67, 73, 76, 82–84, 91, 205, 237 (*see also* governor, leadership)
King Lear (Shakespeare) 20, 39, 41, 47, 59, 67, 90, 99, 107, 115, 118, 120, 123, 140, 144, 164, 177, 201, 203, 205, 222, 226, 228, 237
King's Men (acting company) 4, 90, 206, 207
Kishlansky, Mark 235
Knights, L. C. 240
Knox, John 108, 148
Kott, Jan 154, 176, 196, 200, 223, 241–44
Kyd, Thomas 142, 208

Ladder of Perfection, The (Hilton) 21
leadership 30, 47, 51, 57, 91, 120, 156, 170, 203–5, 208, 211
Legend of Good Women, The (Chaucer) 116, 211, 218
Letter to Octavia (Daniel) 216
lex talionis 144
Locrine (anon.) 102, 203
Lovell, Mary 239
Love's Triumph (Jonson) 124

lower sort, the 121, 199
Lydgate, John 168, 241
Lucretius 189, 243
Luther, Martin 11, 115

Macbeth (Shakespeare) 91, 137, 141, 144, 201, 205
Machiavelli, Niccolo 62–63, 234, 238, 242
Magellan, Ferdinand 20
Malcontent, The (Marston) 208
Malmesbury, William of 154, 223, 233
Malleus Maleficarum (Kramer) 95, 239
Marc Antoine (Garnier) 216
Marlowe, Christopher 58, 127, 203, 207–8
Mars 16, 18, 153, 157, 176, 187, 189, 212
Marston, John 117–18, 172, 205–6, 208
Martin, Thomas 11, 115, 204
Mary I (Mary Tudor, 'Bloody Mary') 11–12
Mary Queen of Scots 68, 177
Mary, the Virgin 17, 19, 23, 41, 95, 115
Massacre at Paris, The (Marlowe) 203
Measure for Measure (Shakespeare) 14, 22, 47, 55, 67, 90–91, 96, 118, 123, 205
Meres, Francis 142
Mermaid Tavern 206
Middleton, Thomas 29, 99, 130, 205–6, 208, 243
middling sort, the 13, 18, 23–25, 32–33, 47, 121
Milton, John 234
mimesis 136
Mirrour for Magistrates, The (Blennerhasset and Higgins) 46, 136
Miseries of Enforced Marriage, The (Wilkins) 117
misogyny 94, 98–99, 107, 114 (*see also* gender relationships)
Monke's Tale, The (Chaucer) 141
Monmouth, Geoffrey of 31
Montaigne, Michel 44, 61, 89, 103, 108, 134, 168, 191, 207, 236, 238, 242
Montagu, Lord 31, 99
More, Sir Thomas 112
Mortimer, Ian 234–35, 239
Moulsworth, Martha 101
Much Ado About Nothing (Shakespeare) 67, 97, 114, 175, 191, 205
Muir, Kenneth 244

Mulcaster, Richard 111, 240
mythos 136

Nashe, Thomas 154, 209, 241
Nemesis 146, 163, 169
Newton, Thomas 144
Nietzsche, Friedrich 191
Nichols, John 235–36, 238
Nichomachean Ethics, The (Aristotle) 23, 235
North, Sir Thomas 165, 210, 228, 241

Octavius 9, 10, 24, 101, 134, 138, 165, 187, 214, 233
Omphale 6, 164, 172, 212, 229
Orgel, Stephen 237, 243
Original Sin 20, 39, 61, 87
Osiris 16, 172, 188, 190
Othello (Shakespeare) 20, 67, 144, 224, 228
Ovid 112, 157, 241

Paglia, Camille 57, 187, 188, 190–96, 224, 243–44
Palladis Tamia (Meres) 241
Paradise Lost (Milton) 234
Paraphrases (Erasmus) 112
Patriarcha (Filmer) 84
patriarchy 84, 94, 104, 115, 117, 172
Peck, Linda Levy 235, 236, 240
Pembroke, Earl of and Countess of 211, 244
Percy, Henry, Earl of Northumberland 51, 100, 236
Pericles (Shakespeare) 22, 75, 115
peripeteia 137, 201
Perkins, William 48
Phaedo (Plato) 236
Philosophers Satyrs, The (Anton) 5, 233
Plato 22, 72, 83, 204, 236
Plutarch 4, 16, 79–80, 91, 134–35, 139–40, 165–66, 168, 170, 178–80, 185, 189, 200, 202, 204, 207, 210–16, 219, 223, 229–32, 242, 243
Poetics, The (Aristotle) 136
Politics, The (Aristotle) 236
Polydore, Vergil 88, 239
Pompey, Sextus 26, 64, 162, 177, 199, 210, 213, 216, 221, 224, 227–28

Pompey, the Great 9, 173, 226, 237
Poor Man's Petition, The 121
Positions (Mulcaster) 111
Praise of Folly (Erasmus) 75, 236
primogeniture 105
Prince, The (Machiavelli) 233–34, 237, 242
probitas 30
Problem Plays 22, 205, 210, 221
Progresses, Processions and Magnificent Festivities of James I, The (Nichols) 235–36, 238
psychomachia 20, 57, 234
Ptolemy (or Ptolemaic System) 19, 166, 189
Purgatory 117, 234
Puritans 10, 12, 61, 67, 69, 97, 126, 128, 192, 195
Pyramid, The Social 26

Raleigh, Sir Walter 29, 42, 62, 136, 234, 238
Reformation, The 11, 48, 58, 67, 74, 104, 114, 128, 240
Republic, The (Plato) 1, 9–10, 24, 58, 162, 165, 184, 203, 215
Revels Office 90
Revenge Tragedies 22, 40, 46, 78, 144, 208, 224, 228
Revenger's Tragedy, The (Tourneur and Middleton) 206, 208
Richard II (Shakespeare) 211
Richard III (Shakespeare) 67, 137, 149, 211
Roaring Boys 212
Romances 22
Romeo and Juliet (Shakespeare) 5, 31, 97, 138, 141, 169
Rota Fortunae 147–48
Rover, The (Behn) 96

Sallust 186, 242
scala naturae 21
Scaramelli, Giovanni 43–44, 236
Schlegel, Karl Wilhelm 6
Schleiner, Louise 239
Scott-Kilvert, Ian 241–44
Secor, Philip 238

Sejanus (Jonson) 25, 78, 203, 207, 238
Seneca 37, 44, 75, 142–43, 154, 238
Seven Deadly Sins of London, The (Dekker) 206
Seven Gifts of the Holy Ghost 74
Sexual Personae (Paglia) 190, 243–44
Shapiro, Susan 233
sibling rivalry (or fraternal rivalry) 67, 242
Sidney, Sir Philip 109, 113, 233
Sins, The Seven Deadly 44, 54, 63–64, 71, 169, 206
Sophocles 143, 160
sophrosyne 134, 192
Southampton, Earl of 43
Spanish Tragedy, The (Kyd) 142, 208
Speght, Rachel 113–14, 240, 244
Spiritual Works of Mercy 29, 32, 74
Star Chamber 20, 235
Starr, Tamara 239
Stationers' Office (or Stationers' Register) 4, 90
Stock, Richard 113–14, 240, 244
Stone, Lawrence 104, 117, 235, 238–40
Stow, John 243–44
Strype, John 236
Stuart, Arbella 68, 109, 130, 208, 211, 243
Stubbes, Philip 122, 240
Sumptuary Laws 122
Swetnam, Ralph 114, 240

Tamburlaine the Great (Marlowe) 127
Taming of the Shrew, The (Shakespeare) 67, 98, 114
Tawney, Richard Henry 240
Tempest, The (Shakespeare) 14, 22, 40, 91, 106, 115
Tertullian 95
Theobalds 121
Tilney, Edmund (Master of the Revels) 209
Timon of Athens (Shakespeare) 91, 204
'*Tis Pity She's a Whore* (Ford) 55, 93, 106
Titus Andronicus (Shakespeare) 115, 137, 204

Tragedy of the Gowrie, The (anon.) 90
tragedy 3, 15, 22, 25, 69, 71, 88, 113–15, 120, 133, 135–37, 141–42, 145–48, 150, 152, 154–55, 160, 166, 169, 193, 196, 201–2, 207–8, 210, 217, 222, 226
Triumvirate, First 9, 135
Triumvirate, Second 9
Troilus and Cressida (Shakespeare) 22, 44, 67, 81, 145, 164, 172, 205
Twelfth Night (Shakespeare) 69, 205

Unfortunate Traveller, The (Nashe) 241
unities, the 145
Utopia (More) 46, 112

Venus 3, 16, 18, 157, 176–77, 187, 189, 212
Virtues, The Seven Cardinal 71, 237
Vives, Juan 112
Volpone (Jonson) 39, 41, 206, 209

Weber, Max 240
Webster, John 41, 203, 208, 236
Weldon, Sir Anthony 234
White Devil, The (Webster) 41, 123, 203, 208, 236
Wickham, Glynne 243
Wife of Bath's Tale, The (Chaucer) 235
Wilkins, George 117
Wilson, John Dover 244
Wilson, Thomas 235
Winter's Tale, The (Shakespeare) 22, 91, 115
Winthrop, Sir John (and Lady) 239
Winwood, Sir Ralph 238
Wither, George 94
Woman's Prize, The (Fletcher) 100
Wootten, David 236, 238
Wroth, Lady Mary 113
Wycliffe, John 237

Xenophon 238

www.ingramcontent.com/pod-product-compliance
Ingram Content Group UK Ltd.
Pitfield, Milton Keynes, MK11 3LW, UK
UKHW041917140426
5217IPUK00013B/189